PENGUIN ANANDA
LEARNING HAPPINESS

Osho defies categorization. His talks, which run into thousands, cover everything from the individual quest for meaning to the most urgent social and political issues facing society today. Osho's books are not written but are transcribed from audio and video recordings of his extemporaneous talks to international audiences. As he puts it, 'So remember: whatever I am saying is not just for you . . . I am talking also for the future generations.'

Osho has been described by *Sunday Times* in London as one of the '1000 Makers of the 20th Century', and by American author Tom Robbins as 'the most dangerous man since Jesus Christ'. *Sunday Mid-Day* (India) has selected Osho as one of ten people—along with Gandhi, Nehru and Buddha—who have changed the destiny of India.

About his own work Osho has said that he is helping to create the conditions for the birth of a new kind of human being. He often characterizes this new human being as 'Zorba the Buddha'—capable both of enjoying the earthy pleasures of a Zorba the Greek and the silent serenity of a Gautama the Buddha.

Running like a thread through all aspects of Osho's talks and meditations is a vision that encompasses both the timeless wisdom of all ages past and the highest potential of today's (and tomorrow's) science and technology.

Osho is known for his revolutionary contribution to the science of inner transformation, with an approach to meditation that acknowledges the accelerated pace of contemporary life. His unique OSHO Active Meditations™ are designed to first release the accumulated stresses of body and mind, so that it is then easier to take an experience of stillness and thought-free relaxation into daily life.

Two autobiographical works by the author are available: *Autobiography of a Spiritually Incorrect Mystic*, St Martin's Press, New York (book and e-book), and *Glimpses of a Golden Childhood*, OSHO Media International, Pune, India.

OSHO

LEARNING HAPPINESS

THE DISCIPLINE OF TRANSCENDENCE

PENGUIN ANANDA

Published by the Penguin Group
Penguin Books India Pvt. Ltd, 7th Floor, Infinity Tower C, DLF Cyber City, Gurgaon 122 002, Haryana, India
Penguin Group (USA) Inc., 375 Hudson Street, New York, New York 10014, USA
Penguin Group (Canada), 90 Eglinton Avenue East, Suite 700, Toronto, Ontario, M4P 2Y3, Canada
Penguin Books Ltd, 80 Strand, London WC2R 0RL, England
Penguin Ireland, 25 St Stephen's Green, Dublin 2, Ireland (a division of Penguin Books Ltd)
Penguin Group (Australia), 707 Collins Street, Melbourne, Victoria 3008, Australia
Penguin Group (NZ), 67 Apollo Drive, Rosedale, Auckland 0632, New Zealand
Penguin Books (South Africa) (Pty) Ltd, Block D, Rosebank Office Park, 181 Jan Smuts Avenue, Parktown North, Johannesburg 2193, South Africa

Penguin Books Ltd, Registered Offices: 80 Strand, London WC2R 0RL, England

First published by OSHO Media International 1976
Published in Penguin Ananda by Penguin Books India 2015

Copyright © OSHO International Foundation 1976, 2014
OSHO® is a registered trademark of OSHO International Foundation, used under licence

All rights reserved

10 9 8 7 6 5 4 3 2

ISBN 9780143424925

For sale in the Indian Subcontinent only
Printed at Repro India Ltd, Navi Mumbai

This book is sold subject to the condition that it shall not, by way of trade or otherwise, be lent, resold, hired out, or otherwise circulated without the publisher's prior written consent in any form of binding or cover other than that in which it is published and without a similar condition including this condition being imposed on the subsequent purchaser and without limiting the rights under copyright reserved above, no part of this publication may be reproduced, stored in or introduced into a retrieval system, or transmitted in any form or by any means (electronic, mechanical, photocopying, recording or otherwise), without the prior written permission of both the copyright owner and the above-mentioned publisher of this book.

A PENGUIN RANDOM HOUSE COMPANY

CONTENTS

Preface vii

1. Desire Cannot Be Fulfilled 1
2. Aloneness Is Your Reality 27
3. The Passion for Truth 53
4. A Rich Man Is Very Poor 79
5. Godhood Is Your Nature 105
6. I Am Not a Perfectionist 131
7. Sex Is the Basic Problem 153
8. The Forbidden Path 181
9. The World Has Never Lacked Buddhas 207
10. Religion Is the Ultimate Luxury 235

OSHO International Meditation Resort 265

PREFACE

Happiness and unhappiness are both present in your life. The happiness may be just a little, perhaps only a glimpse, a hope or even an illusion, but still it is there. And unhappiness is there as well. You want to get rid of the unhappiness, so you approach the one who knows because he offers you some possibility of relief from your unhappiness. But when you approach the man who knows, he tells you to cast off the happiness as well as the unhappiness because only then can knowing happen.

Really, this is where the difficulty lies. You don't want to cast off the happiness that is yours. You have only recently got married; the wife is beautiful, people have been congratulating you, expressing their delight that you are married and now you have the one you wanted. You want to preserve this happiness. The arrangement you are seeking is one in which the unhappiness of the world disappears, but the happiness remains – and this is impossible.

No one has ever been able to manage this, nor ever will, because the happiness and unhappiness of the world are two sides of the same coin. Either you retain the whole coin or you throw the whole coin away. You are trying the impossible, and that is why you are divided within yourself. You want to leave one half and keep the other. But this life cannot be divided. Life is whole; to divide it is impossible.

Osho
Nowhere to Go But In

1

DESIRE CANNOT BE FULFILLED

The Buddha said:
Moved by their selfish desires, people seek after fame and glory.
But when they have acquired it, they are already stricken in years.
If you hanker after worldly fame and practice not the way, your
labors are wrongfully applied and your energy is wasted. It is like
unto burning an incense stick. However much its pleasing odor be
admired, the fire that consumes is steadily burning up the stick.
The Buddha said:
People cleave to their worldly possessions and selfish passions so
blindly as to sacrifice their own lives for them. They are like a
child who tries to eat a little honey smeared on the edge of a knife.
The amount is by no means sufficient to appease his appetite, but
he runs the risk of wounding his tongue.
The Buddha said:
Men are tied up to their families and possessions more helplessly
than in a prison. There is an occasion for the prisoner to be
released, but householders entertain no desire to be relieved from
the ties of family. When a man's passion is aroused nothing

prevents him from ruining himself. Even into the maws of a tiger will he jump. Those who are thus drowned in the filth of passion are called the ignorant. Those who are able to overcome it are saintly arhats.

The way of Buddha is not a religion in the ordinary sense of the term because it has no belief system, no dogma, no scripture. It does not believe in God, it does not believe in the soul, it does not believe in any state of *moksha*. It is a tremendous non-belief, and yet it is a religion.

It is unique. Nothing like it had ever happened in the history of human consciousness, and nothing like it has happened since. Buddha remains utterly unique, incomparable.

He says that God is nothing but a search for security, a search for safety, a search for shelter. You believe in God not because God is there, but because without that belief you feel helpless. Even if there were no God, you would invent one. The temptation comes from your weakness. It is a projection.

Man feels very limited, very helpless, almost a victim of circumstances – not knowing where he comes from and not knowing where he is going, not knowing why he is here. If there is no God it is very difficult for ordinary man to have any meaning in life. The ordinary mind will go berserk without God.

"God" is a prop which helps you, consoles you, comforts you. It says, "Don't be worried, the Almighty God knows everything about why you are here. He is the creator; he knows why he has created the world. You may not know but the Father knows, and you can trust in him." It is a great consolation.

The very idea of God gives you a sense of relief that you are not alone, that somebody is looking after affairs; that this cosmos is not just a chaos, it is really a cosmos, and that there is a system behind it, a logic behind it. It is not an illogical jumble of things, it is not anarchy. Somebody rules it; the sovereign king is there looking after each small detail, and not even a leaf moves without his moving it. Everything is planned. You are part of a great destiny. Maybe the meaning is not known to you, but the meaning is there because God is there.

"God" brings a tremendous relief. One starts feeling that life is not accidental; there is a certain undercurrent of significance, meaning, destiny. "God" brings a sense of destiny.

Buddha says: "There is no God" – it simply shows that man knows not why he is here. It simply shows man is helpless. It simply shows that man has no meaning available to him. By creating the idea of God he can believe in meaning, and he can live this futile life with the idea that somebody is looking after it.

Just think: you are on a flight and somebody comes and says, "There is no pilot." Suddenly there will be a panic. No pilot? "No pilot" means you are doomed. Then somebody says, "Believe the pilot is there, just invisible. We may not be able to see the pilot, but he is there; otherwise how is this beautiful mechanism functioning? Just think of it: everything is going so beautifully there must be a pilot. Maybe we are not capable of seeing him, maybe we are not yet prayerful enough to see him, maybe our eyes are closed, but the pilot is there. Otherwise, how is it possible? This airplane has taken off, it is flying perfectly well; the engines are humming. Everything is a proof that there is a pilot."

If somebody proves it, you relax again into your chair. You close your eyes, you start dreaming again, you can fall asleep. The pilot is there, you need not worry.

Buddha says that the pilot doesn't exist. It is a human creation. Man has created God in his own image. It is man's invention; God is not a discovery, it is an invention. God is not the truth; it is the greatest lie there is. That's why I say Buddhism is not a religion in the ordinary sense of the term. A God-less religion – can you imagine? When for the first time Western scholars became aware of Buddhism they were shocked. They could not comprehend that a religion can exist without God. They had known only Judaism,

Christianity and Islam. All these three religions are in a way very immature compared to Buddhism.

Buddhism is religion come of age. Buddhism is the religion of a mature mind. Buddhism is not childish at all, and it doesn't help any childish desires in you. It is very merciless. Let me repeat it: There has never been a man more compassionate than Buddha, but his religion is merciless. In fact, in that mercilessness he is showing his compassion. He will not allow you to cling to any lie. Howsoever consoling, a lie is a lie, and those who have given you the lie are not your friends. They are enemies because under the impact of the lie you will live a life full of lies.

The truth has to be brought to you, howsoever hard, howsoever shattering, howsoever shocking. Even if you are annihilated by the impact of the truth, it is good. Buddha says that the truth is that man's religions are man's inventions. You are in a dark night surrounded by alien forces. You need someone to hang on to, someone to cling to.

Everything that you can see is changing. One day your father will die and you will be left alone; your mother will die one day and you will be left alone, and you will be an orphan. From your very childhood you have been accustomed to having a father to protect you, a mother to love you. Now that childish desire will again assert itself: you will need a father figure. If you cannot find it in the sky, then you will find it in some politician.

Stalin became the father of Soviet Russia; they had dropped the idea of God. Mao became the father of China; they had dropped the idea of God. But man is such that he cannot live without a father figure. Man is childish. Only a very few rare people grow to be mature.

My own observation is that people remain about the age of seven, or eight, or nine. Their physical bodies go on growing, but their minds remain stuck somewhere below the age of ten.

Christianity, Judaism, Islam, Hinduism are all religions for those below the age of ten. They fulfill whatsoever your needs are; they are not very worried about truth. They are more worried about you, they are more worried about how to console you.

The situation is like this: the mother has died and the child is crying and weeping, and you have to console the child. So you tell lies. You pretend that the mother has not died: "She has gone for a visit to the neighbors, she will be coming home soon. Don't be worried, she will be coming." or: "She has gone for a long journey. It will take a few days but she will be back." Or: "She has gone to visit God – nothing to be worried about. She is still alive: maybe she has left the body, but the soul lives forever."

Buddha is the most shattering individual in the whole history of humanity. His whole effort is to drop all props. He does not say to believe in anything. He is an unbeliever and his religion is that of un-belief. He does not say, "Believe." He says, "Doubt."

Now, you have heard about religions which say believe. You have never heard about a religion which says doubt. Doubt is the very methodology: doubt to the very core, doubt to the very end, doubt to the very last. And when you have doubted everything, and you have dropped everything out of doubt, then reality arises in your vision. It has nothing to do with your beliefs about God. It is nothing like your so-called God. Then arises reality: absolutely unfamiliar and unknown. But that possibility exists only when all beliefs have been dropped and the mind has come to a state of maturity, understanding, acceptance: "Whatsoever is, is, and we don't desire otherwise. If there is no God, there is no God. We have no desire to project a God. If there is no God, then we accept it."

This is what maturity is: to accept the fact and not to create a fiction around it; to accept the reality as it is, without trying to sweeten it, without trying to decorate it, without trying to make it more acceptable to your heart. If it is shattering, it is shattering. If it is shocking, it is shocking. If the truth kills, then one is ready to be killed.

Buddha is merciless. And nobody has ever opened the door of reality as deeply, as profoundly as he has done. He does not allow you any childish desires. He says become more aware, become more conscious, become more courageous. Don't go on hiding behind beliefs and masks and theologies. Take your life into your own hands. Burn bright your inner light and see whatsoever is. And once you have become courageous enough to accept it, it is a benediction. No belief is needed.

That is Buddha's first step toward reality: all belief-systems are poisonous; all belief-systems are barriers.

He is not a theist. Remember: he is not an atheist either because, he says, a few people believe that there is God and a few people believe that there is no God, but both are believers. His non-belief is so deep that even those who say there is no God and believe in it, are not acceptable to him. He says that just to say there is no God makes no difference. If you remain childish, you will create another source of God.

For example, Karl Marx declared: "There is no God," but then he created a god out of history. History becomes the god; the same function is being done now by history that was done previously by the concept of God. What was God doing? God was the determining factor; God was the managing factor. It was God who was deciding what should be and what should not be. Marx dropped the idea of God, but then history became the determining factor, then history became the fate, then history became kismet, then history determined. Now, what is history? Marx says that Communism is an inevitable state. History has determined that it will come, and everything is determined by history. Now history becomes a super-God.

But somebody to determine is needed. Man cannot live with indeterminate reality. Man cannot live with reality as it is: chaotic, accidental. Man cannot live with reality without finding some idea which makes it meaningful, relevant, continuous, which gives it a shape which reason can understand; which can be dissected, analyzed, into cause and effect.

Freud dropped the idea of God, but then the unconscious became the God. Everything is determined by the unconscious of man, and man is helpless in the hands of the unconscious. Now, these are new names for God; it is a new mythology.

The Freudian psychology is a new mythology about God. The name is changed, but the content remains the same; the label has changed, the old label has been dropped; a fresh, newly painted label has been put on it, and it can deceive people who are not very alert. But if you go deeper into Freudian analysis you will immediately see that now the unconscious is doing the same work that God used to do.

So what is wrong with poor God? If you have to invent something, and man has always to be determined by something – history, economics, unconscious, this and that — if man cannot be free, then what is the point of changing mythologies, theologies? It does not make much difference.

You may be a Hindu, you may be a Mohammedan, you may be a Christian, you may be a Jew, it does not make much difference. Your mind remains childish, you remain immature. You remain in search, you continue to search for a father figure: someone somewhere who can explain everything, who can become the ultimate explanation.

The mature mind is one who can remain without any search, even if there is no ultimate explanation of things.

That's why Buddha says, "I am not a metaphysician." He has no metaphysics. Metaphysics means the ultimate explanation about things; he has no ultimate explanation. He does not say, "I have solved the mystery." He does not say, "Here I hand over to you what truth is."

He says, "The only thing that I can give to you is an impetus, a thirst, a tremendous passion to become aware, to become conscious, to become alert; to live your life so consciously, so full of light and awareness, that your life is solved." Not that you come to some ultimate explanation of existence — nobody has ever come. Buddha denies metaphysics completely. He says that metaphysics is a futile search.

So the first thing: he denies God.

The second thing: he denies *moksha*, paradise, heaven. He says, "Your heaven, your paradise, are nothing but your unfulfilled sexual desires, unfulfilled instincts, being projected into the other life, the life beyond, the life after death." And he seems to be absolutely true.

If you see the depiction, the description of heaven and paradise in Islam, in Christianity, in Judaism, you will understand perfectly what he is saying. Whatsoever remains unfulfilled here you project in the hereafter. But the desire seems to be the same.

Hindus say there are trees they call *kalpa-vriksha* — you sit under them and whatsoever you desire is fulfilled without any lapse of time. You desire a beautiful woman, she is there immediately, instantly. Just now in the West instant coffee and things like that have been invented. Down the centuries India has believed in a wish-fulfilling tree that is instantly fulfilling, really instantly without any time lapse. Here the idea arises, there it is fulfilled; not even a single second passes between the two. The idea is its fulfillment. You desire a beautiful woman, she is there. You desire delicious food, it is there. You desire a beautiful bed to rest on, it is there.

Now, it is simple psychological analysis that man is unfulfilled in life. And he goes on, his whole life trying to fulfill it, still he finds it cannot be fulfilled so he has to project in the future. Not that in the future it can be fulfilled; desire as such is not fulfillable.

Buddha has said, "The very nature of desire is that it remains unfulfilled." Whatsoever you do, regardless of what you do about it, it remains unfulfilled – that is the very intrinsic nature of desire. Desire as such remains unfulfilled. So you can sit under a wish-fulfilling tree, and it doesn't make any difference. You can feel many times it is being fulfilled, and again it arises. Ad infinitum it will go on arising again and again and again.

The Christian, the Muslim, the Jewish, the Hindu, all heavens and paradises are nothing but unfulfilled projected desires, repressed desires, frustrated desires. Of course, they console man very much: "If you have not been able to fulfill here, then there. Sooner or later you will reach to God; the only thing you have to do is go on praying to him, go on bowing down before some image or some idea or some ideal, and keep him happy, keep God happy, and then you are going to reap a great crop of pleasures and gratifications. That will be his gift to you for your prayers, for your appreciation, for continuous surrender, for again and again touching his feet, for your obedience. That is going to be your reward."

The reward is, of course, after death, because even cunning priests cannot deceive you in this life. Even they cannot deceive; they know desire remains unfulfilled, so they have to invent an afterlife. Nobody has known the afterlife; people can be deceived very easily.

If somebody comes and says to you, "God can fulfill your desire here and now," it will be difficult to prove it because nobody's desire has ever been fulfilled herenow. Then their God will be at stake. They have tried a very cunning device; they say, "After this life." Isn't your God potent enough to fulfill here? Isn't your God potent enough to create wish-fulfillment trees on the earth? Isn't your God powerful enough to do something while people are alive? If he cannot fulfill here, what is the proof that he is going to fulfill hereafter?

Buddha says, "Look into the nature of desire." Watch the movement of desire – it is very subtle – and you will be able to see two things: one, that desire by its very nature is unfulfillable; and second, the moment you understand that desire is unfulfillable, desire disappears and you are left desireless. That is the state of peace, silence, tranquility. That is the state of fulfillment. Man never comes to fulfillment through desire; man comes to fulfillment only by transcending desire.

Desire is an opportunity to understand. Desire is a great opportunity to understand the functioning of your own mind – how it functions, what the mechanism of it is. When you have understood that in that very understanding is transformation. Desire disappears, leaving no trace behind. And when you are desireless, not desiring anything, you are fulfilled. Not that desire is fulfilled, but when desire is transcended there is fulfillment.

Now see the difference: other religions say, "Desires can be fulfilled in the other world." The worldly people say, "Desires can be fulfilled here"; the Communists say, "Desires can be fulfilled here. Just a different social structure is needed, just the capitalists have to be thrown out, the proletariat has to take over, the bourgeoisie has to be destroyed, that's all, and desires can be fulfilled here, heaven can be created on this earth here."

The worldly people say, "You can fulfill your desires if you struggle hard." That's what the whole West goes on doing: "Struggle, compete, cheat, by any means and methods. Acquire more wealth, more power." That's what the politicians all over the world go on doing: "Become more powerful and your desires can be fulfilled." Scientists say that only a few more technologies have to be invented and paradise is just around the corner. And what do your religions say? They don't say anything different. They say, "Desires can be fulfilled, but not in this life – after death." That is the only difference between the so-called materialists and so-called spiritualists.

To Buddha, both are materialists; and to me also, both are materialists. Your so-called religious people and your so-called irreligious people are both in the same boat. Not a bit of difference. Their attitudes are the same, their approaches are the same.

Buddha is really religious in this way when he says, "Desire cannot be fulfilled." You have to look into desire. Neither here nor anywhere else has desire ever been fulfilled, never. It has never happened and it is never going to happen because it is against the nature of desire.

What is desire? Have you looked into your desiring mind ever? Have you encountered it? Have you tried any meditation on it? What is desire?

You desire a certain house; you work for it, you work hard. You destroy your whole life for it, and then the house is yours. But is fulfillment there? Once the house is yours, suddenly you feel very empty, more empty than before, because before there was an occupation to achieve this house. Now it is yours. Immediately your mind starts looking for something else to get occupied with. Now there are bigger houses; your mind starts thinking of those bigger houses. There are bigger palaces... You desire a woman and you have achieved your desire, then suddenly your hands are again empty. Again you start desiring some other woman.

This is the nature of desire. Desire always goes ahead of you. Desire is always in the future. Desire is a hope. Desire cannot be fulfilled because its very nature is to remain unfulfilled and projected into the future. It is always on the horizon.

You can rush, you can run toward the horizon, but you will never reach: wherever you reach you will find the horizon has receded, and the distance between you and the horizon remains absolutely the same. You have ten thousand rupees, the desire is for twenty thousand rupees; you have twenty thousand rupees, the desire is for forty thousand rupees. The distance is the same; the mathematical proportion is the same. Whatsoever you have, desire always goes ahead of it.

Buddha says, "Abandon hope, abandon desire." In abandoning hope, in abandoning desire, you will be herenow. Without desire you will be fulfilled. It is desire that is deceiving you.

So when Buddha said that these so-called religious people are all materialists, of course Hindus were very, very angry; they had never been so angry against anybody. They tried to uproot

Buddha's religion from India, and they succeeded. Buddhism was born in India, but Buddhism no longer exists in India because the religion of the Hindus is one of the most materialistic religions in the world.

Just look in the Vedas: all prayer, all worship is just asking for more, for more from gods or from God – all sacrifice is for more. All worship is desire-oriented. "Give us more. Give us plenty. Better crops, better rain, more money, more health, more life, more longevity, give us more." The whole Veda is nothing but desire written large, and sometimes very ugly. In the Veda not only do the so-called *rishis* go on praying "Give us more," they also pray, "Don't give to our enemies. Give more milk to my cow, but let the enemy's cow die or let its milk disappear."

What type of religion is this? Even to call it religion looks absurd. If this is religion, then what is materialism? Even so-called ascetic people who have renounced the world... There were many in the days of Buddha. He himself had gone to many masters while he was searching, but from everywhere he came back empty-handed because he could not see that anybody had really understood the nature of desire. They themselves were desiring; of course, their desire was projected in the faraway future, the other life, but still the object of desire was the same, the desiring mind was the same. It is only a question of time.

A few people desire before death, a few people desire after death, but what is the difference? There is no difference. They desire the same things – *they desire*. The desire is the same.

Buddha went to many teachers and was frustrated. He could not see religion flowering anywhere, blossoming. They were all materialistic people. They were great ascetics: somebody was fasting for months, somebody was standing for months, somebody had not slept for years, they were just skeletons. You could not call them worldly and materialistic if you looked at their bodies; but look at their mind, ask them, "Why are you fasting? Why are you trying so hard? For what?" and there arises the desire to attain to paradise, to heaven, to have eternal gratification in the afterlife.

Listen to their logic and they all will say, "Here things are fleeting. This life is temporary. Even if you attain, everything is taken away when you die, so what is the point? This life is not going to be forever. We are searching for something which will remain forever. We are after immortality, we are after absolute gratification. People who are running after desire here, in this life, are fools because death will take everything away. You accumulate wealth, and here comes death and all is left behind. We are searching for some treasure which we can take with ourselves, which will never be lost, which cannot be stolen, no government can tax it, and nobody can take it away, not even death."

You call these people religious people? They seem to be even worldlier than the so-called worldly; they are more materialistic than the materialists. Of course, their materialism is garbed in a disguise; their materialism has a flavor of spiritualism, but it is a deception. It is as if on a dung heap you have thrown some beautiful perfume. The dung heap remains the dung heap; the perfume can only deceive fools.

Buddha was not fooled, he could see through and through. And he could always see that the desire is there. If desire is there you are a materialist and you are worldly.

So he is not preaching any paradise to you, he does not believe in any paradise. It is not that he does not believe in blissfulness, no, he believes in blissfulness, but that is not a belief: when all paradises are lost, when all desires drop, suddenly it is your innermost nature to be blissful. For it, nothing is needed: no virtue is needed, no asceticism is needed, no sacrifice is needed. Just understanding is enough.

The way of the Buddha is the way of understanding.

And the third thing before we enter into the sutras: He does not believe in the soul – no God, no paradise, no soul. Now, this seems to be very difficult.

We can accept there is no God, maybe it is just a projection; who has seen it? We can accept there is no paradise, maybe it is just our unfulfilled desire dreaming about it. But no soul? Then you take the whole ground from underneath. No soul? Then what is the point of it all? If there is no soul in man, if there is nothing immortal in man, then why make so much effort? Why meditate? For what?

Buddha says that this idea of the self is a misunderstanding. You are, but you are not a self. You are, but you are not separate from the universe. The separation is the root idea in the concept of self: if I am separate from you then I have a self; if you are separate from me then you have a self.

But Buddha says, "Existence is one." There are no boundaries. Nobody is separate from anybody else. We live in one ocean of consciousness. We are one consciousness deluded by the boundaries of the body, deluded by the boundaries of the mind. And because of the body and the mind, and because of the identification with the body and mind, we think we are separate, we think we are selves. This is how we create the ego.

It is just like on the map you see India, but on the earth itself there is no India. It is only on the map of the politicians. On the map you see the American continent, the African continent as separate, but deep down, down under the oceans, the earth is one. All continents are together, they are all one earth.

We are separate only on the surface. The deeper we go, the more separation disappears. When we come to the very core of our being suddenly it is universal, there is no selfhood in it, no soul there.

Buddha has no belief in God, in soul, in *moksha*. Then what is his teaching? His teaching is a way of life, not a way of belief. His teaching is very scientific, very empirical, very practical. He is not a philosopher, not a metaphysician. He is a very down-to-earth man.

Buddha says, "You can change your life – these beliefs are not needed." In fact, these beliefs are the barriers for the real change. Start with no belief, start with no metaphysics, start with no dogma. Start absolutely naked and nude, with no theology, no ideology. Start empty. That is the only way to come to truth.

I was reading an anecdote:

A traveling salesman opened the Gideon Bible in his motel room. On the front page he read the inscription: "If you are sick, read Psalm 18; if you are troubled about your family, read Psalm 45; if you are lonely, read Psalm 92."

He was lonely, so he opened to Psalm 92 and read it. When he was through, he noticed on the bottom of the page the handwritten words: "If you are still lonely call 888-3468 and ask for Myrtle."

If you look deep down into your scriptures you will always find a footnote which will be truer. Look for the footnote on every scripture page. Sometimes it may not be written in visible ink, but if you search hard you will always find there is a footnote which is more real.

Buddha says that all your scriptures are nothing but your desires, your instincts, your greed, your lust, your anger. All your scriptures are nothing but creations of your mind. It is bound to be so, that they will carry all the seeds of your mind. Scriptures are man-made. That's why religions try hard to prove that their scripture at least is not man-made.

Christians say the Bible is not man-made; the Ten Commandments were delivered to Moses directly from God, directly from the boss himself. The New Testament is a direct message from his own son, the only begotten son, Jesus Christ. It has nothing to do with humanity; it comes from above. Hindus say the Vedas are not man-made, they are God-made. And the same story goes on being repeated: Mohammedans say the Koran descended on Mohammed from heaven above.

Why do these religions insist this about their scriptures, and only their scriptures, not anybody else's? Mohammedans are not ready to accept that the Vedas are God-made, neither are Hindus ready to accept that the Koran is God-made; only their Vedas are God-made and everything else is just manufactured by man. Why this insistence? Because they are aware that whatsoever man will create will have the imprint of man's mind and man's desires.

Buddha says that all the scriptures are man-made, and it is true. He is not a fanatic at all. He does not belong to any country and he does not belong to any race; he does not belong to any religion, to any sect. He is simply a light unto himself. And whatsoever he has said is the purest statement of truth ever made.

I was reading this beautiful anecdote which Paritosh has sent me:

One of the religious leaders in Ireland was asked by his followers to select a suitable burial place and monument for his mortal remains. A "religious" war was in progress and his life had been threatened.

Three separate plans had been submitted to him, and to the

dismay of the committee he chose the least expensive.

He was asked why he had made this selection, why he had chosen this humble resting-place, when the other two designs were of magnificent tombs.

"Well, my dear friends," he told them, "I appreciate your generosity. But is it worth all this expense when I don't expect to remain in my tomb for more than three days?"

Now, this sort of stupidity you will never find in Buddha. This sort of dogmatic certainty you will never find in Buddha. He is very hesitant. There is only one other who is also so hesitant and he is Lao Tzu; these two persons are very hesitant.

Sometimes, because of their hesitance, you may not be impressed by them. Because you are confused, you need somebody to be so confident that you can rely on him. Hence, fanatics impress you very much. They may not have anything to say, but they beat the table so much, they make such a fuss about it, and their very fuss gives you a feeling that they must be knowing, otherwise how can they be so certain? The witnesses of Jehovah and people like that – stupid people, but they are so dogmatic in their assertions that they create a feeling of certainty. And confused people need certainty.

When you come to a buddha, you may not be immediately impressed because he will be so hesitant, he will not assert anything. He knows better than that: he knows that life cannot be confined to any statement, and all statements are partial. No statement can contain the whole truth, so how can you be certain about it? He will remain always relative.

Buddha and Mahavira, two great masters of India, were both very deep in relativity. Einstein discovered it very late; Einstein brought relativity to the world of science. Before Einstein, scientists were very certain, dogmatically certain, absolutely certain. Einstein in addition to bringing relativity also brought humbleness and truth to science.

The same was done by Buddha and Mahavira in India: they brought relativity, the concept that truth cannot be asserted totally, that we can never be certain about it, that at the most we can hint at it. The hint has to be indirect; we cannot pinpoint it directly – it is so big, so vast. And it is natural that we fragile human beings should hesitate. This hesitation shows alertness.

You will always find stupid, ignorant people to be very dogmatic. The more ignorant a person is, the more dogmatic. It is one of the greatest misfortunes in the world that the foolish are absolutely certain, and the wise are hesitant. Buddha is very hesitant. So if you really want to understand him you will have to be very alert in your listening, very open. He is not delivering truths to you wholesale. He is simply hinting, giving indications at the most, and they too are very subtle.

As I told you, Buddha is very down-to-earth. He never flies high into metaphysics. In fact, he never introduces; he has no preface to his statements. He simply says them directly, immediately, as simply as possible. Sometimes his statements may not look to be of any profound depth. They are, but he does not beat around the bush, he does not make any fuss about it.

I have heard...

She was a sweet young thing; he was a fast-rising account executive with the well-known Madison Avenue advertising agency, Bittner, Berman, Dirstein and Osman. Everyone thought it was an ideal marriage. But alas, there was a problem with sex. The honeymoon hadn't even begun.

"B-b-eing an advertising man," she sobbed to a friend, "all he does every night is sit on the edge of the bed and tell me how wonderful it's going to be."

But it never happens! You can understand about an advertising man: he simply goes on saying how wonderful it is going to be.

Buddha has no preface. He never advertises what he is going to say. He simply says it and moves ahead.

> *The Buddha said:*
> *Moved by their selfish desires, people seek after fame and glory. But when they have acquired it, they are already stricken in years. If you hanker after worldly fame and practice not the way, your labors are wrongfully applied and your energy is wasted. It is like unto burning an*

> *incense stick. However much its pleasing odor be admired, the fire that consumes is steadily burning up the stick.*

A very simple and matter-of-fact statement. *Moved by their selfish desires, people seek after fame and glory.* What is a selfish desire? In the Buddhist way of expression, a selfish desire is one that is based in the self. Ordinarily, in ordinary language, we call a desire selfish if it is against somebody else, and you don't care about others. Even if it harms others, you go ahead and you fulfill your desire. People call you selfish because you don't care about others, you don't have any consideration for others.

But when Buddha says that a desire is selfish, his meaning is totally different. He says: "If a desire is based in the idea of self then it is selfish."

For example: nobody will call it a selfish desire if you donate a million rupees for some good cause: hospitals to be made or schools to be opened, or food to be distributed to the poor, or medicine to be sent to poor parts of the country. Buddha will say it is, if there is any motivation of self. If you are thinking that by donating a million rupees you are going to earn some virtue and you are going to be rewarded in heaven, it is a selfish desire. It may not be harmful to others – it is not – in fact, everybody will appreciate it. People will call you a great man, religious, virtuous, a great man of charity, love, compassion, sympathy. But Buddha will say the only thing that determines whether a desire is selfish or not is motivation.

If you have donated without any motivation, then it is not selfish. If there is any motivation hidden somewhere – conscious, unconscious – that you are going to gain something out of it, here or hereafter, then it is a selfish desire. That which comes out of the self is a selfish desire; that which comes as part of the ego is a selfish desire. If you meditate just to attain to your selfhood, then it is a selfish desire.

Buddha has said to his disciples: Whenever you meditate, after each meditation, surrender all that you have earned out of meditation, surrender it to the universe. If you are blissful, pour it back into the universe, don't carry it as a treasure. If you are feeling very happy, share it immediately, don't become attached to it, otherwise your meditation itself will become a new process of the self. And the ultimate meditation is not a process of self. The ultimate meditation is a process of getting more and more into un-self, into non-self; it is a disappearance of the self. *Moved by their selfish desires, people seek after fame and glory. But when they have acquired it, they are already stricken in years.*

Buddha says that you can attain to fame, to glory, to power, to prestige, respectability in the world, but what are you doing? Are you aware? You are wasting a great opportunity – for something absolutely meaningless. You are collecting rubbish and destroying your own life and life-energy. *If you hanker after worldly fame and practice not the way...*

Buddha always calls his religion "the way" – *dhamma* – just the way, because he says, "Don't be bothered about the goal; the goal will take care of itself." You simply follow the way, not even with the motivation to reach any goal, but just out of the sheer delight of meditating, of praying, of loving, of being compassionate, of sharing. Out of sheer delight you practice the way. Not that you are going to gain any profit out of it; don't make it a business. Ordinarily the mind is a businessman...

I have heard...

The old father was dying and his family was gathered around the bed waiting for him to take his last breath. As the old man wheezed away life, his oldest son said to one and all, "When Papa goes, if it's tonight, we can bury him early tomorrow from the big funeral parlor downtown. Since the funeral will be early in the morning, we won't be able to get in touch with too many people so we won't need a lot of cars or the big room, and it won't cost too much."

His daughter was standing there and she said to the brother, "You know, death to me is a very personal thing. Why do we have to call a bunch of strangers together to witness such a sad scene – if you two boys are there and I'm there, who needs anyone else?"

The youngest son looked at them both and said, "I couldn't agree with you more. In fact, why do we need the expense of taking Papa to an undertaker? He is dying in the house, let's bury him from the house."

All of a sudden the old man's eyes flew wide open. He looked at his three children and shouted, "Give me my pants!"

They answered in a chorus, "Papa, you are a very sick man. Where do you want to go?"

He replied, "Give me my pants. I'll walk to the cemetery — I am a businessman."

Their whole life people simply go on saving, saving, and for what? Life is slipping by; each moment a precious moment is gone and it cannot be reclaimed. Buddha says, "Don't waste it in foolish things."

Fame is foolish, it is pointless, meaningless. Even if the whole world knows you, how does it enrich you? How does it make your life more blissful? How does it help you to be more understanding? To be more aware? To be more alert? To be more alive?

If you are not practicing the way ...your labors are wrongfully applied and your energy is wasted. It is like unto burning an incense stick. However much its pleasing odor be admired, the fire that consumes is steadily burning up the stick.

That's how life is: each moment burning. You are always on the funeral pyre because each moment death is coming closer, each moment you are less alive, more dead. So before this whole opportunity is lost, Buddha says: "Attain to a state of no-self — then there will be no death." And then there will be no misery. And then there will be no constant hankering for fame, power, prestige.

In fact, the emptier you are within, the more you seek fame; it is a sort of substitute. The poorer you are within, the more you seek riches; it is a substitute to somehow stuff yourself with something.

I observe every day: people come to me, and whenever they have a problem with their love, they immediately start eating too much. Whenever they feel that their love is in a crisis, they are not being loved, or they are not able to love, something has blocked their love-energy, they immediately start stuffing themselves with things, they go on eating. Why? What are they doing with the food? They feel empty, and that emptiness makes them afraid. They have to somehow stuff it with food.

If you are feeling happy inside you don't bother about fame; only unhappy people bother about fame. Who bothers whether anybody knows you or not if you know yourself? If you yourself know who you are, then there is no need. But when you don't know who you are, you would like everybody to know who you are. You will collect opinions, you will collect people's ideas, and out of that collection you will try to arrange some identity: "Yes, I am this man. People say, 'You are very intelligent' – so I must be intelligent." You are not certain. If you were certain, who bothers what people say?

You go on looking into people's eyes to see your face because you don't know your face. You beg: "Say something about me. Say, 'you are beautiful.' Say, 'you are lovely.' Say, 'you are charismatic.' Say something about me." Have you seen yourself begging: "Say something about my body, about my mind, about my understanding – say something!"

You immediately grab if somebody says something. And if somebody says something which is shocking and shattering, you become very angry. He is destroying your image if he says something against you. If he says something in favor of you, he helps your image to be a little more decorated, it becomes a little more ornamental, you come home happy. If people applaud you, you feel happy. Why?

You don't know who you are. That's why you go on seeking. You go on asking people "Who am I? Tell me." And you have to depend on them. The beauty of it is, or the irony of it is, that those same people don't know who they are. Beggars begging from other beggars. They have come to beg from you, so there is a mutual deception.

You come across a woman; you say, "How beautiful. How divine." And she says, "Yes, and I have never come across such a beautiful man as you." This is a mutual deception. You may call it love – this is a mutual deception. Both are hankering for a certain identity about themselves. Both fulfill each other's desires. Things will go well until one day one of the two decides that enough is enough and starts dropping the deception. Then the honeymoon is over, and marriage starts. Then things go ugly. Then you think "This woman deceived me" or "This man deceived me." Nobody can deceive you unless you are ready to be deceived, remember. Nobody has ever deceived anybody unless you are ready to be deceived, unless you were waiting to be deceived.

You cannot deceive a person who knows himself, because there is no way. If you say something he will laugh. He will say, "Don't be worried about it, I already know myself who I am. You can drop that subject and go ahead with whatsoever you have to say. Don't be bothered about me – I know myself, who I am."

Once you have an inner richness of life, you don't seek wealth, you don't seek power.

Psychologists have become aware that when people start becoming impotent, they start finding some sexual, phallic symbols. If a person becomes impotent then he wants some phallic symbol to replace it. He may try to have the biggest car in the world – that is a phallic symbol. He would like to have the most powerful car in the world now his own power is lost, his own sexual energy is gone, so now he would like a substitute. While rushing his car to the maximum speed he will feel good, as if he is making love to his woman. The very speed will give him power. He will get identified with the car.

For many years psychologists have been watching the phenomenon that people who have a certain inferiority complex always become ambitious. In fact, nobody goes into politics unless he is deeply rooted in an inferiority complex. Politicians are basically inferiority complex people. They have to prove their superiority in some way, otherwise they will not be able to live with their inferiority complex.

What I am trying to point out is: whatsoever you miss within, you try to accumulate something outside as a substitute for it. If you don't miss your life within, you are enough unto yourself. And only then are you beautiful. And only then you are.

> *The Buddha said:*
> *People cleave to their worldly possessions and selfish*
> *passions so blindly as to sacrifice their own lives for them.*
> *They are like a child who tries to eat a little honey*
> *smeared on the edge of a knife. The amount is by no*
> *means sufficient to appease his appetite, but he runs the*
> *risk of wounding his tongue.*

Nothing is enough in this life to fulfill your desires, to fulfill your appetite. This world is a dreamworld, nothing can fulfill because only reality can be fulfilling.

Have you watched? You feel hungry in the night and in a dream you go to the fridge and open it and eat to your heart's desire. Of course, it helps in a way. It does not disturb your sleep, otherwise the hunger will not allow you to sleep, you will have to wake up. The dream creates a substitute; you continue to sleep, you feel "I have eaten enough." You have deceived your body.

The dream is a deceiver. In the morning you will be surprised that you are still hungry because a feast in the dream is equivalent to a fast. Feast or fast, both are the same in a dream because a dream is unreal. It cannot fulfill. To quench real thirst, real water is needed. To fulfill, a real life reality is needed.

Buddha says, "You go on taking the risk of wounding yourself, but no fulfillment comes out of this life." Maybe here and there you have a taste of honey – sweet, but very dangerous, unfulfilling. And the honey is smeared on the edge of a knife; there is every danger you will wound your tongue.

Look at old people: you will not find anything but wounds; their whole being is nothing but wounds: ulcers and ulcers and ulcers. When a person dies you don't see blossoming flowers in his being; you simply see stinking wounds.

If a person has really lived and not been deceived by his dreams and illusory desires, the older he grows the more beautiful he becomes. In his death he is superb.

Sometimes you may come across an old man whose old age is more beautiful than his youth ever was. Then bow down before that old man – he has lived a true life, a life of inwardness, a life of "interiorness." Because if life is lived truly, then you go on becoming more and more beautiful and a grandeur starts coming to you, a grace; something of the unknown starts abiding in your surroundings. You become the abode of the infinite, of the eternal. It has to be so because life is an evolution.

If when you are no longer young and you become ugly, that simply means in your youth you tasted honey on too many knives – you have become wounded. Now you will suffer these cancerous wounds. Old age becomes a great suffering. And death is very rarely beautiful, because very rarely have people really lived.

If a person has really lived – like a flame burning from both ends – then his death will be a tremendous phenomenon, an utter beauty. When he is dying you will see his life aglow at the maximum, at the optimum. In the last moment he will become such a flame; his whole life will become a concentrated perfume in that moment, a great luminosity will arise in his being. Before he leaves, he will leave behind him a memory.

That's what happened when Buddha left the world. That's what happened when Mahavira left the world. We have not forgotten them, not because they were great politicians or great people of power – they were nobodies, but we cannot forget them. It is impossible to forget them. They had not done anything as far as history is concerned. We can almost omit them from history, we can neglect them from history, nothing will be lost. In fact, they never existed in the main current of history, they were by the side of it, but it is impossible to forget them. Their very last moment has left such a glory to humanity. Their last glow has shown us our own possibilities, our infinite potentialities.

> *The Buddha said:*
> *Men are tied up to their families and possessions more helplessly than in a prison. There is an occasion for the prisoner to be released, but householders entertain no desire to be relieved from the ties of family. When a man's passion is aroused nothing prevents him from ruining himself. Even into the maws of a tiger will he jump. Those who are thus drowned in the filth of passion are called the ignorant. Those who are able to overcome it are saintly arhats.*

Buddha says: "Those who are lost into the filth of passion and never transcend it, those who never transcend as the lotus transcends the mud it is born into, they are the ignorant people, the worldly people. Those who transcend lust and desire, those who understand the futility of desire, and those who become understanding about the whole nonsense that the mind creates and the dreams that it manufactures, they are the great arhats."

Arhat, the very word means "one who has overcome his

enemies." Buddha says that desire, desiring, is your enemy. Once you have overcome your desire, you have overcome your enemy, you have become an arhat. Arhat is the goal: to become desireless because only when you are desireless is there benediction.

Our so-called religions are based in fear. Buddha's religion is based in an inner benediction. We worship God because we are afraid, because we don't know what to do with our lives. We are continuously trembling, scared, death is coming and we don't know what to do, how to protect ourselves. We need a protector. It is out of fear. Buddha's religion is based in an inner benediction, in an inner blessing; it has nothing to do with fear.

Let me tell you one anecdote:

Henry went on his first hunting trip. When he got back to his office his partner Morris couldn't wait to hear all about his trip. Henry told him, "Well, I went into the woods with the guide. You know me, two minutes in the woods, I get lost. I'm walking extra quiet, when all of a sudden the biggest bear you ever did see is standing right in front of me. I turn around and run just as fast as I can and that bear is running even faster. Just when I feel his hot breath on my neck, he slipped and fell. I jumped over a brook and kept running, but I was losing my breath and sure enough there was that bear getting close to me again. He was almost on top of me when he slipped again and fell. I kept on running and finally I found myself in the clearing of the woods. The bear was running as fast as he could and I knew I didn't stand a chance. I saw the other hunters and shouted for help, and just then the bear slipped and fell again. My guide was able to take aim and he shot the bear and killed him."

Morris said, "Henry, that was quite a story. You are a very brave man. If that would have happened to me, I would have made in my pants."

Henry looked at him and shrugged, "Morris, what do you think the bear was slipping on?"

The so-called religions come just out of fear. And anything based on fear can never be beautiful. Your gods, your churches, your temples, if they have come out of your fear they stink; they are bound to stink of your fear.

Buddha's religion is not based in fear at all. That's why he says the first step is to drop all beliefs. Those beliefs are because of the fear. Dropping the beliefs you will become aware of your fear, and that is good, to become aware of your fear. You will become aware of your death. You will become aware of this whole infinite cosmos – nowhere to go, nobody to guide, nowhere to find any security. In that fear, in that awareness of fear, the only place left will be to start going withinward because there is no point in going anywhere. It is so vast.

The interior journey starts when you have dropped all beliefs and you have become aware of the fear, death, desire. And once you are in, suddenly you see fears are disappearing; because in the deepest core of your being there has never been any death, there cannot be. Your innermost core is absolutely a non-self.

A self can die. The no-self cannot die. If there is something, it can be destroyed. That's why Buddha says that there is nothing inside you; you are a pure nothing. That nothing cannot be destroyed. And once you have understood it, that death cannot destroy, that this nothingness is in itself so beautiful, there is no need to go on stuffing it with money, power, prestige, fame. This nothingness is so pure and so innocent and so beautiful that you are blessed in it. You start dancing in that nothingness. That nothingness starts a dance. Buddha hints you toward that dance.

When Buddha was dying, Ananda started crying and he said, "What will I do now? You are leaving and I have not yet become enlightened."

Buddha said, "Don't cry, because I cannot make you enlightened, only you can do that miracle to yourself. Be a light unto yourself – *appa deepo bhava.*"

Buddha throws humanity into the interiormost core. Buddha says: "Go within, and there is nowhere else to go. You are the shrine. Go within." And there is no other God anywhere to worship. The more you move inward, the more a worshipping consciousness will arise. Without any object for worship; a prayer will arise, not addressed to anybody. A pure prayer, out of bliss, out of being, out of inner benediction.

Enough for today.

2

ALONENESS IS YOUR REALITY

The first question:

> Osho,
> Your lecture yesterday was ruthless, sharp and
> shattering. I felt throughout the lecture that a deep
> surgical operation was happening within my psyche.
> What is this, Osho? Along with the verbal talk what
> else do you transmit to the listener?

The word, the verbal, has nothing to do with transferring anything to you. The verbal is just a toy, so you can play with it. When you are absorbed with the words I have an opportunity to do something to your being; otherwise you won't allow me.

So whatsoever I am saying is just to keep you engaged. Once your mind is engaged with the words you are available to me, your heart is available to me. When the mind is not engaged it functions like a barrier, and the heart becomes unavailable.

So the real work is not through the words; the real work is

through the presence. If you stop thinking and you can put aside your mind, then there is no need for me to talk at all, then silence will do because that which is going to happen is going to happen through silence. It is going to happen not through any verbal communication, it is going to happen on a deeper level than words can reach, on a deeper level of your being where mind has nothing to say.

The mind is only the surface, the circumference of your being. It is not your center. But the circumference has become too strong. It surrounds you like a hard crust, it has become your prison. You need something so intriguing, so interesting, that your mind gets totally absorbed in it.

And sometimes I will be shattering – I have to be. Sometimes I have to be merciless because that is the only way to help you, the only way to destroy you, annihilate you, and give you an opportunity to be reborn. As you are you have to disappear. As you are you have to die, only then can the new arise out of you. The ego has to disappear for your real being to be. The mind has to cease for godliness to be. The known has to be dropped for the unknown to be welcomed.

Sometimes I am persuasive. Sometimes I am shattering. Sometimes through affection and love I try to seduce you to drop the mind. Sometimes I hammer hard on it. I change like the climate around the year. You have to be with me in all the climates, only then will you be able to know me. You have to be with me in all of my forms, only then will you be able to see the formless.

Once I have accepted you as my disciple it is my responsibility that you should be transformed. If you allow me easily, then the operation is very easy. If you don't allow me easily, if you struggle, resist, don't cooperate, you create conflict, then the operation is still going to happen, but then it will be hard. The hardness will come because of your resistance, remember it. I have to be shattering sometimes only because you resist too much.

Let me tell you one anecdote:

Joe Levy went to a leading mountain resort for a week's vacation. That night, when he ordered dinner, the waiter told him that he highly recommended the chicken soup. Joe replied, "I hate soup. I never eat soup. I couldn't care less." He ate his dinner, played cards, and retired to his room early and fell asleep.

In the middle of the night, the man in the room below his took sick suddenly and the house doctor recommended that they get a nurse and give an enema. The nurse arrived and in error entered Joe Levy's room, and before he even realized what was happening to him, gave him the enema and left.

When he got back to New York, his friends asked him how he had liked the hotel. He said, "It was very nice, but if you ever go there and the waiter suggests that you eat soup, eat it, otherwise they shove it into you anyway."

So please cooperate with me...

The second question:

Osho,
You tell us so many jokes – what is the basic secret of
a joke and why do you tell them?

I have to tell jokes to you, otherwise you will fall asleep. A joke shocks you back into awareness. It is a small electric shock. That's the beauty of a joke, and that's the secret of a joke. It is impossible even for the dullest mind not to remain alert when a joke is being told. Even the dullest, the most stupid, will become interested, even one who is snoring will come out of his snoring and will start listening to what is going on.

That's the beauty of a joke. A joke is something that brings a subtle awareness in you. The awareness comes because you have to listen to the joke very alertly otherwise you will miss the punch line. If you miss a single word in a joke, it is lost. A joke is a very small thing – a few lines. You cannot afford to be unaware. If you miss one line, you will not be able to catch hold of it.

A joke takes a sudden turn – that is its secret – a very unexpected turn. A joke is not logical, that's why I love jokes. They are illogical, still, they have a logic of their own. A joke is illogical and yet logical – very paradoxical. A joke takes such an illogical turn that you could never have expected. If you can expect, then that much pleasure will be lost.

If a joke is a simple syllogism, an Aristotelian syllogism, that you can simply go on and you can feel what conclusion is coming, and you can conclude because the premises are given already; if you can conclude logically, as if two plus two is four, this cannot be a joke because two plus two is four. When somebody is saying "two plus two" you have already known the conclusion: it is going to be four. If a joke is absolutely logical and the conclusion is not absurd, then it is not a joke, and it will not shock you into awareness.

The joke takes a very unexpected turn. Yet, when you have listened to the punch line, you suddenly realize that there is a logic in it – not Aristotelian, non-Aristotelian. When you have heard the punch line, then you suddenly recognize, yes, everything becomes clear. If a joke is absolutely absurd, then too it will be meaningless, because then the conclusion will not be in continuity with the whole story; then there will be discontinuity and you will not be able to know how to connect them.

The joke has not to be absolutely logical, the joke has not to be absolutely illogical, it has to be somewhere in the middle, very ambiguous, vague, surrounded by mist. You cannot figure out where it is going, and that's why it becomes intriguing. And it takes the turn so suddenly that in a single line it is there in its totality.

Let me tell you one joke:

A Jewish synagogue was collecting money for a new building for the synagogue as the old one was rotten and falling apart. They were doing everything that can be done to collect more money.

They had sold lottery tickets, and then the lottery was opened and the president of the community declared the third prize: it was a beautiful TV set, and the man who got it was very happy.

Then he declared the second prize – of course, the man whose name was declared was hoping for something like a Cadillac, Impala, Mercedes, something like that. But when he came the president gave him a small box. He immediately opened it as he was very puzzled as to what was there in the box. And there was nothing much: chocolates, cookies. He said, "What is this? You must have forgotten, you must have misplaced something. For the third prize you have given a TV set, and second prize, just cookies? This is nonsense!"

The president said, "You don't understand: the rabbi's wife herself has prepared it for you."

The man was annoyed. He said, "Screw the rabbi's wife!"

The president said, "That's the first prize."

Now this is a joke. You cannot expect, it is impossible, but once it is there then everything becomes clear. The conclusion makes the whole story clear. But if the conclusion has not been given to you, you will not be able to come to it logically.

Logic proceeds in steps, from the beginning to the end. A joke spreads backward, from the end to the beginning – that is the beauty of it. And it brings laughter, because when the story is going on you become tense, you want the conclusion immediately. You become very curious about it, what is going to happen. You start throbbing with energy. You become alert, more alert, more alive, and the energy is there; you cannot release it. It becomes a crescendo. Then comes the shattering punch line and the whole energy spreads all over your being. That's what laughter is.

I have to tell jokes, because the things that I am saying are so subtle, so deep and profound, that if I simply go on telling you those things, you will fall asleep and you will not be able to listen or to understand. You will remain almost deaf.

The profounder the truth I have to tell you, the worse the joke I choose for it. The highest the truth I am trying to relate, then the lowest I have to go in search for a joke. That's why I don't even bother about dirty jokes. Even a dirty joke can be helpful – more so because it can shock you to the very roots, to the very guts. And that's the whole point. It helps you to come again and again to your alertness. When I see you are alert, I again go relating that which I would like to relate to you. When I see again you are slipping into your sleep, I have to bring in a joke again.

If you really listen with alertness, there will be no need – I can say the truth directly. But it is difficult. You start yawning and it is better to laugh than to yawn.

The third question:

> Osho,
> I am going soon to the West. If I call you there, will your help be available to me as it has been available here?

Call me only when it is absolutely needed, when you find that now nothing can be done. First try to do all that you can do. And out of a hundred cases, ninety-nine you will not need to call me. And if you have not called me for ninety-nine cases – you have earned for the hundredth case – you can expect me in every possible way. But don't make it an everyday thing.

Let me tell you one anecdote, a true anecdote. It has already happened. And I say it is true because it comes to me from a very reliable source: Kamal has sent this story to me.

One day, Swami Arup Krishna, alias Chinani, and Sadar Gurudayal Singh were coming toward this place. It had rained for two, three days, and the roads were muddy and dirty water had collected everywhere and the gutters were overflowing. Gurudayal slipped on a banana peel. Not only that: a small coin fell from his pocket and was lost into the gutter.

He immediately cried, "Satya Sai Baba, Satya Sai Baba, help me!"

Of course, Arup Krishna was very surprised. He said, "Gurudayal, have you gone crazy? You are Osho's disciple!"

Gurudayal said, "What do you mean? Should I call Osho in this dirty water in the gutter?"

So remember it: whenever you really need, and it is not dirty water and a gutter, and not only a small coin is lost – then follow Gurudayal.

The fourth question:

> *Osho,*
> *Can the mind commit suicide?*

The mind cannot commit suicide, because whatsoever the mind can do will strengthen the mind. Any doing on the part of the mind makes the mind stronger. So suicide is impossible.

Mind doing something means mind continuing itself, so that is not in the nature of things. But suicide happens. Mind cannot commit it – let me make it absolutely clear: mind cannot commit it, but suicide happens. It happens through watching the mind, not by doing anything.

The watcher is separate from the mind, it is deeper than the mind, higher than the mind. The watcher is always hidden behind the mind. A thought passes, a feeling arises – who is watching this thought? Not the mind itself, because mind is nothing but the process of thought and feeling. The mind is just the traffic of thinking. Who is watching it? When you say, "An angry thought has arisen in me," who are "you"? In whom has the thought arisen? Who is the container? The thought is the content, who is the container?

The mind is like when you print a book: on white, clean paper, words appear. That empty paper is the container and the printed words are the content. Consciousness is like empty paper. Mind is like written, printed paper.

Whatsoever exists as an object inside you, whatsoever you can see and observe, is the mind. The observer is not the mind, the observed is the mind. So if you can go on simply observing, without condemning, without in any way creating a conflict with the mind, without indulging it, without following it, without going against it, if you can simply be there indifferent to it, in that indifference suicide happens. It is not that mind commits suicide: when the watcher arises, the witness is there – mind simply disappears.

Mind exists with your cooperation or your conflict. Both are ways of cooperating – conflict too. When you fight with the mind, you are giving energy to it. In your very fight you have accepted the mind, in your very fighting you have accepted the power of the mind over your being. So whether you cooperate or you conflict, in both the cases the mind becomes stronger and stronger.

Just watch. Just be a witness. And, by and by, you will see gaps arising. A thought passes, and another thought does not come immediately, there is an interval. In that interval is peace. In that interval is love. In that interval is all that you have always been seeking and never finding. In that gap you are no longer an ego. In that gap you are not defined, confined, imprisoned. In that gap you are vast, immense, huge. In that gap you are one with existence. The barrier no longer exists, your boundaries are gone. You melt into existence and the existence melts in you. You start overlapping.

If you go on watching and you don't get attached to these gaps either because that is natural now, to get attached to these gaps. If you start hankering for these gaps because they are tremendously beautiful, they are immensely blissful. It is natural to get attached to them, and desire arises to have more and more of these gaps; then you will miss, then your watcher has disappeared. Then those gaps will again disappear, and again the traffic of the mind will be there.

So the first thing is to become an indifferent watcher. The second thing is to remember that when beautiful gaps arise don't get attached to them, don't start asking for them, don't start waiting for them to happen more often. If you can remember these two things – when beautiful gaps come, watch them too, and keep your indifference alive – then one day the traffic simply disappears with the road, they both disappear. And there is tremendous emptiness.

That's what Buddha calls nirvana: the mind has ceased. This is what I call suicide, but mind has not committed it. Mind cannot commit it. You can help it to happen. You can hinder it, you can help it to happen – it depends on you, not on your mind. All that mind can do will always strengthen the mind.

So meditation is not really effort of the mind. Real meditation is not effort at all. Real meditation is just allowing the mind to have its own way and not interfering in any way whatsoever, just remaining watchful, witnessing. By and by, it becomes still and silent. One day it is gone. You are left alone.

That aloneness is what your reality is. In that aloneness nothing is excluded, remember it. In that aloneness everything is included – that aloneness is godliness. That purity, that innocence, uncorrupted by any thought, is what godliness is.

The fifth question:

> Osho,
> I hoo my guts out in the Dynamic, I laugh with you in the lecture, I dance for you in Nataraj, I cry and scream after Nadabrahma, I watch my tensions in Kundalini, and listen to the birds which come together specially for the meditations with music – they enjoy tremendously.
> I provide dinner for the mosquitoes in Gourishankar. In and between the meditations it seems I am doing all the groups at once. I feel very, very crazy. I know you love it – how can I love it too?

Then you are not very, very crazy; otherwise the question would never arise. When you are very, very crazy, you have already fallen in love with it.

A crazy person is one who is still resisting. A very, very crazy person is one who has surrendered to it. That's the only difference. A crazy person is one who feels that there is something which is going crazy but he is still fighting it, resisting it, repressing it, is still against it, not allowing it. If you do that, then one day you will really go crazy. And when I say "really go crazy," I mean it will not be a spiritual growth; it will be simply a fall.

If you go on repressing craziness... Everybody has craziness, because God himself is crazy. He never creates anybody without a certain streak of craziness in him. And the greater the person is, the more crazy, more eccentric. Buddha, Mahavira, Krishna, Christ are eccentric people. And psychologists are right in a way: they call them abnormal. They are abnormal because they are supernormal. They are abnormal because they are not the common lot.

If a Buddha walks on the earth, he is absolutely unique. No precedent, never has it happened before, and never is it going to happen again. He happens only once. He is unrepeatable, irreplaceable. He is a unique moment in the consciousness of humanity. Of course, eccentric, bound to be a little crazy. People will think that he has gone mad: he was the son of a king; he renounced the palace, his beautiful wife, all comforts and became a beggar. Does it seem normal?

The normal is just the reverse: a beggar wants to become an emperor. That is normal, every beggar wants to become an emperor. Everybody wants to become an emperor. Ambition is very ordinary. To become rich, to become famous, to become known to the world, to become very powerful is an ordinary phenomenon, nothing special in it. But an emperor getting down from his throne and moving like a beggar is eccentric, crazy, very, very crazy.

If you go on suppressing your craziness... Craziness is your uniqueness. Craziness is simply that element in you which cannot fit with anybody else in the world, which can never become part of the machinery of society, which can never be a cog in the wheel. That's what craziness is. Your individuality is your craziness.

Society does not want your individuality: it wants efficient mechanisms, robots. It does not want crazy people. It does not want Picassos, it does not want Buddhas, it does not want Wagners, Nietzsches, no. Once in a while they are good just for a change, but the world does not need too many of them. And they are very disturbing people, they shatter many ideals; they go on pulling humanity ruthlessly toward some unknown goal. They are never for the ordinary. Something extraordinary has to happen, only then can man feel at home. The usual and the ordinary and the common are futile, frustrating.

Society does not want them. Society can tolerate a few and that it has learned with much difficulty. Otherwise, why should Jesus be crucified? Society could not tolerate the man. He was risking not only his own life, he was risking other people's lives. He was opening some crazy door, not only for himself but for others also. Society was afraid.

Society wants people almost dead. Society only needs one requirement of living people and that is that they should be efficient. They should work hard, produce more, be obedient, good citizens, live comfortably, and die silently. They should not create any noise in the world. They should not even sing a song. They should not dance on the streets. They should simply live as if they never existed. They should live as numbers not as individuals. They should not assert their individuality in any way. They should not say "I am." They should be slaves. They should not be free people.

Society represses all sorts of individuality. And that repressed individuality, if it becomes too much, one day explodes, and then a person is crazy. This is my observation: that the crazy people who are confined in mental asylums are very sensitive people, more sensitive than the ordinary lot. They could not tolerate their inner individuality and it exploded. They tried hard, they forced it as deep as possible, but they were fragile people, sensitive people; they were not dull.

To be crazy, some intelligence is needed. To be just a part of the collective, no intelligence is needed; any stupid person can become a perfect citizen. In fact, the more stupid you are, the more obedient you will be, the less rebellious you will be. Always you will be ready to fall in line with any fool who comes to command. Anybody who shouts loudly, you will fall at his feet; he will become your leader.

But to be an individual you need intelligence, sharp consciousness, because it is very difficult to live an individual life. Surrounded by so many stupid people, surrounded by the crowd, surrounded by the dull and the dead, it is very difficult to remain alive, throbbing, streaming. Then you are very alone.

So those who are very sensitive... And now in the West, modern psychiatrists have become aware of the fact that whomsoever you call crazy are the cream. You ask R.D. Laing. Now they say the crazy people are the cream; they should have been allowed more freedom, they should have been helped to be individuals and then humanity would have risen higher than ever because they are the vanguard.

Have you ever heard about any stupid person going mad? I am not talking about retarded people; when I say "mad," I don't mean the retarded. The retarded person is physically retarded; the problem is not of the mind. A crazy person is one who is not retarded. In fact, crazy people have higher IQ's than ordinary people. Crazy people have higher IQ's than your politicians. A mad Nietzsche has a greater IQ than Richard Nixon. A mad van Gogh has a higher IQ than Lenin, Mao, Stalin. A Picasso has greater intelligence than any Adolf Hitler. But they are all crazy people. In fact, they look crazy because the world is very dull.

If everybody is allowed individuality, crazy people will not be found anywhere. If everybody is allowed to be rebellious and to be himself, authentically to be himself, there will be no need for mental asylums. Mad people are victims of the society, of a repressive society. First the society forces sensitive people to go crazy and then forces them into mental asylums or forces them into hospitals, gives them electric shocks, insulin shocks, forces them onto the psychiatrist's couch for years together – a sheer wastage of potential, and of the purest potential.

In primitive societies, crazy people don't exist. The more primitive a society is, the less is the possibility of anybody going mad because in a primitive society individuality is accepted. In a primitive society, craziness is accepted as individuality. Somebody wants to live in this way, somebody else wants to live in some other way. If somebody walks naked in a primitive society, people accept it. It is his choice, nothing is wrong in it. But if you walk naked in London, or in New York, you are mad.

Just think of Mahavira: he was very clever – he chose India to be born in, and he chose a right time. If he had to choose the twentieth century and he was to be born in New York, can you think what would have happened to him? He would have been under psychiatric treatment. Naked! They would have given him shocks, electric shocks; they would have dulled his mind. They would not have been able to accept his individuality.

What is wrong? A man wants to live naked under the sky, with the wind, with the sun; a man wants to be open to nature, what is wrong in it? Why should a man be forced to wear clothes? If he likes to – perfectly good. There is no need to force him to remain naked, because then you do the same again. But if somebody likes to be naked, what is wrong in it?

Just think of yourself sitting naked in your drawing room, and a guest comes, and you welcome him. He will escape and he will not come again. He will go directly to the police station. And you were not doing anything to anybody: just sitting in your drawing room, naked, enjoying, listening to music. You don't allow even small children to be naked. Such a repressive and violent society! The byproduct is craziness, madness.

I accept you as you are. I have never come across any crazy person, because the very word is meaningless. People are different, that's all. And the difference is beautiful. That's what makes life rich. That's what gives life variety. That's what gives life spice. Crazy people are the very salt of the earth. But if you reject it, if you become afraid of it, if you choose the social structure rather than your own individual freedom, then you will go on accumulating your craziness in the basement of your being. One day or other, if you are an intelligent person, a sensitive person, that will explode. You are sitting on a volcano and once it explodes, then you will not be capable – then you will go mad.

The only way not to go mad is to accept your individual forms, individual styles, to accept so totally that you never repress anything, and you will always remain sane.

Now the questioner says: "I feel very, very crazy. I know you love it, how can I love it too?"

Accept it, enjoy it. Love will arise by and by if you start enjoying it. Something great is happening to you; something very significant, spiritual. Your individuality is asserting itself. You are starting to feel that you are individual, not just a cog in the wheel of the mechanism that surrounds you. You are throbbing again with life. You are being reborn. This is going to be a new birth, the second birth. Enjoy it!

My whole effort in this place is to give you absolute space to be yourself. It is very difficult, because this place also has to exist in society. But let it be difficult – it has to be done. Even if a few pockets, a few oases on the earth exist where a person is not condemned as crazy, we will be creating a new sort of world and a new sort of society.

This is going to be the society of the future. This is going to be the shape of things to come. This small place is just a miniature world of the future and you are pioneers, Feel blessed that you are creating a new sort of human being, who lives in freedom and yet with tremendous responsibility.

One thing more I would like to say about this question: when you feel crazy you are completely allowed to be crazy, but your craziness should not be forced upon anybody else, that's all. Otherwise you start repressing the other person.

You want to sing a song loudly in the middle of the night – nothing is wrong – but then go far away from the town, because you are not allowed to disturb others' sleep. Your idea is perfectly beautiful: the middle of the night is so beautiful who would not like to sing a song? It's perfectly okay. Nothing is wrong in it, but others are sleeping. You need not disturb anybody. This is what I call responsibility.

Freedom for you and responsibility toward others. If you can keep yourself between these two, a balance will arise. And if you are responsible, society will not force you too much because you will not be getting in its way. If you are irresponsible, then the society will immediately catch hold of you and will not allow you to be crazy. So to be responsible is a good policy also.

If you really want to be free, then responsibility has to be taken care of, otherwise you will not be allowed freedom. And what are you against this big society? They can crush you. If they can kill Jesus, they can poison Socrates, they can kill anybody, they can poison anybody, it is very simple. A man is so fragile, a man is like a flower and can be crushed very easily.

So if you really want to be free, then never be irresponsible. The more a person wants to be free, the more he has to learn the ways of responsibility. If you can remain alert about responsibility, you will have more and more freedom available to you. Even in this society you can remain absolutely free. I have remained, that's why I say it to you. I have never done anything that I did not want to do. I have done only that which I always wanted to do. But then you have to be very, very intelligent, and you have to be very, very alert. I am a crazy person – very, very crazy. But there is no problem in it. I don't suffer from it, I celebrate it.

Start enjoying it, rejoicing in it, and love will arise. Love always follows joy, and joy always follows love; they are together. Either start by loving, or, if it is difficult, then start by rejoicing. If you can love your craziness, good – joy will come out of it. If the question has arisen: "How to love it?" then forget about loving. Enjoy it and love will follow it. They go together, they are one phenomenon.

The sixth question:

> Osho,
> Are all desires the same? What is my desire for love?

In the ultimate sense, all desires are the same because desire means you are not contented with yourself as you are. Desire is a discontent.

Essentially, desire is a longing for that which is not. Essentially, desire is a complaint against existence. You say: "This is not the way I want to be. This is not the house I want to live in, and this is not the woman I want to love and be loved by. This is not the world, this is not the society, this is not the body, this is not the mind that I can be content with."

Desire means discontent, and desire means a hope in the future, that somewhere there must be a place where everything will fall in tune with you. Desire means that, "I am not in tune with the world as it is, so I hope for another world with which I can be in tune." But you are not going to be in tune anywhere, because all the time you are learning only one thing: not being in tune with.

Yesterday you were not in tune with, the day before yesterday you were not in tune with. In childhood, there was no harmony between you and the world. Young, you were not in harmony. Old, you are not in harmony. And you are hoping: "Tomorrow I will be in tune with things and things will be in tune with me." And the whole life is disciplined, trained, for not being in tune with. Tomorrow will always be the same as yesterday.

In Hindi, we have the same word for both, for yesterday and tomorrow. That is something very significant – the same word for both. Yesterday we call *kal*, and tomorrow, also we call *kal*. It simply means that your tomorrow is going to be nothing but a repetition of your yesterday, your future is nothing but a repetition of your past. So don't wait for the future because then the future will only be a repetition of the past.

To be desireless means to be herenow, contented: whatsoever is, is good; whatsoever is, is the only way for things to be – there is no other way, it cannot be otherwise. It is the way life is and life is meant to be. Suddenly you are surrounded by peace.

Just look: this very moment I can see peace surrounding you. This moment being with me, there is no yesterday, no tomorrow. The past is not there, the future is not there, you are just herenow. This nowness, this hereness, this is what desirelessness is. You are just happy being with me.

This is the way to live your whole life. Let this be your *dhamma* – the way. Each moment, whatsoever is, enjoy it, celebrate it, feel thankful for it.

So, ultimately, all desires are the same, because the nature of desire is the same. But if we don't think about the ultimate meaning of desire, then there are differences, then there are many differences.

You have asked: "What is my desire for love?" Now the desire for love can have three meanings – it depends on you. The ultimate meaning is certainly one, and that meaning is that you are not happy with yourself. You think you will be happy with somebody else. Now this is stupid, now this is not possible. You are not happy even with yourself? How can you be happy with someone else? You can manage to find somebody else to live with you only if that someone else is also not happy with himself or herself, otherwise why should she or he bother about you?

You can manage and persuade somebody to live with you only because he or she is also in the same trap of desire. Now two unhappy persons meet. Now two persons who are not happy with themselves meet. You are asking for miracles, and miracles don't happen. Two unhappy persons meeting cannot make each other happy; they will become doubly unhappy, that's all. It is simple arithmetic. They will become very, very unhappy. Not only doubled, in fact, their unhappiness will be multiplied because their unhappinesses will clash. They will be angry at each other. They will take revenge on each other. They will think the other has been a cheat because, "The other promised me a garden of roses, and there seems to be no possibility of any delivery."

All promises prove false because out of unhappiness, how can you promise? Out of unhappiness, how can you give? You don't have it in the first place, how can you share? You share only that which you have. If you are happy, you share happiness. If you are unhappy, you share unhappiness. If you are sad, you share sadness.

So you ask me: "What is my desire for love?" It will depend on you.

First thing: it can be just a desire for sex. That is simple, not very complicated – very gross. In fact, to call it love is not right. But we call everything love. Somebody says, "I love ice-cream." Somebody says, "I love my house. I love my dog. I love my wife. I love golf." So what to do?

"Love" is one of the most misused words. We use it for a thousand and one things. So when people need sex, they call it love. Sex is a very rudimentary form of love, very primitive, just the *ABC* of love. It cannot go very deep and it cannot be very fulfilling. Or you can really mean love by "love." Then it means that you are a happy person and you would like to share your happiness. You are burdened with your happiness.

When your love means sex, you are simply burdened with sexual energy and you would like to release it. It is going to be a relief. You want somebody to help you relieve it. The sexual love is very physical.

If you really mean love by "love," then you have to be happy, content, rejoicing in your life. Then celebration is needed in your heart so that you can share. This is sharing of the heart. Sex is sharing of the body: love is sharing of the heart.

There is still another possibility I call prayerfulness. When you have even gone beyond the heart, your whole being is in deep need to flower, bloom, needs to be shared, then it is prayerfulness.

Sex exists between two bodies; it can exist even with a dead body. That's what happens when you go to a prostitute. The prostitute is not there; just the body is there. The prostitute makes her body available to you and she simply escapes from the body because she never loved you, how can she be there? She becomes absent. That is the whole art of being a prostitute. She becomes absent to you, she simply forgets all about you. She may start thinking about her boyfriend; she may create a dream about her boyfriend and she will completely forget you and leave the body at your disposal. It is a dead body. You can use it, but it is just a means. It is ugly, it is tremendously ugly, to make love to a dead body.

But I am not saying that it happens only with prostitutes, it may be happening to you with your wife. Your wife may not be there. If love is not there, how can she be there? Your wife may not be present to you when you are making love to her, or your husband may not be present there, he may be simply fulfilling a duty. Then again it is prostitution. Maybe marriage is a more permanent sort of prostitution, more institutional, more convenient and secure, but the difference is not of quality – maybe of quantity, but not of quality.

Whenever you love a person and the person is not present, you love a person and you are not present, then only bodies are there. It is a mechanical thing. When you love a person you have to be present to the person, you have to be present to the presence of the person. Two presences meet, overlap, merge, and there is tremendous joy, there is peace, silence.

So many religious people are against sex because they have not yet understood what love is. They have understood love only as the first gross thing: sex. So they go on talking against it. They have not understood the beauty of love; they have known only ugly sex. If you find a saint still talking about sex and being against it, you can be certain he has never known love. And a person who has never known love cannot know prayer, whatsoever his pretensions because sex becomes refined in love, and love becomes refined in prayer. It is a hierarchy, it is a pyramid. The base is sex and the peak is prayerfulness, and between the two is the expanse of love.

When you are present to another's presence, and fulfilled in the presence, and happy in the presence, there is a sharing. Love may become sexual, love may have a sexual dimension too, but then sex is elevated, then sex itself is no longer gross, then sex itself has come to a higher altitude. Then it has a different quality to it.

When you love a person and sex happens spontaneously, just as a sharing – not that there is any greed for it, not that you have been desiring it, not that you have been planning it, not that it has been in your mind, it has not been there at all – you were simply sharing the presence, and out of that sharing even bodies started meeting and merging into each other, then sex is also different.

In love, either sex disappears or is transformed. First it is transformed, then by and by it disappears. Then arises another, higher quality of love that is prayerfulness. In prayerfulness there is no sex left. Love is just in the middle between prayerfulness and sex.

In love, both are possibilities: love may spread to the very roots, to sex, and love may sometimes rise to the very peak of prayer. Loving a person, sometimes you may love in a sexual way, and sometimes you may love in a prayerful way. Love will spread to both the banks. Love is the river; it touches both the banks. Sometimes even the body, and sometimes the person, will be so transfigured that you will see a god or a goddess. Unless your love starts feeling the presence of the other as divine, then there is no prayer.

When you move to prayerfulness then sex completely disappears. From prayer there is no fall to sex, that is impossible. Prayer is the other shore. From sex there is no contact with prayer – sex is the other shore. They are far apart. They meet in love, so love is the most complex thing in human experience, because in love there is a meeting of two shores. In love, matter and spirit meet, body and soul meet, the creator and the creation meet. Never miss any opportunity to grow into love.

But it depends. You ask me: "Are all desires the same? What is my desire for love?" You will have to watch. I cannot give you an answer for it right now. You will have to observe. Be very clear about your own feelings. If it is sexual, nothing to hide, nothing to be worried, it is natural. It has to rise from that natural source, you have to begin from there. Don't hide it, don't rationalize it – let it be whatsoever it is. If it is sex, it is sex. Try to understand it. Help it to move toward more loving, more and more toward the person, less and less toward the body.

If you feel it is love, then help it to move in the direction of prayer. Then love the person, but remember God. Then hug the person, but remember God. Then hold the person of your love, the hand of your beloved, your lover, but remember that that hand belongs to God. Then let this remembrance go deeper and deeper.

I cannot give you an answer – you will have to find it. Even if I give you an answer, you will interpret it in your own way. I may talk about prayer, but if your energy remains stuck at sex you will interpret it in a sexual way.

I have been saying for years that religion is a bridge from sex to superconsciousness. All sorts of people have heard it. Those who are obsessed with sex, they think: "Very good, so *samadhi* is also sex." They reduce *samadhi* to sex. Those who are really flowing into *samadhi* become very happy, so they say, "Good, so now there is no need to condemn anything, even sex has an element of *samadhi* in it. We can accept it, absorb it, and can be deep in peace, because when there is no conflict there is peace."

I have talked to many people, but they understand always in their own way. Let me tell you one anecdote before you fall asleep:

Mulla Nasruddin went to his doctor. He was old, very old, almost ancient, and he was looking very weak. And the doctor said, "Nasruddin, tell me about your love life, because it seems you are wasting too much energy."

He said, "My love life is very simple: four times a week I make love to my wife, four times a week I make love to my secretary, and four times a week I make love to my typist."

The doctor was horrified. He said, "Nasruddin, you will kill yourself! It is time you should take yourself in hand."

Nasruddin said, "That too I do four times a week."

Your understanding is your understanding. Even if I talk about prayerfulness, you will understand whatsoever you can understand. It is better you observe, it is better you go into your own mind, its functioning.

Just one thing I would like to tell you: don't condemn, never condemn. A condemnatory mind will never be able to understand life. Never judge, never evaluate, just be a simple observer, because once you have a judgment then you don't allow your mind to open itself completely to you, your judgment becomes a barrier. If you are already convinced that sex is sin, then how can you face your own sexuality? You will clothe it; you will deceive yourself. You will rationalize it. You will find ways and means and words and philosophies to hide it.

Never keep any prejudice, let your existence become transparent to you. And whatsoever it is, at least with me, everything is good – whatsoever it is, it is good. It is your mind, it is your body, it is your energy. The first basic requirement is to see it clearly, and from that vision things start moving.

If it is sex, there is nothing to be worried about. It is good that you are not impotent, think of that. It is sex, it is good – you have energy. Now you can use that energy. Have you ever heard of any person who was impotent and became enlightened? I have not heard. And, believe me, it has not happened, it cannot happen. An impotent man is the poorest man in the world because enlightenment cannot happen to him. Even if he tries it cannot happen, because he has no energy in the first place to transform.

Let me tell you another truth: whenever enlightenment has happened it has always happened to a very sexual person. Because that high energy you can ride on. It has not happened to so-called lukewarm people – nothing happens to them; they are stuck with their lukewarmness. It has happened to very hot people.

Buddha was very hot. He had lived a very sexual life and out of that he became more and more understanding. And one day, when he became aware of how much energy he was throwing unnecessarily, he started channeling that energy into a different direction – toward love, prayer, compassion, meditation.

It is the same energy. There is only one energy in the world and that energy is sexual energy. Even if God has to create something, he has to do it through sexual energy. A child is born, life is born, out of sex. A flower blooms out of sexual energy. The cuckoo goes on singing a crazy song – it is out of sexual energy. Just look all around. The whole world is throbbing with sexual energy. It is the only energy there is. Sex is the stuff the universe is made of. So don't condemn it, ride on the waves, the roaring waves of sex and you will start feeling new dimensions, new altitudes.

The first entry will be in love, and the second door will be of prayer. But you can start only from where you are. So the first thing to be absolutely certain about is where you are, and only you can be certain about that.

Watch, just go on noting. And if you are not condemning, if you are not justifying, if you are not saying good or bad, if you are not a puritan moralist, if you are simply a pure observer, you will be able to see because it is within you, where your energy is. And once you have known where it is, start working.

If it is hanging around the sex center, then don't be worried. Just remember one thing: never make love to a person you don't love. That is a perversion, because then you will remain obsessed with sex. Make love to a person you really love, otherwise wait – because when you love a person, the very love will pull the energy upward. And once the energy has started moving toward love, love is so satisfying that who bothers about sex? Sex has never satisfied anybody. It creates more and more dissatisfaction. Sex has never fulfilled anybody, it knows no fulfillment.

Have a sexual relationship only when you have a loving relationship, so love and sex become associated. Love is a greater center, a higher center. Once sex is hitched to love, it starts moving upward. Once you feel that you are loving, then never go to pray in a temple or in a mosque or in a church, that is foolish. Then again do the same as you did in the first place: your first prayer has to happen with your beloved or with your lover. Either before you make love, let there be prayer; or, after you have made love, let there be prayer; or – and the third is the best – while you are making love, let there be prayer.

If love becomes joined with prayer then it can hitchhike, then it can be pulled by prayer. Love has to pull sex energy up, and then prayer has to pull love energy up. Once you are at the point of prayerfulness, *sahasrar* – the one-thousand-petaled lotus in your head – opens. It only opens at the moment of prayerfulness.

These are the three basic centers: the sex center, the heart center, and the *sahasrar* – the one-thousand-petaled lotus. The heart center is just in the middle, between the *sahasrar* and the sex center. From the heart center the roads go to both the centers. From sex nobody can jump directly to *sahasrar*; one has to pass through love, through the heart center. From the heart center you can spread both ways – nothing is wrong in it. Once you have reached *sahasrar*, the ultimate flowering of your inner lotus, then sex completely disappears. Then there is no sex left.

In sex there is no prayer. In prayer there is no sex. In love both meet and mingle. That's why I repeat again: love is the door of entering into this world, or entering into the other world. Love is the door which opens both ways.

Jesus is right when he says: "God is love." But I would like to say – and I feel my statement is better than Jesus' – I would like to say to you: "Love is God." Jesus says: "God is love." I say: "Love is God."

A small child asked me, "What is your name?"
I said, "My name is love."

Let that be your name also. Once you understand what love is, you have understood life. You have understood all that is needed to be understood.

The seventh question:

> Osho,
> Do you give the lady sannyasins a more difficult time than the men, or am I imagining things again?

Lady – you are imagining.

The last question:

> Osho,
> The day before yesterday you parted with your old companion hand-towel, celebrating the silver jubilee of the friendship. You had said that everybody should remain sitting at his or her place in meditation, and let the towel land on some sannyasin as God descends in the same way. Then with a historic, loving gesture you tossed the towel, but strangely enough, it struck the wall beam and landed on the empty floor in front of you about two feet away from Maitreya and Teertha. Maitreyaji stretched his hand and took it. You played this mysterious joke and you witnessed it too. Now to whom does the towel go? It remains unsolved! To approach Mulla Nasruddin is not possible. Who knows where he is? – in Iran, Iraq, in Baghdad or maybe in Osho's room! I did approach Chinmaya with the puzzle. He redirects me to you. Osho, help me with your comments!

Now let it remain a puzzle. It will be good for centuries to come to think about it. It is a koan.

Let me tell you one anecdote:

A mailman was delivering letters on a new route in the heavily Irish south side of Boston. At one house there was such a racket from an argument going on inside that he was afraid to approach. Suddenly a little boy appeared on the porch. "What is all the noise about, sonny?" the mailman asked.

"It is my parents fighting," answered the boy. "They are always fighting."

The mailman glanced at his letters. "What is your father's name?" he asked.

"That's just what they're always fighting about," said the boy.

Now there is no way... It is good that it should remain a mystery. Let people fight about it. Let people think about it.

And the towel did well, it landed on the floor. If it had landed on somebody's head I would not have believed it, because godliness never descends on anybody's head. It would have been absolutely wrong. It did well. It descended on the floor, the empty floor. Whosoever is as humble as the floor, only on him does godliness descend.

Enough for today.

3

THE PASSION FOR TRUTH

The Buddha said:
There is nothing like lust. Lust may be said to be the most powerful passion. Fortunately, we have but one thing which is more powerful. If the thirst for truth were weaker than passion, how many of us in the world would be able to follow the way of righteousness?

The Buddha said:
Men who are addicted to the passions are like the torch-carrier running against the wind; his hands are sure to be burnt.

The lord of heaven offered a beautiful fairy to the Buddha, desiring to tempt him to the evil path. But the Buddha said: Be gone! What use have I for the leather bag filled with filth which you have brought to me?

Then, the god reverently bowed and asked the Buddha about the essence of the way, in which having been instructed by the Buddha, it is said, he attained the srotapanna fruit.

The essence of the religion of Buddha is awareness. There is no prayer in it, there cannot be, because there is no God. And there cannot be any prayer in it because prayer is always motivated. Prayer is a form of desire, a form of lust.

Hidden deep down in prayer is the very cause of misery. The cause of misery is that we are not contented as we are. The cause of misery is that we would like a different type of life, a different situation, a different world, and the world that is before us pales before our imagination. The cause of misery is imagination, desire, hope, and in prayer all the causes are present, so there is no possibility for prayer in Buddha's religion. Only awareness is the key. So we have to understand what awareness is.

When you pray, you ask for something. When you meditate, you meditate upon something. But when you are aware, you are simply centered in your being. The other is not important at all, the other is irrelevant. You are simply aware.

Awareness has no object to it. It is pure subjectivity. It is a grounding in your being, it is a centering in your being. Standing there inside your being, you burn bright. Your flame is without any smoke. In your light the whole life becomes clear.

In that clarity is silence. In that clarity, time ceases to be. In that clarity, the world disappears. Because in that clarity there is no desire, no motivation. You simply are, not wanting anything whatever. Not wanting any future, not wanting any better world, not wanting heaven, *moksha,* not wanting God, not wanting knowledge, liberation. You simply are.

Awareness is a pure presence, a centered consciousness. Buddha's whole effort is to make you centered, grounded, a flame without smoke, a flame which knows no wavering. In that light, everything becomes clear and all illusions disappear and all dreams become nonexistential. And when the dreaming mind stops, there is truth.

Remember it: only when the dreaming mind has stopped is there truth. Why? Because the dreaming mind continuously projects and distorts that which is. If you look at a thing with desire, you never look at the thing as it is. Your desire starts playing games with you.

A woman passes by, a beautiful woman, or a man passes by, a handsome man – suddenly there is desire to possess her, to possess him. Then you cannot see the reality. Then your very desire creates a dream around the object. Then you start seeing the way you would like to see. Then you start projecting – the other becomes a screen and your deepest desires are projected. You start coloring the object; then you don't see that which is. You start seeing visions, you start moving into fantasy.

Of course, this fantasy is bound to be shattered; when the reality erupts, your dreaming mind will be shattered. It happens many times. You fall in love with a woman; one day suddenly the dream has disappeared. The woman does not look as beautiful as she used to look. You cannot believe how you were deceived. You start finding faults with the woman. You start finding rationalizations, as if she tricked you into it, as if she deceived you, as if she pretended to be beautiful while she was not. Nobody is cheating you, nobody can cheat you, except your own desiring and dreaming mind. You created the illusion. You never saw the reality of the woman. Sooner or later reality will win over.

That's why all love affairs are always on the rocks. And lovers become afraid, by and by, to see the reality – they avoid it. The wife avoids the husband, the husband avoids the wife. They don't look direct. They are afraid. They are already aware that the dream has disappeared. Now, don't rock the boat. Now, avoid each other.

I have heard...

A man was very worried about his wife. He had heard rumors that she was moving with somebody. Naturally, he was disturbed. He asked a detective to follow the woman and to make a film: with whom she is moving, what they are doing.

Within a few weeks, the detective was back with the film ready. The film was shown to the man. He watched it; again and again he would shake his head as if he could not believe it. The wife was swimming with somebody, was going to a movie, hugging, kissing, making love to the man, and he was shaking his head in tremendous disbelief. The detective could not contain himself: "Why does he go on shaking his head?"

Finally, when the film was over, the man said, "I cannot believe it!"

The detective said, "This is too much. You have seen the film, now what more proof do you need?"

He said, "Don't misunderstand me. I cannot believe that my wife can make somebody so happy. Now try to find out what that man sees in my wife, because I have lived with her and I don't see anything at all. What does this man see in her?"

Husbands stop seeing things that they used to see in their wives. Wives stop seeing things in their husbands that they used to see. What happens? The reality remains the same, only against the reality the dream cannot win forever. Sooner or later the dream is shattered. And that happens in all directions.

You are after money, you are dreaming about money; you never look at the people who have money, you don't see them. You are just after money. You think when the money is there everything will be beautiful. Then you will rest and then you will enjoy, and then you will celebrate and sing and dance, and do whatsoever you always wanted to do when there was no money to do it and no opportunity to do it.

But have you ever looked at people who have money? They are not dancing, they are not celebrating. They don't look happy. It is possible that sometimes you may come across a beggar who looks happy, but it is impossible to come across a rich man who looks happy. It is almost impossible to find a rich man who is happy. Because the beggar can still dream, that's why he can be happy. The beggar can still hope, that's why he can still be happy. He can believe that tomorrow things will be better, or the day after tomorrow things are going to be better.

There is future for the beggar, but for a rich man the whole future has disappeared. He has attained whatsoever he wanted to attain, and there is nothing in it. When the money is piled up he suddenly feels frustrated. Whatsoever it was that he saw in the money he can no longer find, that dream has disappeared.

Man continuously dreams of power, prestige, respectability, and whenever he gets it, there is frustration. The happiest people are those who never attain to their desires. The unhappiest people are those who have succeeded in attaining their desires because then there is frustration.

The nature of desire is dreaming, and you can dream only when things are not there. You can dream about the neighbor's wife – how can you dream about your own wife? Have you ever dreamed about your own wife? It never happens. You can dream about somebody else's wife. He may be dreaming about your wife. Whatsoever is far away looks beautiful. Come closer, and things start changing. Reality is very shattering.

Buddha says that to be aware means not to dream, to be aware means to drop this unconscious sleep in which we live ordinarily. We are somnambulists, sleepwalkers. We go on living, but our living is very superficial. Deep down there are dreams and dreams and dreams. An undercurrent of dreaming goes on, and that undercurrent goes on corrupting our vision. That undercurrent of dreaming goes on making our eyes cloudy. That undercurrent of dreams goes on making our heads muddled.

A person who lives in a sort of sleep can never be intelligent. Awareness is the purest flame of intelligence. A man who lives in sleep becomes more and more stupid. If you live in stupor, you will become stupid, you will become dull.

This dullness has to be destroyed. And it can be destroyed only by becoming more aware. Walk with more awareness. Eat with more awareness. Talk with more awareness. Listen with more awareness.

I have heard...

Once there was a mother monkey who had a philosophic turn of mind. This would make her forgetful and often inattentive to her baby, whose name was Charles. Like many modern mothers, she just did not take enough care, distracted as she was by her thoughts. Nevertheless, she went through the routine as her mother had done before her, but not in the same spirit. She just hitched him on her back and absently scaled the palms. So there it was. And as she rummaged among the more middling nuts, revolving matters in her mind, the baby just slipped off, with all his young life before him too.

On the way down, Charles, who also tended to brood, called up, "Mother, why are we here?"

"We are here," she observed, "to hang on."

We are here to hang on – all his life a sleepy person is doing only that. He goes on trying to hang on with hope, with dreams, with the future. He goes on somehow hanging around, as if that is the only goal in life, as if just to be here is enough. It is not enough. Just to be alive is not enough, unless you come to understand what life is. Just to be here is not enough, unless you are so fully aware of being here that in that awareness is ecstasy, in that awareness is contentment, in that awareness is peace.

A man can live in two ways. One is just to go on hanging around. Or, to be more aware: "Why am I here," and "Who am I." Buddha says the whole of religion is nothing but a tremendous effort to become aware.

The first sutra:

> *The Buddha said:*
> *There is nothing like lust. Lust may be said to be the most powerful passion.*

People can be divided into two categories very easily and very scientifically. The first: people whose whole life is sex-oriented. Whatsoever they do, whatsoever they say, is just superficial: deep down remains their obsession with sex. It starts when one is a small child not even aware of what sex is. Children start playing around, and children start learning things. And it continues the whole life. Even when people are dying in their old age, then too they remain sex-obsessed.

This is one of my observations, that when a person is dying you can see in his face, in his eyes, what type of life he has lived.

If he is dying in a reluctant way, resistant, fighting against death, does not want to die, feels helpless, wants to cling to life, then his has remained a sex-obsessed life. And in that moment of great crisis, in that moment of death, all his sexuality will surface in his consciousness.

People die thinking of sex; ninety-nine percent of people die thinking of sex. You will be surprised that only rarely is there one person who dies not thinking of sex. A person who dies thinking of sex is immediately reborn because his whole idea is nothing but an obsession with sex. Immediately he enters into a womb. This has to be so because in the moment of death your whole life becomes condensed. Whatsoever you have lived for simply has to be encountered in the moment of death.

If you have lived a life of awareness, then death is very relaxed, peaceful, graceful, then there is an elegance and grace to it. Then one simply slips into it, welcoming it. There is no resistance; there is beauty. There is no conflict; there is cooperation. One simply cooperates with death.

A sexual person is afraid of death because death is against sex. This has to be understood. Sex is birth; death is against sex, because death will destroy whatsoever birth has given to you. Death is not against life, let me remind you. In your mind this is the dichotomy, life and death. That is wrong. Death is not directly opposed to life. Death is directly opposed to sex, because sex is synonymous with birth; birth is out of sex. Death is against birth; death is against sex. Death is not against life.

If you live a life of awareness, by and by the energy that was moving in sexuality is transformed. Not that you have to transform it – just by being aware, dreams disappear; exactly as you bring a burning torch into the room and the darkness disappears. Sex is like darkness in your being. It can exist only if you are unaware. And Buddha says: "There is nothing like that," ...*nothing like lust. Lust may be said to be the most powerful passion.*

It starts very early. If you listen to the Freudians, and they have to be listened to because they are more right than your so-called saints – your saints may be telling you convenient and comfortable truths, but truth is never convenient and never comfortable. Only lies are convenient and comfortable. Freud is telling very uncomfortable truths. Truth is uncomfortable, because you have lived a life of lies.

Whenever somebody says a truth it shocks you, it hits deep, it hits on your lies, it makes you uneasy, uncomfortable. You start protecting your lies. When Freud asserted this, that from the very beginning a child is sexual, he was opposed all over the world. All so-called religious people opposed him. Now, I cannot believe it, that a religious person can oppose such a tremendous truth.

A child is born in sex, *has* to be sexual. A child is out of sex, *has* to be sexual. And children start preparing for their sexual life. I was reading a beautiful story:

A little four-year-old girl and a three-year-old boy walked hand in hand up to the front of their neighbor's house. "We are playing house," the little girl said when the neighbor opened the door. "This is my husband and I am his wife. May we come in?"

The lady was enchanted with the scene. "Do come in," she said.

Once inside, she offered the children some lemonade and cookies, which they gracefully accepted. When a second glass of lemonade was offered, the little girl refused by saying, "No thanks, we have to go now. My husband just wet his pants."

It starts very early: the husband and the wife and playing house. They are preparing. And it goes to the very end.

Another story:

The octogenarian went to the psychiatrist to complain about her husband's impotence.

"And how old is your husband?" the doctor asked.

"He's ninety."

"And when did you first notice his disinterest in you physically?"

"Well," she said, "the first time was last night – and again this morning."

A ninety-year-old man, and the wife is worried about his impotence, and she has noticed it last night and this morning too. It goes on – the whole life is obsessed with sex, from beginning to end.

You gain energy by eating food, by breathing oxygen, by

exercise; by living you create energy. Man is a dynamo. He continuously creates energy. And when this energy accumulates in your being you are uneasy, you want to throw it out because it feels like a burden. Sex is simply used as a relief. Now this is foolish.

On one hand, you go on working hard to have better food, to have more nourishment, to have a better house, more rest. On the other hand, you want to have better air, more sun, more of the beach, more of the sky, more greenery: you work hard. Then you accumulate energy, you generate energy, and then you are worried how to throw it somewhere, how to throw it down the drain. And when you have thrown it, again you are accumulating. This is a vicious circle.

From one end you go on accumulating energy, from another end you go on throwing it out. This is the whole life: gathering energy, throwing energy; gathering energy, throwing energy. If this is all, then what is the point of it all? Why should one live? It is a repetition. It is a vicious circle. When energy is lost you are hungry for the energy; when energy is there you are ready to lose it. You find ways and means to lose it.

Buddha says that this is the most powerful thing in man's life. And if life is lived according to this, then life is a wastage, a sheer waste. Nothing comes out of it. So much running, and never arriving anywhere. So much work, and no fulfillment. In the end comes death, and one finds one's hands are empty. Can this be the sole purpose of life? If this is the sole purpose of life then life has no meaning, then life in itself is just accidental.

One of the most profound thinkers of the West was G. K. Chesterton. He used to say that either man is a fallen god, or some animal has gone completely off his head. Only two are the possibilities: either man is a fallen god, or some animal has gone completely off his head. If sex is the only story, then some animal has gone completely off his head. There must be something more to it. There must be something more to life, otherwise it is meaningless. Your parents lived to give birth to you. You will live to give birth to a few more children, and they will live to give birth to somebody else. And this goes on and on, but what is the purpose of it all?

Buddha says, "By becoming aware, you open another door to energy." Sexual energy moves downward; sexual energy moves toward the earth; sexual energy moves according to gravitation. When you become aware there comes a change, a change of direction. The more aware you become, the more the sexual energy starts moving upward against gravitation. It starts moving toward the sky. It starts moving on the lines of grace, not on the lines of gravitation.

If sexual energy moves downward, it is a wastage. If sexual energy starts moving upward, you start exploding new worlds, new plenitudes of being, new altitudes of consciousness.

Now, there are two possibilities to have this energy move upward. You can force it upward. That's what Hatha yoga does. That's why standing on the head became meaningful. Do you understand the meaning of standing on the head? It is a trick to use gravitation for sexual energy to come toward the head, but you still live under gravitation. You stand on your head; head comes lower than the sex center; energy can start moving toward the head. But how long can you stand on your head? Again you will have to stand on your feet. You don't go beyond the law of gravitation. You simply use the law of gravitation. In fact, you cheat the law of gravitation. That is doing something illegal in a legal way. But you don't change, you are not transformed. Your being remains the same.

Hatha yoga has developed many methods to prevent sexual energy from going downward and to force it upward, but they are all violent, a sort of enforced conflict. The growth is not natural. You can see it on the Hatha yogi's face. His face will be always tense. You will not find grace there. You will not find beauty, grandeur. You will not find godliness there; you will find a subtle egoism. He has cheated, he has cheated nature itself. But you cannot cheat; it cannot be a real thing.

Buddha developed a totally different methodology – the methodology of elegance, grace. For that Buddha became the symbol. Have you seen statues of Buddha? – so graceful, so divine, so peaceful; not a single flaw, not a single tension on his face, so innocent. What did he do with his energy? He never enforced it, he never fought against it, and he never cheated nature.

Buddha became aware of one very subtle thing – now science knows it very well – that every law has its opposite whether you know it or not. If there is positive electricity there must be negative electricity, otherwise the positive cannot exist. If there is a law we call gravitation, the pull toward the earth, then there must be another law – whether we know it or not – that goes against gravitation. Laws are opposed to each other, and only because of their opposition do they create a balance. Because of their opposition and contrast, they create a situation where life becomes possible.

Man exists because woman exists. Man cannot exist alone and woman cannot exist alone. The downward exists because the upward exists, and the outward exists because the inward exists. Life exists because death exists. If sex exists, then there must be a law which can go beyond sex. And if sex moves downward, there must be a law which has to be sought and discovered that moves upward, that helps energy to move upward.

Buddha found that the more aware you become, energy automatically starts moving upward.

In the human body there are many centers, and each center changes the quality of the energy. Have you not seen every day that electricity can be changed into many forms? Somewhere it becomes light, somewhere it runs a fan, somewhere it runs a motor. Just different mechanisms are needed for it and it can be used in millions of forms.

In the human personality many centers exist. The sex center is the lowest. When energy moves into that center it becomes a generative force; you can give birth to a child. It is the lowest use of the sexual energy. If it starts moving a little higher, then different qualities start coming to it. When it comes to the heart center, it becomes love. And love gives you a totally different world.

A man whose energy is moving at the sex center can never know many things. If a woman passes by, he will only see the physical form. If your energy is moving at the heart center, when a woman passes by you will be able to see her subtle body which is far superior, which is far more beautiful. If a woman passes by your side and your energy is moving at the heart center, you will be able to feel her heart, not only her body. And sometimes it happens that a beautiful heart can exist in a very homely body. And the contrary is also true: a very ugly heart can exist in a very beautiful body.

If you can only see the physical body you will be in trouble sooner or later because a man does not only live with a woman's body; he lives with the woman's heart. Life is of the heart. You can choose a woman who looks beautiful and is ugly. If her heart is not beautiful, if her subtle form is not beautiful, then you will be in trouble. You can choose a man who looks very handsome, very powerful, but may be just a beast, may not have any inner beauties, may not have any inner qualities, may be just a body and nothing else – then you are bound for trouble. Then sooner or later you will have to encounter the beast and you will have to live with the beast. And you will be wondering always "What happened to such a beautiful man? What happened to such a beautiful woman?"

If your energy moves still higher, then the highest peak is *sahasrar* – where it becomes prayerfulness, where suddenly your innermost eyes open and you can not only see the body, you can see the heart, you can see the soul. A man whose *sahasrar* has opened looks into the world, but the world is totally different because he never sees just the body. Even if he looks at a tree, he looks at the soul of the tree. The form is not the only thing; it is there, but now it is luminous from an inner light.

A man who lives at his *sahasrar* lives in a totally different world. You may think that Buddha is walking with you on the road, but he is walking on a different road, he is walking in a different world. He may be just walking with you, but that doesn't mean anything because his vision is different. His energy is at a different altitude. He looks at the world from a different clarity.

Buddha says that lust is the most powerful thing in man's life because it is the reservoir of all his energies. But there is no need to feel despondent:

> *There is nothing like lust. Lust may be said to be the most powerful passion. Fortunately, we have but one thing which is more powerful. If the thirst for truth were weaker than passion, how many of us in the world would be able to follow the way of righteousness?*

He says that there is one thing which is higher than lust, and that is the thirst for truth. There is one thing which is higher than life and that is the search for truth. People can sacrifice their life for it. They can sacrifice their passion for it. The highest passion is for truth;

Buddha calls it the passion for truth – you can call it the passion for the divine – it means the same thing.

That's why the person who has lived only a sexual life cannot understand the story of a Meera, the story of a Chaitanya, the story of Christ, Buddha, Krishna – he cannot understand. What type of people are these? When Jesus was alive, many were wondering: "What type of man is this Jesus? What manner of man?" because they know only one life, that is of lust and sex. And this man seems to be in a totally different world. It seems as if his whole sexual energy is arrowed somewhere high in the skies. His target seems to be somewhere else, it is not in this world. It is not visible: it is invisible. You cannot touch it. You cannot measure it, you cannot see it. But his life is of great passion, his life is of great adventure.

Buddha is not in favor of renunciation, remember. He is in favor of transformation. The energy that is moving into sex has to be moved toward truth.

Ordinarily, people just want to explore each other: a woman wants to explore a man; a man wants to explore a woman. It seems their whole life is just an exploration into each other's being. The thirst for truth means that one wants to explore into the being of this whole existence. It is a great passion, the greatest passion. And it has to be more powerful than sex, otherwise, Buddha says: "How will anybody ever move toward it?"

People have moved, but how do they come to know this thirst for truth? Let me explain it to you. Much depends on how you come to feel the thirst for truth. You can come by listening to me, you can come by reading a book, you can come by seeing a man of insight, but that will not be of much help, because that will be borrowed and thirst can never be borrowed. Either it is there, or it is not there – you cannot pretend that you are thirsty. By your pretensions thirst will not be created, and that creates much misery in the world.

Many people come to me and they say they would like to search and seek what truth is. I ask them only one thing: Has your life, as you have lived it up to now, proved an illusion? If it has not proved an illusion, then the real thirst for truth cannot arise. When you have seen the illusoriness of your life, only then does a real thirst arise to know what truth is. If you are still in the illusion of life, if you are still enchanted by it, if you are still hallucinated by it, if you are still in that hypnosis of desiring and dreaming, then talking about truth will again be only another illusion, another desire. It will not help.

Truth cannot be one of your desires. Truth can only be there when all the desires have proved to be futile, and your whole energy is available and you don't know where to go, because the whole life seems to be meaningless. You are stuck. You are tremendously frustrated. You have failed and all your dreams have disappeared. You are shattered to the very roots. You are standing there throbbing with energy not knowing where to go. Then that energy becomes a pool and creates a new thirst in you: the thirst to know the truth. When the world has been known as an illusion, only then...

So experience the world as deeply as you can. Don't escape from anywhere, not even from sex. Never escape from anywhere. Just do one thing: wherever you are and wherever your dreams are moving, go with alertness, awareness. Even if you go into sex, make it a meditation, be watchful about what is happening. And by and by you will be able to see the illusoriness of it, the futility, the meaningless repetition, the boredom, the dullness, the death that goes on coming closer through it. The more you waste your energy, the closer you are to death.

I have heard...

A friend of mine tells the story about a traveling salesman who was passing through a small hick town in the West when he saw a little old man sitting in a rocking chair on the stoop of his house. The little man looked so contented the salesman couldn't resist going over and talking to him.

"You don't look as if you have a care in the world," the salesman told him. "What is your formula for a long and happy life?"

"Well," replied the little old man, "I smoke six packs of cigarettes a day, I drink a quart of bourbon every four hours, and six cases of beer a week. I never wash and I go out every night."

"My goodness," exclaimed the salesman, "that's just great! How old are you?"

"Twenty-five," was the reply.

You can go on wasting energy...

Each step taken in illusion is taken toward death. Each move which you take into lust you have taken toward death. So take it carefully and be aware. Be aware of what you really want through it. Is it just a habit? Is it just a natural hypnosis? Is it just that you go on doing it because you don't know what else to do? Is it just an occupation? Is it just a forgetfulness from the worries of life? Or what is it?

And don't go with any prejudice. Don't listen to what the saints have said. They may say it is bad, but don't listen to it. They may be right, but you have to find it out by your own experience. Then, and only then, do you start moving toward truth. Only your experience can bring you to truth; nobody else's experience.

Once you have seen the truth of it, that there is nothing in it, energy is relieved from the burden, energy is relieved from the old patterns, and energy goes on gathering inside you.

Scientists have discovered a law that quantitative change becomes qualitative at a certain stage. For example, if you heat water it evaporates only when the heat is one hundred degrees, never before it. At ninety degrees it may be hot, but not evaporating. At ninety-nine degrees it is very hot, but not evaporating. And just one degree more, at one hundred degrees, and a sudden jump, a leap, and the water starts moving.

Have you seen the change? Water naturally flows downward, but when it evaporates it starts flowing upward – it has taken a different route. And you have not done anything but simply heated it to a certain degree. A certain quantity of heat and a qualitative change happens. Water is visible; vapor becomes invisible. Water goes downward; vapor goes upward.

Exactly the same happens in the sexual energy: a certain amount, a certain quantity, has to be accumulated before the change happens. You have to become a reservoir of energy, and out of sheer quantity at a certain moment there is a jump; energy no longer moves downward, energy starts moving upward, exactly like vapor.

When energy moves downward, sex is very visible. That's why scientists cannot discover what happens when the energy moves upward – it becomes invisible. It becomes immaterial. It certainly moves, but there is no passage for it. If you dissect the body of a buddha, you will not find a certain passage for sexual energy to move upward. There is no passage, a passage is not needed. If water moves downward a channel is needed, but when water becomes vapor no channel is needed, it simply moves and becomes invisible. Exactly the same happens with sexual energy.

Awareness is heat. In India, we have called it precisely that: *tap* – *tap* means heat. *Tap* does not mean that you stand under the hot sun; it simply means you bring more fire of awareness inside you. That fire of awareness heats your sexual energy: this is the inner alchemy, and energy starts going upward.

First your sex will become love, and then it will become meditation or prayerfulness. If you follow the terminology of devotion, you can call it prayerfulness; if you follow a more scientific terminology, then you can call it meditation. And once your energy is moving upward, then you see things in a totally different light.

I have heard...

A little old man was sitting on a bus humming, "Dee dee dum dum, dee dee dum."

The bus driver turned around and noticed a suitcase blocking the aisle. He turned to the old man and said, "Would you mind moving the suitcase?"

To which the old man replied, "Dee dee dum dum, dee dee dum."

In complete frustration, the bus driver jumped up and took the suitcase and threw it out the bus window and glared at the old man and shouted, "Now what do you have to say?"

The old man looked at him and smiled and said, "Dee dee dum dum, dee dee dum – it's not my suitcase."

Once you have started moving even death is not your death, even the body is not your body, even the mind is not your mind. You can go on singing: Dee dee dum dum. Even when death approaches, you can go on humming because the suitcase is not yours.

A man of awareness can die so easily, so peacefully. He lives peacefully, he dies peacefully. A man of sexuality lives restlessly, dies restlessly. It is your choice.

Buddha is not for repression – he cannot be, notwithstanding what Buddhist interpreters have said down the ages. I don't agree with them. The interpretation must be wrong because I know it from my own experience that repression cannot help a person, repression can never become a transfiguration. Repression drags you down. It is not repression: it is awareness.

Of course, from the outside it may look like repression. You are rushing toward money; suddenly on the road you come across a treasure, and somebody else is passing by. He also looks at it but is not interested. What will you think about that man? You were afraid that he might claim the treasure, he might start asking that it has to be divided in two parts, but he simply goes on, he does not bother about it. You will think he is either mad or he is a renunciate, he has renounced the world and repressed the desire for money.

You cannot understand that there can be a man who cannot see anything in money. You will think it is impossible because you see so much in it. Your whole life seems to be meaningless if there is no money. Money seems to be your whole life. How can you believe that there can be a man for whom money is simply meaningless? Only two are the possibilities: either the man is so stupid that he does not know the difference between money and no money, or he has repressed his desire – he has repressed his desire, his greed, his ambition.

When a man like Buddha happens in the world, people interpret it according to their own minds. He looks so faraway. Only two are the possibilities: those who are against him will say he is crazy; those who are for him will say he has disciplined his life, skillfully he has dropped his greed, lust. But both are wrong. Both have to be wrong because both are unable to understand a buddha. You can understand a buddha only when you are a buddha; there is no other way to understand. If you want to understand somebody who is standing on the peak of a Himalayan hill you have to go to that peak, only then will his vision become your vision.

I would like to say that all the interpretations about Buddha are wrong in the sense that they all imply that it is as if he is teaching repression. He is not teaching repression. He is simply teaching awareness. In awareness, things change. Through repression, you may manage somehow but things remain the same.

I was reading about a church and about a priest:

A topless girl tried to enter the church. The vicar stopped her at the door. "But, Vicar, you can't stop me from going to church," she protested. "I have a divine right."

"They're both divine," he said, "but that is not the question. You'll have to go home and put on something that is more respectable."

Now she says, "I have a divine right," and the priest says, "They both are divine." The priest's repressed mind – he must be looking at her breasts. He says, "They both are divine, but still you will have to go home and put on something that is more respectable."

You can repress a desire, but you cannot uproot it. It will come in subtle ways. It will surface in many forms. It may take such disguises that you may not even be able to detect it. A repressed person is not a transformed person, he remains the same, he simply manages to be somebody else who he is not.

Buddha is not for repression. Buddha is for transformation. Repression is very easy. You can repress your sex – that's what so many saints are doing. You can drop out of society, you can run away from women. You can go to the Himalayan caves and sit there and you may think that you have attained celibacy, but this is not celibacy. Sitting there in your Himalayan cave you will still dream about women – even more so, because you will be so far away from women. Your fantasy will become more psychedelic and colorful. Of course, you will fight with it, but by fighting you will force the desire deep into your unconscious, you cannot uproot it. By fighting nobody is ever changed. Only by awareness is a person changed. Awareness is not a fight. What is awareness? Awareness is neither accepting nor rejecting.

There is a famous saying of Tilopa: "Truly, because of our accepting and rejecting, we have not the suchness of things" – we miss the suchness of things. We cannot become aware of what reality is because we accept or we reject. When we accept, we indulge. When we reject, we repress. Buddha says, "Don't accept, don't reject – just be alert, just see. Look, with no prejudice for or against."

If you can be in such an indifferent *udasin* – in such nonvaluing, nonjudging awareness – things start changing of their own accord.

Tilopa says:

> It never leaves this place and is always perfect.
> When you look for it, you find you can't see it.
> You can't get it, you can't be rid of it.
> When you do neither – there it is!
> When you are silent, it speaks.
> When you speak, it is silent.

You cannot get it, you cannot get rid of it, it is always there. "When you do neither – there it is!"

Awareness is not something that you have to do. Awareness is not something that you have to force upon yourself, impose upon yourself. When you do nothing, it is there. Your doing is your undoing.

> Fortunately, we have but one thing which is more
> powerful. If the thirst for truth were weaker than passion,
> how many of us in the world would be able to follow the
> way of righteousness?
> The Buddha said:
> Men who are addicted to the passions are like the torch-
> carrier running against the wind; his hands are sure to be
> burnt.

You can look: everybody's hands are burned. But you never look at your own hands. You always look at others' hands and you say, "Yes, their hands seem to be burned, but I will be cleverer, I am cleverer: I will carry the torch and run against the wind, and I will show you that I am an exception." Nobody is an exception. Existence does not allow any exceptions. Your hands will also be burned if you are running, rushing against the wind and carrying a torch, a burning torch. Lust is rushing against the wind. Nobody has come out of it unburned.

But people go on looking at each other. Nobody looks at himself. The moment you start looking at yourself you have become a sannyasin.

I was reading:

Mrs Cantor suspected her husband of playing around with the maid. Having to spend a few days with her sick mother, she told her small son, Harvey, to keep an eye on Papa and the maid. As soon as she returned she asked: "Harvey, did anything happen?"

"Well," said the boy, "Papa and the maid went into the bedroom and took off their clothes and..."

"Stop! Stop!" shouted Mrs Cantor. "We will wait until Papa comes home."

Papa was met at the door by his irate wife, cringing maid and confused son. "Harvey, tell me what happened with Papa and the maid," stormed Mrs Cantor.

"As I told you, ma," said Harvey. "Papa and the maid went into the bedroom and took off their clothes."

"Yes! Yes! Go on, Harvey!" said Mrs. Cantor impatiently. "What did they do then?"

Replied Harvey, "Why, mother, they did the same thing you and Uncle Bernie did when Papa was in Chicago."

Everybody goes on looking, everybody goes on seeing others' faults, flaws, foolishnesses. Nobody looks at himself. The day you start looking at yourself you are a sannyasin. The day you start looking at yourself a great change is on the way. You have taken the first step against lust, toward love; against desire, toward desirelessness because when you see your own hands, they have been burned so many times, you are carrying so many wounds.

Looking at others is just a way of avoiding looking at oneself. Whenever you criticize somebody else, watch: it is a trick of the mind so that you can forgive yourself. People go on criticizing others; when they criticize the whole world they feel very good. In comparison, they can think they are not worse than other people; in fact, they are better. That's why when you criticize somebody you exaggerate, you go to the very extreme, you make a mountain out of a molehill, you go on making the mountain bigger and bigger and bigger, then your own mountain looks very small. You feel happy.

Stop this. This is not going to help you. This is very suicidal. Here you are not to think about others. Your life is yours. Thinking about others is not going to be of any benefit. Think about yourself, meditate about your own self. Become more aware of what you are doing here. Are you just hanging around or are you really doing something? And the only thing that can be relied upon is awareness. Only awareness can you carry through death, through the door of death, nothing else.

A beautiful parable comes:

> *The lord of heaven offered a beautiful fairy to the Buddha,*
> *desiring to tempt him to the evil path. But the Buddha*
> *said: Be gone! What use have I for the leather bag filled*
> *with filth which you have brought to me?*
> *Then, the god reverently bowed and asked the Buddha*
> *about the essence of the way in which having been*
> *instructed by the Buddha, it is said, he attained the*
> *srotapanna fruit.*

A beautiful parable: Brahma came to Buddha... Hindus have never forgiven Buddhists for inventing such beautiful tales because Hindus think that Brahma is the creator of the world. And Buddhists say Brahma came to Buddha to be instructed on the path. Of course, as a test he brought a beautiful fairy.

It is significant because there are only two types of man: the man of sex and the man of truth. So if Buddha is really the man of truth then he cannot be deluded, then you cannot create any hallucination for him. The most beautiful fairy will not mean anything to him. And that is going to be the touchstone as to whether he has attained to truth. When a person is absolutely beyond sex, only then; otherwise his energy is still moving, still moving into the direction of lust, still going downward.

The lord of heaven – Brahma – *offered a beautiful fairy to the Buddha, desiring to tempt him to the evil path.*

That temptation is a test, and temptation comes only at the very end. In all the world religions you must have come across stories like this. When Jesus is just close, arriving home, the devil tempts him. When Buddha has reached just very close, Brahma comes and tempts him. Such stories are there in the life of Mahavira, in the life of everyone who has attained to truth. There must be a meaning to these parables.

I don't mean to say that it happened exactly as it is told in the parable. These are symbolic parables, they are not historical facts, but they are very meaningful.

I was reading about Baal Shem, a Hasid mystic, the founder of Hasidism. A disciple came to him one day and said, "Master, how can I avoid temptation? How can I avoid the devil tempting me?"

Baal Shem looked at him and said, "Wait! There is no need for you to avoid any temptation because right now temptation cannot be given to you – you are not worthy of it."

He said, "What do you mean?"

Baal Shem said, "Temptation comes only at the last moment. Right now the devil is not worried about you. In fact, the devil is not chasing you at all – you are chasing the devil – so don't be worried about temptation. It is not going to happen to you so soon. And when it happens, I will take care of it. I will tell you what to do."

The temptation comes only at the last moment. Why? Because when the sexual energy is coming to a point, the hundred-degree point, then the whole past, millions of lives lived in sexuality, pull you back. The devil is not a person somewhere; the devil is just your past. Many lives of mechanical sex pull you back. You hesitate for a moment whether to take the jump or not.

Just as when a river comes to the ocean she must be hesitating for a moment before she loses herself into the ocean, she must be looking backward with nostalgia: the beautiful mountains, the snow-peaked mountains, the forests, the valleys, the song of the birds, the banks, the people, the journey – the past thousands of miles. And suddenly now here comes a moment: you jump and you are lost forever. The river must be thinking: "To be, or not to be?" – a hesitation, a trembling, a shaking to the very foundations.

That's what temptation is. When Buddha has come to the point where the energy is ready to take the ultimate jump and become nonsexual, when desire is ready to dissolve into desirelessness, when the mind is ready to die and the no-mind is ready to be born – it is such a great jump that it is natural one should hesitate. That is the meaning of the parable.

...the Buddha said: Be gone! What use have I for the leather bag filled with filth which you have brought to me? When a man

has come to that point, then body is meaningless; then body is nothing but a bag, a skin bag filled with filth. In fact, that's how the body is. If you don't believe it, go to the surgeon some time and see a body being opened, and then you will believe Buddha. Or go to the hospital to see a postmortem, when the whole body is dissected, and then you will see what he is saying.

In my town once it happened: a man was shot dead and there was a postmortem. I was just a small child but somehow I managed to persuade the doctor. His son was my friend, so I succeeded in persuading him: "Just allow me to see, I would like to see."

He insisted, "But why do you want to see?"

I said, "I have come across the saying of Buddha that the body is nothing but a bag full of filth. Just let me have one glimpse."

He allowed me, and he said, "Okay, you can stay."

But I said, "Now there is no need to stay and I cannot stay anyhow." It was stinking so much, and the stomach was open – and just filth and nothing else.

Each child should be brought to the postmortem. Buddha used to send his disciples to the burning place, where bodies are burnt, just to watch and meditate there. He said, "Unless you are completely aware of what the body is you will not drop your illusion about the beauty of the body and dreams about the body." He's right.

He said: *Be gone! What use have I for the leather bag filled with filth which you have brought to me? Then, the god reverently bowed and asked the Buddha about the essence of the way...*

The touchstone proved that Buddha was real gold.

Then the god reverently bowed down... In Buddhist mythology even gods are as lustful as man – even more so. Their whole life is nothing but one of lust. The Brahma, the Lord of Heaven, bowed down and asked *...about the essence of the way, in which having been instructed by the Buddha, it is said, he attained the srotapanna fruit.*

Srotapanna means one who has entered the stream – *srotapanna*: one who has entered into the stream of consciousness, awareness, alertness. That is the essential message of Buddha: no prayer, no ritual; no priest, no temple. You are the priest, you are the ritual, you are the temple. Only one thing is needed. Buddha has reduced the requirement to the minimum; he is absolutely mathematical. He said awareness is enough. If you can be aware, everything will take care of itself.

Two drunks were weaving along the railroad tracks. One said, "I never saw so many steps in my life."
The other said, "It's not the steps that bother me, it's the low railing."

The only thing that is needed somehow is to bring them out of their drunkenness.

Two other drunks were riding a rollercoaster, when one turned to the other and said, "We may be making good time, but I've got a feeling we're on the wrong bus."

Everybody is on the wrong bus – unconsciousness is the wrong bus. Then wherever you are makes no difference, and whatsoever you do makes no difference. In your unconsciousness, whatsoever you do is going to be wrong. Wrong is that which is done in unconsciousness, and right is that which is done consciously.

Edwin Arnold has written one of the most beautiful books about Buddha, *The Light of Asia*. A few lines to sum up:
"This is peace – to conquer love of self and lust of life, to tear deep-rooted passion from the breast, to still the inward strife; for love, to clasp eternal beauty close; for glory, to be lord of self; for pleasure, to live beyond the gods; for countless wealth, to lay up lasting treasure of perfect service rendered, duties done in charity, soft speech, and stainless days: These riches shall not fade away in life, nor any death dispraise. This is peace – to conquer love of self and lust of life..."

This is the whole essence of Buddha's message. Peace is not to be practiced, it is a by-product of awareness. Love is not to be practiced, it is a by-product of awareness. Righteousness is not to be practiced, it is a by-product of awareness.

Awareness is the remedy for all ills because awareness makes you healthy, whole, and of course holy.

Enough for today.

4

A RICH MAN IS VERY POOR

The first question:

> Osho,
> We have learned from you that freedom lies in the transcendence of the mind, and it is the knowledge and the understanding of the mind which brings about its transcendence. The major part of religion deals with the mind, and so does psychology.
> As modern psychology has successfully discovered and revealed the structure and process of the mind, would you call it a religion? Or a branch of religion? Or a parallel religion?
> How do psychology and religion differ from each other? Kindly point out whether psychology and religion can be helpful to each other.

Religion understands mind in a totally different way from psychology. Their approach is different; their goal is different; their methodology is different.

Psychology studies the mind as an object, from the outside. Of course, it misses much. In fact, the most essential is missed. Only the periphery can be understood that way. The innermost is not objective, the innermost is subjective. You can study it from the within, not from the without.

Psychology is as if somebody wants to study love and watches two lovers hugging each other, holding hands, sitting together, making love, collecting data about how two lovers behave. This won't give him any idea of what love is because love is not on the surface. The surface can be very deceiving, the appearance can be very deceiving. Love is something very inner. Only by being in love do you know it; there is no other way to know it.

Psychology tries to understand mind from the outside. The very approach makes mind material. Only matter can be understood from the outside because matter has no inside to it. The first thing is that mind can only be understood from the inside because mind has no outside to it.

That's why psychology is becoming more and more behavioristic, more and more materialistic, more and more mechanical, and more and more suspicious about the soul of man. The soul is completely denied by psychology. Not that the soul does not exist, but because the very approach prohibits it, the very approach becomes a limitation. The conclusion depends on the approach. If you start wrongly, you end wrongly.

The second thing to be understood is that psychology tries to understand mind, not to go beyond it because psychology thinks there is no beyond to it, it is the end. Religion also tries to understand mind – not to understand mind itself, but to go beyond it. The understanding is to be used as a stepping-stone.

So religion is not concerned with the details of the mind. An essential understanding of the functioning of the mind will do. If you go into details there is no end to it. Religion also studies dreaming, but just to make you awake, that's all. Dreaming itself is not the concern. It does not go deep into the dreaming structure, and it does not go on ad infinitum analyzing dreams. It simply tries to find the essential structure of the dream in order to transcend it, so you can become a witness. It is totally different.

For example, if I give you a seed of a beautiful tree and you become overly concerned with the seed and you try to understand it, and you dissect it, and you go on and on trying to understand and dissect, and dissect more – the chemical structure, the physical structure, the atomic structure, the electrons, the neutrons – and you go on and on, you completely forget that the seed was meant only to become a tree.

And howsoever deep your dissection, by dissecting a seed you are never going to come to the tree. You will come to the atomic structure of the seed, you will come to the chemical structure of the seed; you may come to the electrical structure of the seed, but that has nothing to do with the tree. The more you dissect the seed, the farther away you are from the tree. Your dissection is not going to bloom. Your dissection is not going to spread its fragrance. And one day, if you have dissected it too much and then you put it in the soil, it won't sprout. It is already dead. In dissection you killed it, you murdered it.

Psychology is interested in mind just like one being obsessed with the seed. Religion is also interested in the seed, but not for itself. It is interested in the seed because it carries in it a potentiality, a possibility of becoming a beautiful tree, a possibility of blossoms, a possibility of fragrance, a possibility of song and dance, a possibility that many birds can come and make their nests on it and many travelers can rest under its shade. But the concern is not the seed; the concern is the tree.

I hope you can see the difference. Religion's concern about the mind is only as a stepping-stone. The mind has to be understood because we are entangled in it. Let us take another example.

You are thrown into jail, in a prison cell. The religious person tries to understand the structure of the jail only to find out ways to escape from it. Is there a gutter that can be used to escape? Is there a stupid guard who can be befooled? Is there a window which can be broken? Is there a wall you can climb over? Is there a right moment when guards change and the gap exists? Is there a right time in the night when guards fall asleep? Or are there other prisoners who are also interested in getting out of the prison, so you can be together and help each other? Climbing alone may be difficult, getting out of it alone may be difficult. A group can be created and the group can become a power. You try to understand the structure of the jail just to get out of it.

But if you get too interested in it and you completely forget the goal, and you go on studying the jail – the walls and the warden and the prisoners and the guards, and you go on making maps about the structure – then it is stupid. Modern psychology is a little stupid.

In the East we had also developed a tremendously significant psychology. I call it the psychology of the buddhas. But their whole interest was in how to get out of the prison of the mind, how to use its structure to go beyond it. Modern psychology is absolutely obsessed with the structure of the mind and has completely forgotten the goal.

These two differences are very vital. Religion understands from within. Of course, then it is a totally different thing. When you study mind from the outside, you study somebody else's mind. It is never yours. And if you go to the labs of psychologists you will be surprised: they go on studying the minds of rats to understand the human mind. It is humiliating, it is very disrespectful. The understanding that is based on the rat's mind cannot be of much help.

When a meditator watches his own mind, he watches the human mind alive, throbbing, beating. And he watches his own mind because that is the closest you can get to the mind. From the outside you can never get very close to the mind; from the outside you can infer, but it will remain inference. It can never become knowledge because even rats can deceive you, and they have been found to deceive. Even rats are not just on the surface; their innermost core remains inaccessible.

Why do psychologists go on studying rats? Why not man directly? Because man seems to be so complex. They study elementary structures. It is as if you want to study Einstein and you go to a primary school and you study a small child; and from that understanding you develop the understanding of an Einstein. It is simply absurd. It is not right at all, the direction is wrong. Every child is not going to become an Einstein. If psychologists were right, then every child would develop into an Einstein. But every child is not going to become an Einstein. Only a certain child has flowered as Einstein. If you want to understand Einstein, the only way is to understand Einstein.

But how does one understand an Einstein? From the outside he is as ordinary as anybody else. His distinction is inner, his uniqueness is inner. If you study his blood, his blood is just like anybody else's. If you study his bones, they are just like anybody else's. In fact, Einstein's brain was studied after his death, and it was found to be nothing special. That is something to be noticed. Nothing special has been found, but certainly he was a unique man, you cannot deny it. Maybe there has never before existed such a subtle mind on the earth. Nobody ever had such glimpses as he had, but the brain seems to be as ordinary as anybody else's.

Brain is not the mind. It is as if one day I am gone and you go into my room and you study the room and you try to find out what type, what manner of man this was who lived in this room. Mind is the guest, the brain is the host. When the mind is gone, the brain is left. The brain is just the room you used to live in. If you study from the outside you can dissect, but you will find only the brain, not the mind. And to study the brain is not to study the mind.

Mind is elusive, you cannot hold it in your hand. You cannot force it into a test-tube. The only way to know it is to know it from within, from your witnessing self. The more you become aware, the more you can watch your mind and its subtle functioning. The functioning is tremendously complex and beautiful. Mind is the most complex phenomenon on the earth, the most subtle flowering of consciousness. If you want to really understand what the mind is, then you will have to detach yourself from your mind and you will have to learn how to be just a witness. That's what meditation is all about.

Psychology can become helpful to religion, but then psychology will have to change tremendously. A radical change will be needed. And psychology will have to become more meditative, introspective; and psychology will have to listen more to the East, to the great meditators: Patanjali, Buddha, Mahavira. It will have to listen to their understanding.

One thing more I would like you to notice, to keep in mind: psychology has developed through the study of the pathological mind. That too is something unbelievable, ridiculous. Psychology has developed through the study of the neurotic, psychotic, schizophrenic – the ill mind. Because who goes to the psychoanalyst? A healthy person never goes to a psychoanalyst. Why would you go to a psychoanalyst if you are healthy? You go only when something goes wrong, you go only when some illness takes possession of your mind. When you are not normal, then you go to the psychoanalyst. Then he studies the pathological mind. Studying the pathological mind he comes to certain conclusions. Those conclusions are applicable only to the ill mind. They are not applicable to the normal mind, and certainly not to a mind which has gone beyond mind. They don't say anything about a buddha, they cannot. No Freud, no Jung, no Adler, has ever studied a buddha. In fact, the fault is with the psychoanalysts because buddhas have always existed.

When Carl Gustav Jung came to the East there was a buddha alive – Ramana Maharishi – but Jung wouldn't go to see him. It was even suggested, many friends suggested to him that he go, but he wouldn't go. Maybe he had a subtle fear that his knowledge would prove futile there, a certain ego that he is a great psychoanalyst – why should he go to anybody?

But buddhas are certainly not going to come to your laboratories; you will have to go to them. You will have to be respectfully close to them to understand them. They are not going to lie down on your couch. You will have to develop different methods, you will have to develop different structures, to understand them. And if you don't go, they are not at a loss – psychology suffers.

Psychology has remained at the level of the pathological. It is not even at the level of the normal man.

For example, if you ask a psychoanalyst, "What do you say about Mahavira who threw away his clothes and became naked?" Certainly they will say, "He is a certain type of psychotic. Many mad people suffer from that disease." Or, "He is an exhibitionist; he wants to show his naked body to people – a sexual pervert."

Is this right about Mahavira? And whatsoever they are saying, they are saying after a long study, but they have studied mad people. And about them, they are right. The wrong comes only because they are stretching their understanding too far. Mahavira used to pull his hair out, he wouldn't go to a barber, because he said, "Even to depend for that on a barber is a dependence." So when the hairs were too long he would simply pull them out and throw them away.

Now ask the psychoanalyst what he says. He will say, "This is a sort of madness. There are mad people who pull their hair out." You may have also observed that when your wife goes mad she starts pulling her hair – becomes angry and wants to pull her hair. A certain craziness – and they are right! And yet not right. Their understanding remains at the pathological level.

Ask them about Jesus. Many books have been written about Jesus because Jesus seems to be closer to them than Mahavira. They have neglected Mahavira, and it is good for Jainas that they have neglected Mahavira, otherwise they will certainly prove that he is a neurotic. Many books have been written about Jesus saying that he is mad, that he is a megalomaniac. Why do they say this? Because there are cases in madhouses where somebody says, "I am the only prophet of God."

Have you heard the famous anecdote? In Baghdad it happened:

A man declared, in the days of Caliph Omar, "I am the real prophet. After Mohammed I have been sent to the world." Of course, Mohammedans cannot tolerate such a thing – certainly not Mohammedans. If he had been in India he would have been tolerated, but Omar could not tolerate it. The man was thrown in the jail.

But after seven or eight days another man declared that he was God himself. Now this was going too far. That man was also thrown into jail.

After a few days Omar went to the jail to see them because both were beaten badly, punished badly. He thought, "Now they may have come to their senses." He went, and the man who was declaring himself the new prophet was laughing. His whole body was covered with wounds, blood was flowing out of the wounds, but he was laughing loudly. Omar asked, "Why are you laughing?"

He said, "When God told me, 'You are going to be my last prophet, the final prophet,' He told me also that 'They will treat you badly – they always treat prophets very badly.' And now the prediction has come true. So I am laughing – it simply proves that I am the prophet!"

While this dialogue was going on the other man, who was tied to another pillar, started laughing even more loudly. Omar asked, "What is the matter with you?"

He said, "This man is a liar. I never sent him. "In fact, I have not appointed any prophet to the world after Mohammed. Mohammed is my last prophet."

You can find many people in madhouses, and the psychoanalysts' understanding depends on them. And when Jesus declares: "I am God's only son, the only begotten son," of course he is mad. Certainly because there are mad people who declare such things, he is also mad.

When Krishna declares: "I am the creator and the destroyer of the world" certainly he is mad. This is the ultimate in being an egoist. How can you be more egoistic than this: "I am the creator and the destroyer of the world"?

And Buddha says, "I have attained to the ultimate, and even gods come to my feet to have instructions from me." Now these are mad people.

Psychoanalysis still remains at the level of the pathological. It has not even known the normal human mind, and it has not even touched the supernormal. But sooner or later a great revolution is going to happen, because if psychology does not change itself then it will be in a rut, then it will go stale and die. It has to move. Everything alive has to move ahead. And this much I can say about psychology: it is very much alive and there is hope. Much work is going on, and psychoanalysts, psychologists, psychiatrists, are becoming more and more interested in meditation.

You will be surprised. I have all sorts of people here. People have come from different professions, but the most sannyasins from any field have come from the profession of psychology, psychoanalysis. I have hundreds of psychotherapists as my sannyasins. This is very significant. Not so many doctors have come, not so many engineers have come, not so many bankers have come, not so many politicians have come. The greatest number from any single profession is that of psychotherapists. That is a great indication.

That shows psychology is moving beyond itself, psychology is moving into religion slowly, slowly. Sooner or later, psychology will become a very firm foundation for a religious leap. And unless it becomes a firm foundation for the religious jump, it will not have any meaning. It will get its meaning only when it becomes a step to the temple of God.

But when I say "When it becomes a step toward religion," I mean simply religion. I don't mean Hinduism, Christianity, Judaism; I don't mean Mohammedan, Jaina, Buddhist. Those are not really religions, they have become politics. They are political organizations.

A religion is very much individual. Religion is basically individual. It is a transformation of the individual consciousness; it has nothing to do with organizations. You are a Mohammedan or a Hindu or a Christian because you are born into that organization. Nobody can be born into a religion. Religion has to be consciously chosen. In the very conscious choice it becomes significant; otherwise it is meaningless.

You have been brought up as a Christian. You can't have any personal relationship with Christ. You don't know Christ. You know only the Pope and the church. And the Pope and the church, and the priests, and the *shankaracharyas* – they are not religious people. They have very subtle politics hidden behind them: racial, national, sectarian. Once a religion becomes an organization and people start being born into it without any personal contact, without any personal search, without any personal encounter with the master, when they are simply born into it, when religion becomes accidental, it is no longer religion. Then it becomes a sort of opium for the people, an exploitation.

So I don't mean Jew, Hindu, Christian. I mean simply religion. Religion has no adjective to it.

Let me tell you an anecdote. Listen to it very carefully.

Sigmund Steinberg, the well-known importer of ladies' gloves, paid an unexpected call on the rabbi of his temple. The rabbi was more than pleased to see his fabulously wealthy Congregationalist, who more than made up in contributions what he lacked in attendance and religious zeal. This time, however, the trip to the temple was for a completely religious, if rather unusual, reason.

"Rabbi," Steinberg commenced after the usual amenities, "I am here to see you about someone most near and dear to me. Mine own, mine darling, mine three-times-a-champion Westminster Abbey the Third, mine little poodle-la, is this coming Tisha Bov thirteen years old, and I want, Rabbi, you should Bar Mitzvah.

The rabbi was completely taken aback. "But my dear Mr Steinberg, that is impossible! Who has ever heard of a dog being Bar Mitzvahed? There has never in the history of the Jewish religion been any mention of such a thing. It would be a scandal. The temple would be a laughing-stock. My orders would be revoked, the sisterhood would be abandoned, the building campaign would be halted, the gentiles would be hysterical, and the board of directors would have my neck!"

Steinberg was unmoved. Without so much as the bat of an eyelash, he addressed the rabbi again. "For the occasion, I am donating to the temple the amount – in cash – of five thousand dollars."

"Mr Steinberg," the rabbi beamed, "why didn't you tell me in the first place the dog is Jewish?"

When it comes to money then even a dog becomes Jewish. When it comes to money and politics, then your popes and your *shankaracharyas* are no longer religious. Their religion consists only of rituals, dead rituals. It is a facade, it is not the reality. A real religious person has always found it difficult to exist in any organization.

Jesus was born a Jew, but could not remain in the Jewish fold. It was impossible. The priests wouldn't allow him. He was thrown out of it. Not only that, they killed him. Buddha was born a Hindu, but Hindus wouldn't allow him, the priests wouldn't allow him because whenever there is a religious person he is such an alive revolution, he is rebellion incarnate. The priests wouldn't allow him. He was thrown out of the Hindu fold. Buddhism was destroyed from India.

Jews killed Christ; Hindus killed Buddhism which was more subtle and more cunning. By killing Christ nothing was killed. Hindus were cleverer. They never killed Buddha. Had they killed Buddha, it would have been very difficult to destroy Buddhism in India. You can see: Christianity is there, and Christianity has flowered out of the crucifixion. Without the cross there would not have been any Christianity. By crucifying Jesus, they made Jesus important, historical.

Hindus are more clever and cunning. They say Buddha is our tenth avatar, but they do it in a very clever way. They have a story in their puranas that when God created hell and heaven, millions of years passed. And then the devil went to God and said, "Sir, why have you created hell? Nobody comes there, it remains empty. Not a single soul has turned up; people are so religious that everybody dies and goes to heaven. So what is the point of keeping it? Relieve me, I am just getting fed up and bored."

God said, "Wait, I will do something." And he sent an avatar who descended on the earth, and became Buddha to destroy people's religion, to destroy people's honesty, to destroy people's truth. To confuse them he became Buddha. And since then hell is overflowing.

Now this is very tricky. On one hand they accept that Buddha is an avatar, an incarnation of God. On the other hand they say, "Beware of him because he has come only because the devil had appealed. So if you listen to him you will go to hell. Of course, he is a god."

You see the cunningness? Even Jews have been defeated by Hindus. They raised Buddha to the tenth avatar and they destroyed Buddhism completely.

This has always happened. This will always happen. Try to understand it. Just being born into a household, in a certain religion, is accidental. You have to choose, you have to move on your own. It is an arduous journey, it is a great challenge and adventure, and there is great risk.

The second question:

> Osho,
> If I am God, how come I wake up every morning to find myself in this body?

For a God everything is possible.

> Osho,
> Oh, dear, last night I dreamed of thousands of orange elephants all wearing malas of their white elephant king. What can this mean?

This simply shows that not only man but elephants can also go mad.

The fourth question:

> Osho,
> After each of your discourses on Hasidism, I would leave glowing and feeling life is a leela to be lived fully and enjoyed. Yet when you talk about the Buddha I feel despairing and everything seems futile.
> Does the Buddha ever laugh?

He laughs, but never before his disciples. He laughs when he is alone.

Listening to me on Hasidism is half of the *leela*. And unless you can go with laughter while listening to me on Buddha, your laughter is not very deep. Listening to me on Hasidism, of course you were laughing and enjoying and you were thinking that life is *leela*. Immediately I have chosen Buddha. There is a mathematics to it. It is a dialectics. I never choose haphazardly.

Things were going too sweetly with Hasidism. You need a little bitter medicine also. It was daylight with Hasidism, now it is night. With Buddha it is night. But unless you can enjoy the night also, your enjoyment of the day is not complete. Unless you can be happy even seeing the futility of life, you have not learned what *leela* means. If you are happy only when you are happy, you have not learned anything. When you are happy even when there is no happiness, then you have learned the secret of it.

Do you follow me? It is a very simple mathematics. When I am singing a song of life, you enjoy it. But when I start singing a sad song about death, then you cannot enjoy it. Then you will remain partial; then you will choose the good, the sweet, the light part. What will happen to the bitter part? What will happen to the dark part? Then you will never be a whole, and if you are not whole you can never be holy.

With me, sometimes it is life singing and sometimes it is death. And I would like you to learn both. I would like you to become so happy, so playful, that even when there is despair there is no despair. Even when things are going rough you can laugh; even when things are going very heavy you can dance. So try to laugh with Buddha also.

To laugh with Hasids is very easy, to laugh with Buddha is difficult. It is an uphill task. But to laugh with Hasids, anybody can do that. It requires no effort on your part; it requires no growth on your part. To laugh with Buddha great growth, maturity is needed.

Life consists of these polarities: good and bad, success and failure, day and night, summer and winter, birth and death, marriage and divorce, love and hate. The whole life consists of these diametrically opposite polarities – and you are the whole. You cannot choose half of it. If you choose half of it you will remain half, and the other half will remain repressed. And the other half will take revenge some day or other. And if you cannot be really sad – happily sad, I say – then your happiness cannot go very deep, because you will become afraid of depth. In depth, the other is waiting. So your happiness will be shallow; you will not allow it to go very deep, because the other is waiting there. You know that if you go a little deeper, you may touch sadness.

Have you seen it? In villages in India, mothers say that a child should not be allowed to laugh too much, because if he laughs too much then he starts crying. It is a great insight. Have you seen that if you laugh too much your laughter tends to turn into tears?

All happiness tends to turn into unhappiness. All life tends to turn into death. Youth tends to turn into old age. Health tends to turn into illness, disease. This is how things are. And if you learn only: "I will be happy while I am happy," what will you do with your unhappiness that is also there? If you say, "I will be happy only with the roseflowers," what will you do with the thorns which are almost always there and more than the flowers? They are part of the game.

With Hasidism I talked about the roses, now let me talk about the thorns. And if you can understand both and still be playful, then you know what *leela* is. *Leela* means playfulness – playfulness in success, playfulness in failure; playfulness when you are winning, playfulness when you are being defeated.

The fifth question:

Osho,
Am I okay?

You cannot be, certainly not. Otherwise the question will not arise. The very question says something is wrong somewhere, otherwise who will bother to ask it? "Okayness" is such a feeling that when it is there you know it. It is just like a headache: you never ask anybody else, "Have I got a headache?" And if you ask they will laugh. They will say, "Have you gone mad?" If you have, you have, and you know. If you don't have, you don't have, and you know.

Okayness is an inner well-being. A great, beautiful feeling arises in your being, and goes on spreading ripples upon ripples. Everything seems to be light. Everything seems to be weightless. You don't walk, you run. You don't run, you dance. You feel as if gravitation does not exist. You start flying. You move in unknown bliss. You go on drifting, very peacefully, toward the shore of the unknown. Everything seems to be beautiful, a blessing. You are blessed and you can bless others.

When it is there, there is no question. When it is there, you need not have any certificate from anybody. You know it. It is self-evident. And if okayness is also not self-evident, then nothing can be self-evident.

Mulla Nasruddin and his wife were on a rowboat. The wife was shivering in the rowboat while Nasruddin was fishing: "Tell me again," she cried between blue lips, "how much fun we are having – I keep forgetting."

Nobody can go on forgetting if there is bliss.

A man purchased a secondhand car, and then after seven days he went back to the place he had purchased it from and he asked the salesman, "Please tell me again about this car.
He said, "Why?"
He said, "I go on forgetting. You praised it so highly, and it gives me so much trouble. Just to encourage me, tell me again. I need a little encouragement."

Why do you ask, "Am I okay?" Do you need some encouragement? Remember: I am not a secondhand car salesman. I am not going to encourage you. If you are unhappy, then my suggestion is: be unhappy, there is no need to be okay. Be unhappy. Go into it to the very rock bottom of it. Let it be there. Listen to its message – there must be a certain message in this unhappiness, because existence never sends anything without any message in it. Don't try to hide it.

Unhappy? Then be unhappy. Be truly unhappy; go to the very hell of it. And if you can go without any rejection on your part, without any fight on your part, if you can simply relax and let it happen, you will gain tremendously out of it. You will see that unhappiness is there, but you are not unhappy – you are the witness of it, you are the observer. It is there, certainly it is there, but it is like a cloud that surrounds you. You are not the cloud, and once you realize that, you have transcended. Then a totally different kind of okayness arises in you which is spiritual, which cannot be taken away from you.

But people don't go deep in their unhappiness. This is what I call real *sadhana*: to go into your unhappiness. Don't avoid, don't escape. People don't look into their moods; people try to deceive themselves. People want somehow to carry on smiling always and always. But do you know? – even in heaven, angels don't sing all the time. There are moments when they cry and weep. And you can believe me, I am an eye-witness. But nothing is wrong with tears. Tears can be beautiful, if you welcome them.

Go deep in your unhappiness; it is going to reveal many things to you.

I have heard...

A farmer was driving his horse laboriously along a dusty road. He came to a man sitting beside the road, pulled his team to a halt and called out: "How much longer does this hill last?"

"You ain't on no hill," the stranger called back. "Your hind wheels are off."

But people don't look deep down in their being. They think they are on a hill, but the hind wheels are no longer there. You can go on a flat road, on a superhighway, and you will feel you are on a hill, always going up, and it is difficult and more difficult. And, of course, without wheels you will always be in turmoil; rough will be the road.

Don't ask me whether you are okay or not. The very question decides that you are not. But people are such questioners; they go on asking everything. Maybe you are okay, but you cannot remain without a question; that too is a possibility.

Mulla Nasruddin went to the hills on the suggestion of his psychotherapist, and from there he wired back after a week: "I am feeling happy – why?"

Now you cannot even feel happy without asking; now analysis is needed – why?

The mother went to see the analyst and asked, "Tell me – I gotta daughter in college. She doesn't use drugs, she's not pregnant, she doesn't drink, she got the highest marks in her class and she writes to us every day. Tell me – where did we go right?"

Where did we go right? Now that becomes the problem. Questioning has become such a deep-rooted habit that sometimes, when it is not needed at all, then too you go on asking questions.

You cannot allow your being to remain without questions. Allow it because that is the moment when the answer will come to you – when there is no question.

Don't go on questioning and questioning and questioning. It is meaningless. I answer you only so that you learn how not to question. I don't answer you so that you can become more knowledgeable. I answer you only as a help, so that one day you can remain without questions. That very day a great revelation will open its doors to your being.

When there is no question, the answer arises from your innermost depths. If you are too concerned with the question the answer will never arise – you won't allow it space to arise.

The sixth question:

Osho,
Is dirt really dirty?

It depends. It depends on your outlook. Nothing is good, nothing is bad. It depends on your interpretation, on how you interpret. It depends on your mind.

Mind always divides things in two – the good/the bad, the clean/the dirty, God/the Devil. The mind continuously divides. Mind is a divider. The truth is undivided, the truth is one. It is neither good nor bad, neither clean nor dirty.

I have heard...

A priest went into a tailor's shop and ordered a new suit. When he asked how much it cost, the tailor said, "There is no charge. I never charge the clergy." So the next day the priest sent the tailor a beautiful crucifix.

Then a rabbi went into the tailor's shop and ordered a new suit. When he asked how much it cost, the tailor said, "There is no charge. I never charge rabbis." So the next day the rabbi sent the tailor two more rabbis.

It depends on you, on how you look at things. Your mind is finally the decision maker.

A successful cloak-and-suiter had finally found the girl of his dreams, and he made preparations for a wedding the garment district would never forget. His own designers prepared a wedding gown for the bride of the finest imported silks and satins, and his own marital raiment was truly a sight to behold.

The affair was nothing less than breathtaking. No expense had been spared. Then, as the newlyweds were about to embark on their honeymoon trip to Canada, an urgent message arrived in the form of a telegram.

"It is from my partner," the groom explained. "Urgent business. I'll have to attend to it immediately."

"But what about our honeymoon?" the bride asked tearfully.

"Business comes first," he said. "But you go ahead. I'll catch a later plane and be there by tonight."

"But what if you can't make it by tonight?" she moaned.

"Then..." he blustered, "start without me."

A businessman is a businessman. His whole outlook about life is that of a businessman.

Nothing is good, nothing is bad; nothing is beautiful, nothing is ugly. It is you who decide.

In India we have a certain stage of consciousness called *paramahansa*. The state of *paramahansa* means the state of no division – when ugly and beautiful, clean and dirty, good and bad, both are alike. You can find a *paramahansa* eating, sitting by the side of the road – the gutter is overflowing, the dogs are running around him. Or even the dogs are eating from the same bowl. This is very difficult for the mind to understand. The mind will say "What type of man is this? How dirty!"

But you don't know the state of a *paramahansa*. Don't condemn, don't be in such haste. There is a state of consciousness where divisions disappear, when the mind is totally dropped. Then one simply lives in a oneness with existence.

But, I am not telling you to become *paramahansas* – remember. You cannot become a *paramahansa*, it descends on you. If you try to become a *paramahansa*, you will simply go mad. I am not saying to drop distinctions. I am saying become more and more aware so one day distinctions disappear. You can drop distinctions without becoming aware — then you will be a madman, not a *paramahansa*. And sometimes *paramahansas* and madmen look very alike.

The seventh question:

> Osho,
> Today's discourse is the most wonderful thing I have ever heard.

It is from Vandana. But about the same discourse somebody else has said:

> Why do you go on chattering continuously? I am fed up with you, I am bored, and I don't want to listen to you anymore.

It is from Maneeshi.

Now what to do? Whom to answer? The same discourse can be tremendously beautiful to one; to another it can be terribly boring. It depends on you; it has nothing to do with the discourse. You are not saying anything about the discourse — Vandana or Maneeshi. You are saying something about you.

Vandana must have been in a flowing state. Vandana must have been in a "beatitude." Vandana must have been open; I could enter into her. My words went deep into her heart and became songs.

Maneeshi must have been closed — too much in the head. Maneeshi must have been without heart, at least in that discourse. Then everything went wrong. It depends on you. Whenever you feel something like that, always remember it depends on you.

Now Maneeshi asks: "Why do you go on chattering?" I go on chattering because there are Vandanas also, so I have to go on chattering for them.

And you say: "I am fed up with you and I am bored...." But, who forces you to be here? This is something beautiful. There are two guards on two gates and Shiva with his big nose is there to smell you. And you have to pay to listen to me! Have you ever heard of a such a thing? In the history of India it has never happened, religious discourses are always free. And you ask me: "Why do you go on chattering?" Why do you pay in the first place? You need not come. All the management that I can make to prevent you, I have made.

It is your mind. But I know Maneeshi, I know his heart also. The heart goes on pulling him here; the head does not allow. That is the conflict. When heart and head meet there is a synchronicity. When head and heart meet there is a harmony. That's what happened to Vandana.

Maneeshi has lost contact with his heart. His heart goes on pulling him, so he cannot escape. Because he cannot escape he is annoyed with me, as if I am doing something to him, as if I don't allow him to escape. You are completely free, Maneeshi, though I know you cannot escape. It is impossible because wherever you are, you will hanker for this chattering. I will haunt you because as far as your heart is concerned, I am in possession of it. The head will not allow you totally to be here, but it cannot help you to go away either.

Listen from the heart because what I am saying has nothing to do with the head. What I am saying is not logical, what I am saying is not rational.

Just the other day I was reading a letter in *Current,* written from some Rationalist Association in South India, saying that they would like me to become a member of their association.

Now, I am overwhelmed. This is such a great honor. Even if a Nobel Prize was given to me I would not have been so overwhelmed because Nobel Prizes have been given to so many people, hundreds. Who has ever heard about this Rationalist Association ever inviting anybody else to become a member? This is without precedent. In fact I have never heard the name of the village either. Must be a very esoteric association. There are esoteric groups who work completely hidden, who don't believe in publicity.

Such a great privilege. I hope the village has a post office and a primary school, and at least a bus stop because in India every village that has a bus stop and a primary school and a post office starts wanting a university. It is enough to open a university. That's why every day universities are being opened, hundreds of universities. Sooner or later every village is going to have its own university.

Just one condition they have made that is very simple, and I can fulfill it immediately, at the drop of a hat. One condition they have made: If you drop being called Bhagwan. That I am ready to do, absolutely ready. Because in the first place I am a *bhagwan*, so whether you call me or not makes no difference. A rose is a rose is a rose; you can call it by another name, that makes no difference. I can pretend that I am not a *bhagwan* – there is not much of a problem in it – but I cannot lose this membership.

The trouble arises not by their condition; the trouble arises because it is a rationalist association. And I am absolutely an irrationalist. I am almost absurd. I play with reason, certainly, as a toy. I enjoy reason certainly, but as a toy. I am not a rationalist.

Those who hear me from their heads will go on missing me. And when you hear me and you miss me, of course you will be fed up. You won't be able to see: "What is the point of it all? Why does this man go on talking?" You don't get anything out of it. I go on nourishing you, and you are there without being nourished. Then certainly you will feel bored.

But boredom is your problem, and you have to learn how to listen from the heart. If you listen to me from the heart you can go on listening to me eternally and there will be no boredom at all. The more you listen to me, the more you will enjoy, because from the heart a tremendous revolution happens.

Have you observed small children? You tell them one story, next day they come; they say, "Again, tell the same story!"

And you say, "But I have told you."

They say, "Okay, but you tell me again."

And they are so thrilled. Again listening to the same story, and they know, and sometimes they will tell you ahead what is going to happen. But they are so thrilled, so enthusiastic about it. What is happening? They hear it from the heart; they hear from innocence, not from knowledge. They hear from a tremendous purity, from love. They hear for the hearing's sake.

Howard, who was one of New York's leading custom tailors, went to Rome for a vacation. While there, his wife, who was a firm believer in "when in Rome do as the Romans," insisted that they have an audience with the Pope. It was arranged through the American Embassy and they were granted their audience.

When they returned to New York they told one and all of their trip and of course about the visit to the Pope. Howard's father asked, "Howard, tell me, what is the Pope really like?"

His son replied, "He's a 42 short."

A tailor is a tailor. That is his understanding – 42 short.

Jack came home in the middle of the afternoon. He was met at the door by his wife and his son. His son exclaimed, "Dad there is a bogeyman in the closet."

Jack rushed to the closet and flung the door open. There huddled among the coats was his partner Sam.

"Sam," shrieked Jack, "why in hell do you come here in the afternoon and scare my kid?"

Get it? It depends on your mind, on you, what attitude you will take. You can listen to me year in, year out, and you can remain thrilled.

But I am not worried about that. At least I am always thrilled. If nobody comes to listen to me I will go on talking here. I love to say that which has happened to me, and I love to say it a thousand and one times. And that is the only way to convey it. Because one time you may miss, second time you may miss, but how many times can you miss? One day out of sheer boredom you will say, "Let us now listen to this man."

The last question:

> Osho,
> I hate to do this to you, but I can't resist the
> temptation. What about the robe?

This is from Maneesha. The first thing:

Morris came home from work early one day and found his wife in bed. She said she was not feeling well. He went to the closet to hang up his hat and coat, and to his surprise he found a man hiding in the closet.

He looked at him and shouted, "What are you doing in my closet?"

The man shrugged and said, "Everybody has to be somewhere."

So what about my robe? I have to be in my robe! Everybody has to be somewhere. But the question was going to come, whether from Maneesha, or from somebody else. I was waiting for it.

The towel was like a buffer state. Let me tell you about a buffer state first. In diplomacy, in politics, the clever nations always have buffer states around them. For example, the Britishers in India used to have Tibet as a buffer state between China and India.

China is the largest power close to India. They always maintained a buffer state: Tibet was the buffer state. If China ever wanted to attack India, first China would have to attack Tibet. It could not approach directly. And once it attacked Tibet, the British would fight on Tibetan ground; so India remained untouched.

When India became free, China attacked Tibet, and Pandit Jawaharlal Nehru missed. He was not a diplomat, he was a poet, he was a visionary – a great soul, but not a politician at all. He thought, "It doesn't matter to us. Why should we be worried about it? It is between China and Tibet."

Britishers wouldn't have allowed that. It was not between China and Tibet. Basically it was between India and China, Tibet is nothing. Once China took possession of Tibet, of course, the next step was bound to be India.

If, instead of Pandit Jawaharlal Nehru, Indira had been there, she would not have allowed it. She is more down-to-earth, less visionary, less of a poet. She would have fought there in Tibet. But Jawaharlal thought, "There is no point. It is for them to decide." Once Tibet was possessed, of course India became vulnerable; the next step was India. And China attacked India. It was just natural, it was simple diplomacy.

My towel was my buffer state. I knew it well, that once I dropped it you would ask about the robe. So it is better that

I should take my towel back. Vivek will bring a towel. It is better to keep it, it is safe, it is my Tibet.

The joke has already been stretched too far – three days have passed – and a joke should not be stretched too far, otherwise it becomes dangerous.

Maneesha, are you satisfied?

Enough for today.

5

GODHOOD IS YOUR NATURE

The Buddha said:
Those who are following the way should behave like a piece of timber which is drifting along a stream. If the log is neither held by the banks, nor seized by men, nor obstructed by the gods, nor kept in the whirlpool, nor itself goes to decay, I assure you that this log will finally reach the ocean. If monks walking on the way are neither tempted by the passions, nor led astray by some evil influences, but steadily pursue their course for nirvana, I assure you that these monks will finally attain enlightenment.
The Buddha said:
Rely not on your own will. Your own will is not trustworthy. Guard yourselves against sensualism, for it surely leads to the path of evil. Your own will becomes trustworthy only when you have attained arhatship.

The way of the Buddha is known as *via negativa* – the path of negation. This attitude, this approach has to be understood. Buddha's approach is unique. All other religions of the world are positive religions, they have a positive goal – call it God, *moksha*, liberation, salvation, self-realization, but there is a goal to be achieved, and positive effort is needed on the part of the seeker. Unless you make hard effort you will not reach to the goal.

Buddha's approach is totally different, diametrically opposite. He says that you are already that which you want to become, the goal is within you, it is your own nature. You are not to achieve it. It is not in the future, it is not somewhere else. It is you right now, this very moment. But there are a few obstacles, and those obstacles have to be removed.

It is not that you have to attain godhood – godhood is your nature – but there are a few obstacles which have to be removed. Once those obstacles are removed, you are that which you have always been seeking. Even when you were not aware of who you are, you were that. You cannot be other than that, you cannot be otherwise.

Obstacles have to be eliminated, dropped. So nothing else has to be added to you. The positive religion tries to add something to you: virtue, righteousness, meditation, prayer. The positive religion says you are lacking something; you have to be in search of that which you are lacking. You have to accumulate something.

Buddha's negative approach says you are not lacking anything. In fact, you possess too many things which are not needed. You have to drop some things.

It is like this: You go trekking in the Himalayas. The higher you reach, the more you will feel the weight of the things you are carrying with you. Your luggage will become heavier and heavier. The higher the altitude, the heavier the luggage will become. You will have to drop things. If you want to reach to the highest peak, you will have to drop all.

Once you have dropped all, once you don't possess anything, once you have become a zero, a nothingness, a nobody, you have reached.

Something has to be eliminated, not added to you. Something has to be dropped, not accumulated.

When Buddha attained, somebody asked him, "What have you attained?"

He laughed. He said, "I have not attained anything because whatsoever I have attained was always with me. On the contrary, I have lost many things. I have lost my ego. I have lost my thoughts, my mind. I have lost all that I used to feel I possessed. I have lost my body – I used to think I was the body. I have lost all that. Now I exist as pure nothingness. But this is my achievement."

Let me explain it to you because this is very central.

According to Buddha's approach, in the beginningless beginning of existence there was absolute sleep; existence was fast asleep, snoring, what Hindus call *sushupti*, a state of dreamless sleep. The whole existence was asleep in *sushupti*. Nothing was moving, everything was at rest, so tremendously, so utterly at rest, you can say it was not existing at all.

When you move into *sushupti* every night, when dreams stop, you again move into that primordial nothingness. And if in the night there are not a few moments of that primordial nothingness, you don't feel rejuvenated, you don't feel revitalized. If the whole night you dream, and turn and toss in the bed, in the morning you are more tired than you were when you went to bed. You could not dissolve, you could not lose yourself.

If you have been in *sushupti*, in a dreamless state, that means you moved into that beginningless beginning again. From there is energy, from there you come rested, vitalized, new, again full of juice, full of life and zest. That, Buddha says, was the beginning; but he calls it the beginningless beginning. It was like *sushupti*, it was tremendously unconscious; there was no consciousness in it. It was just like *samadhi*, with only one difference: in *samadhi* one is fully awake. In that *sushupti*, in that dreamless deep sleep, there was no consciousness, not even a single flame of consciousness – a dark night. It is also a state of *sat-chit-anand*, but the state is unconscious.

In the morning when you become awake, then you say, "Last night was beautiful, I slept very deeply. It was so beautiful and so full of bliss." But this you say in the morning. When you were really in that sleep you were not aware; you were absolutely unconscious. When you awake in the morning, then you look retrospectively backward and then you recognize: "Yes, it was beautiful."

When a person awakes in *samadhi*, then he recognizes that: "All my lives of the past, they were all blissful. I have been in a tremendously enchanted, magic world. I have never been miserable." Then one recognizes, but right now you cannot recognize – you are unconscious.

The primordial state is full of bliss, but there is nobody to recognize it. Trees still exist in that primordial state; mountains and the ocean and the clouds and the deserts still exist in that primordial consciousness. It is a state of unconsciousness. This Buddha calls nothingness, pure nothingness, because there was no distinction, no demarcation. It was nebulous: no form, no name. It was like a dark night.

Then came the explosion. Now, scientists also talk about this explosion; they call it the Big Bang. Then everything exploded. The nothingness disappeared and things appeared. It is still a hypothesis, even for scientists, because nobody can go back. For scientists it is a hypothesis, the most probable hypothesis at the most.

There are many theories proposed, propounded, but the Big Bang theory is generally accepted – that out of that nothingness things exploded like a seed explodes, becomes a tree. And in the tree then millions of seeds; and then *they* explode. A single seed can fill the whole earth with greenery. This is what explosion means.

Have you observed the fact of this mystery, that a small seed, barely visible, can explode and fill the whole earth with forests? Not only the whole earth: all the earths possible in existence. A single seed! And if you break the seed what will you find inside it? Just nothingness, just pure nothing. Out of this nothingness, the whole has evolved.

For scientists it is just a hypothesis, an inference. For a buddha it is not a hypothesis, it is his experience. He has known this happening within himself. I will try to explain it to you, how one comes to know this beginningless beginning because you cannot go back, but there is a way to go on moving ahead. And, just as everything moves in a circle, time also moves in a circle.

In the West the concept of time is linear; time moves in a line, horizontal; it goes on and on and on. But in the East we believe in a circular time. And the Eastern concept of time is closer to reality, because every movement is circular. The earth moves in a circle, the moon moves in a circle, the stars move in a circle. The year moves in a circle, the life moves in a circle: birth, childhood, youth, old age, and again birth. What you call death is again birth. Again childhood, again youth, and the wheel goes on moving. And the year goes round and round: summer comes, and the rains, and the winter and again summer.

Everything is moving in a circle. So why should time be an exception? Time also moves in a circle. One cannot go backward, but if you go on ahead, moving ahead, one day time starts moving in a circle. You reach to the beginningless beginning, or now you can call it the endless end.

Buddha has known it, experienced it.

What the scientists call the Big Bang, I call "cosmic orgasm." And that seems to me more meaningful. "Big Bang" looks a little ugly, too technological, inhuman. Cosmic orgasm – the cosmos exploded into orgasm. Millions of forms were born out of it. And it was a tremendously blissful experience, so let us call it cosmic orgasm.

In that orgasm three things developed. First, the universe; what we in the East call *sat*. Out of the universe developed life; what we call *ananda*. And out of life developed mind, what we call *chit*. *Sat* means being, *ananda* means celebrating the being – when a tree comes to bloom it is celebrating its being. And *chit* means consciousness – when you have become conscious about your bliss, about your celebration. These three states: *sat-chit-anand*.

Man has come up to the mind. The rocks are still at the first stage: universe – they exist but they don't flower, they don't celebrate; they are closed, coiled upon themselves. Some day they will start moving, some day they will open their petals, but right now they are caved within themselves, completely closed.

Trees, animals, have come to the next stage: life – so happy, so beautiful, so colorful. The birds go on singing, and the trees go on blooming. This is the second stage: life. The third stage, only man has reached: the state of mind, the state of *chit* – consciousness.

Buddha says that these three are like a dream. The first, the beginningless beginning, the primordial state, is like sleep – *sushupti*. These three are like a dream; these three are like a drama that goes on unfolding. If you move beyond mind, if you start moving toward meditation, that is toward no-mind, again another explosion happens, but now it is no longer explosion – it is implosion. Just as one day explosion happened and millions of things were born out of nothingness, so when implosion happens, forms, names disappear – again nothingness is born out of it. The circle is complete.

The scientists talk only about explosion, they don't talk about implosion yet – which is very illogical. Because if explosion is possible, then implosion is also possible.

A seed is thrown into the earth. It explodes. A tree is born, then on the tree again seeds are born. What is a seed now? When the seed explodes, it is a tree. When the tree implodes, it is again a seed. The seed was carrying a tree; it opened itself and became a tree. Now the tree again closes itself, caves in, becomes a small seed.

If explosion happened in the world, as scientists now trust, then the Buddhist idea of implosion is also a reality. Explosion cannot exist without implosion, they both go together. Implosion means again mind moves into life, life moves into universe, universe moves into nothingness – then the circle is complete. Nothingness moves into universe, universe moves into life, life moves into mind, mind again moves into life, life again into universe, universe again into nothingness. The circle is complete.

After implosion, when it has happened, when everything has again come to nothingness, now there is a difference. The first nothingness was unconscious; this second nothingness is conscious. The first was like darkness; the second is like light. The first was like night; the second is like day. The first we called *sushupti*; the second we will call *jagriti* – awareness, fully awake.

This is the whole circle. The first, scientists call the Big Bang theory because there was such an explosion and so much noise. It was a big bang. Just a moment before everything was silent, there was no noise, no sound, and after one moment, when the existence exploded, there was much sound and much noise. All sorts of noises started.

What happens when the explosion disappears into an implosion? The soundless sound. Now there is no longer any noise. Again everything is silent. This is what Zen calls the sound of one hand clapping. This is what Hindus have called *anahat nad, omkar* – the soundless sound.

The first Hindus have called *nadavisphot* – Big Bang, the sound exploded. And the second is again when the sound moves into silence; the story is complete. Science is still clinging to the half story; the other half is missing. And one who watches this whole play – from *sushupti*, dark night of the soul, to dream, and from dream to awareness – the one who watches it all is the witness. The fourth state we call *turiya* – the one who witnesses all. That one known, you become a buddha; that one known, experienced, you become arhat, you have attained.

But the whole point to be understood is this: that all the time, when you are asleep or dreaming or awake, you are that. Sometimes not aware, sometimes aware – that is the only difference – but your nature remains the same.

T. S. Eliot has written a few beautiful lines:

> *We shall not cease from exploration*
> *and the end of all our exploring*
> *will be to arrive where we started*
> *and know the place for the first time.*
> *Through the unknown, remembered gate*
> *when the last of earth left to discover*
> *is that which was the beginning;*
> *at the source of the longest river*
> *the voice of the hidden waterfall*
> *and the children in the apple-tree*
> *not known, because not looked for*
> *but heard, half heard, in the stillness*
> *between two waves of the sea.*

> *Quick now, here, now, always –*
> *a condition of complete simplicity*
> *costing not less than everything...*

"...a condition of complete simplicity" – utter simplicity – "costing not less than everything..." This is the meaning of Buddha's renunciation, his path of *via negativa*. You have to come to the point from where you started. You have to know that which you are already. You have to achieve that which is already achieved. You have to achieve that which, in the nature of things, *cannot* be lost; there is no way to lose contact with it. At the most we can become unconscious about it.

Religion means becoming conscious of that which you are. It is not a search for something new, it is just an effort to know that which has always been there, is eternal. From the beginningless beginning to the endless end it is always there.

Because the path is negative there are a few difficulties about it. It is very difficult to be attracted to Buddhism because ordinarily the mind wants something positive to cling to, the mind wants something to achieve and Buddha says there is nothing to achieve, rather, on the contrary, you have to lose something. Just the idea of losing something is very unappealing, because our whole concept is of having more and more and more. And Buddha says that having is the problem. The more you have, the less you are because the more you have, the less you can recognize yourself; you are lost.

Your emptiness, your space is covered too much by things. A rich man is very poor because he has no space left, poor because everything is occupied, poor because he does not know any emptiness in his being. And through emptiness you have the glimpses of the primordial and the ultimate, and they are both the same.

It is very difficult to be attracted to Buddhism. Only very, very rare people who have a quality of tremendous intelligence can be attracted to it. It cannot become a mass religion. And when it did become a religion, it was only after it lost all its originality, when it compromised with the masses.

In India, Buddhism disappeared because the followers of Buddha insisted on its purity. There are people who think that it is because Hindu philosophers and Hindu mystics refuted Buddhism, that's why Buddhism disappeared from India; that is wrong. It cannot be refuted. Nobody has ever refuted it. There is no possibility of refuting it because in the first place it is not based on logic.

If something is based on logic, you can destroy it by logic. If something is based on logical proof, you can refute it. Buddhism is not based on logic at all, it is based on experience, you cannot refute it. It is very existential. It does not believe in any metaphysics so how can you refute it? And it never asserts anything about any concept. It simply describes the innermost experience. It has no philosophy, so philosophers cannot refute it.

But it is true that Buddhism disappeared from India. The cause of its disappearance, the basic cause is that Buddha and his followers insisted on its purity. The very insistence on its purity became an unbridgeable gap. The masses could not understand it. Only very rare people, very, very cultured, intelligent, aristocratic, few, a chosen few could understand what Buddha meant. And those who understood it, in their very understanding they were transformed. But for the masses it was meaningless. It lost its hold on the masses.

In China, it succeeded. In Tibet, in Sri Lanka, in Burma, in Thailand, in Japan, it succeeded because the missionaries, the Buddhist missionaries who went out of India, seeing what had happened in India, became very compromising, they compromised. They started talking in the positive language, they started talking about achievement, bliss, heaven. From the back door they brought everything that Buddha had denied.

Again the masses were happy. The whole of China, the whole of Asia was converted to Buddhism except India. In India, they tried to give just the pure, without any compromise; that was not possible. In China, Buddhism became a mass religion, but then it lost its truth.

Let me tell you one anecdote:

A junior devil has been sent to earth to look around and see how things are progressing. He quickly returns to hell, horrified, and obtains an interview with Beelzebub, the chief devil himself.

"Sir," he splutters, "something awful has happened! There is a man with a beard walking around on earth, speaking truth, and people are beginning to listen to him. Something has to be done immediately."

Beelzebub smiles pleasantly, puffing on his pipe but making no comment.

"Sir! You don't realize the seriousness of the situation," continues the distraught junior devil. "Pretty soon all will be lost!"

Beelzebub removes his pipe slowly, taps it out on the ashtray, and sits back in his swivel chair, hands behind his head.

"Don't worry, son," he counsels. "We will let it go on a little longer and when it has progressed far enough we will step in and help them to organize."

Once a religion is organized it is dead, because you can organize a religion only when you compromise with the masses. You can organize a religion only when you follow the desires of the common mass. You can organize a religion only when you are ready to make it into politics and you are ready to lose its religiousness.

A religion can be organized only when it is no longer a religion. That is to say: a religion cannot be organized as religion. Organized, it is no longer religion. A religion basically remains unorganized, remains a little chaotic, remains a little disorderly because religion is freedom.

Now the sutras:

> *The Buddha said:*
> *Those who are following the way should behave like a piece of timber which is drifting along a stream. If the log is neither held by the banks, nor seized by men, nor obstructed by the gods, nor kept in the whirlpool, nor itself goes to decay, I assure you that this log will finally reach the ocean.*

A very significant sutra. The first thing Buddha says is "Surrender." The most basic thing is: surrender to reality. The more you fight, the more you are in conflict with it, the more you will create obstructions. The more you fight with reality, the more you will be a loser. Of course, through fighting you can attain to the ego, you can become a very strong ego, but your ego will be the hindrance.

Those who are following the way should behave like a piece of timber which is drifting along a stream. They should be completely surrendered to the river of life, completely surrendered to the river of existence. In deep surrender, the ego disappears. And when the ego is not there, for the first time you become aware of that which has always been there.

The ego functions as a blindfold on your eyes. The ego keeps you blind; it does not allow you to see the truth. It creates too much smoke and the flame tends to be lost in it. The ego is like too many dark clouds around the sun – the sun gets lost. Not that those clouds can destroy the sun, but they can hide it.

Those who are following the way should behave like a piece of timber... They should become driftwood. Have you watched a piece of timber moving in the river with no idea of its own, not even trying to reach anywhere, not even knowing where this river is going? If it moves north, the timber moves north. If it moves south, the timber moves south. The timber is totally in tune with the river. This tuning with the river is what surrender is all about.

But the idea of becoming driftwood has no appeal. People come to me and they say: "Help us, Osho, to have more willpower. Help us to become more self-confident. Why are we missing willpower? How can we have a stronger will?"

Everybody! If you watch inside yourself you will find the same desire hidden there: how to have more willpower. Everybody wants to become omnipotent, omniscient, omnipresent; everybody wants to become powerful. Somebody wants to become powerful through having more money; of course, money brings power. Somebody wants to have power by becoming a prime minister or a president of a country; of course, politics brings power. Somebody wants to become powerful by becoming virtuous because virtue brings respectability. Somebody wants to become powerful by becoming religious because religion gives you a halo of power, of divine forces. Somebody wants to gain power by becoming more knowledgeable; knowledge is power. But it seems that everybody wants to be powerful. This seems to be the ordinary desire of the human mind.

And Buddha says, "Become driftwood." What does he mean? What does he want to convey? He is saying to drop this idea of becoming powerful. That is your hindrance. That's why you have become powerless. The very idea: "I should become powerful" proves nothing but your impotence. All impotent people want to become omnipotent; they would like to have all the power there is in their hands. But why? Ego is an illness, a megalomania.

Buddha says to become driftwood – powerless, helpless. Watch timber going down the stream: how helpless, no struggle, no conflict, simply cooperating. In fact, to say cooperating is also not right. The driftwood is not there in any ego sense, so there is no point in saying it cooperates. It has no conflict, it has no cooperation. It is simply not there. Only the river is there. The timber is completely surrendered. This is how a disciple should be. And when somebody becomes so surrendered, Buddha says he has become a *srotapanna*. *Srotapanna* means one who has entered the stream.

In the East, the concept of surrender has been developed very minutely, in details. But this example of driftwood is almost perfect; you cannot improve upon it. Sometimes, sitting by the side of the river, watch timber flowing down. See how peacefully, how relaxed, how very trusting the driftwood is. No doubt. If the river is going south, it must be good to go to the south. There is none of its own desire, no private goal – "the river's goal is my goal." The river is already going toward the ocean. The river is going to dissolve into the vast infinity of the ocean. If you can surrender to it, that will be enough.

Coming to a master and surrendering to a master is nothing but entering into the stream. The master is one who is surrendered to the river of existence. It is difficult for you to see the river of existence, it is very invisible. It is not material, it is very immaterial. It is difficult to hold it in your hands, but when you stand by the side of Buddha at least you can hold Buddha's hand. And he has become driftwood. He is floating in the river. You cannot see the river right now; you don't have that much refined consciousness yet. Your eyes are not yet ready to see that river. But you can see Buddha, you can hold his hand. You can see Christ, you can hold his hand.

Buddha is surrendered to the infinite river of life. You can at least take courage and be surrendered to Buddha. By surrendering to Buddha you will be surrendering to the river to which Buddha is surrendered. A master is just a midway passage, a door.

That's why Jesus said again and again "I am the door." Jesus is reported to have said: "Nobody achieves unless he passes through me." Christians have misinterpreted it. They think nobody reaches to God unless one follows Christ. That is not the meaning. When Jesus says, "Nobody reaches unless he passes through me," he is saying: "unless he passes through one who has already attained." He is not talking about Jesus the son of Mary and Joseph; he is talking about Christ – not about Jesus. He is talking about a state of consciousness.

"Christ" is the name of a state of consciousness. "Buddha" is also a name for a state of consciousness. When somebody is enlightened, he is no more, he is just a door. If you surrender to him you will be able to surrender in a roundabout way, in an indirect way, to the stream of life itself.

To become a disciple means to be ready to float with the master. And if you can float with a man, with a master, you will start enjoying, you will start celebrating because all anxiety will disappear, all anguish will disappear. And then you will be ready to surrender totally.

First a little taste is needed. That taste can come through a master – the taste of *tao*, the taste of *dhamma*, the taste of the way.

Those who are following the way should behave like a piece of timber which is drifting along a stream. If the log is neither held by the banks...

Now, Buddha says that a few things have to be remembered. You should surrender, surrender should be total, but there are a few obstacles which have to be continuously watched.

If the log is neither held by the banks, nor seized by men, nor obstructed by the gods, nor kept in the whirlpool, nor itself goes to decay, I assure you that this log will finally reach the ocean.

Now, you can start clinging to the master. Rather than surrendering you can start clinging, and they look alike, but the difference is vast. To cling to a master is not surrendering to him. To cling to a master means you are still clinging to your ego because all clinging is of the ego.

Clinging is of the ego. To what you cling is immaterial. If you cling, then you are trying to save yourself. I watch it. If I say to somebody to "do this," if it is just according to his desire he says, "Osho, I am surrendered to you, whatsoever you say I will do." And if it is not according to his desire, then he never says, "I am surrendered to you." Then he says, "It is difficult." And then he brings a thousand and one reasons why he cannot do it. Now he is playing a game with himself.

You cannot deceive me; you can only go on deceiving yourself. When it fits with your desire, then you say, "I am surrendered to you – whatsoever you say." When it does not fit your desire, then you completely forget about surrender. But the real question arises only when it doesn't fit with your desire. If you can say yes, then too when your ordinary mind goes on saying no, then there is no clinging, then it is real surrender. Otherwise, you can hide behind the master and that hiding itself can become a protection, a security.

A master is a danger. A master is insecurity personified. A master is an adventure.

Buddha said: *I assure you that this log will finally reach the ocean. ...If the log is neither held by the banks, nor seized by men, nor obstructed by the gods...* Buddha does not believe in any gods. He says that people who believe in gods are only obstructed by their ideas; their very idea of "God" becomes their obstruction. If somebody is obstructed by philosophies, dogmas, words, theologies...

For example, a young woman came just two, three days ago, and she said to me, "I love you, Osho, but I am a disciple of Christ. You have helped me tremendously. You have strengthened my religion. Whatsoever I used to believe, now I believe more deeply. You have helped me tremendously. I have come to give you my thanks."

Now, I am not here to strengthen your religion. I am not here to fulfill your philosophies. If you think that I am strengthening your religion, then you must be hearing something else than what I am saying.

Yes, I can bring you close to Christ, but the only way is if you go through me – there is no other way. If you think you already know Christ, if you think that your Christ is the right Christ, then Christ will become the barrier. How can you interpret Christ? Two thousand years have passed, two thousand years of misinterpretations are there; thousands of treatises, thousands of interpretations – how can you interpret Christ now? Those interpretations will never allow you.

A Protestant has a different idea of Christ; a Catholic again a different idea of Christ; a Mohammedan has a totally different idea of Christ. From where will you get your idea? Those ideas will be from the past. You will not attain to Christ because Christ is not a person who happened two thousand years ago. Christ is a state of consciousness which is always available for those who really want to seek.

I say to you: My consciousness is a state of Christ. If you listen to me and still you think that I am fulfilling *your* idea of Christ, you are missing me. If you have understood what I am saying, then you will immediately be able to see Christ in me. Christ will become a presence – *herenow*. It has nothing to do with the Christ who happened two thousand years ago. That was one man, Jesus, coming to the state of christhood. Here is another man who has come to the same state.

Now, you come and listen to me and you think I am here fulfilling your idea of Christ? Your idea is bound to be your idea, it cannot be bigger than you, it cannot be higher than you. It will be as foolish as you are. It will be as idiotic as you are. It will be as dull and stupid as you are. It will be as ignorant as you are. Your idea is, of course, bound to be *your* idea.

I am not here fulfilling your ideas. I am not helping you to become better Christians and better Hindus and better Mohammedans. I am trying to drop all obstacles from your path so you can become that which you are. If you can flower to your totality you will be a christ, you will be a buddha.

But there are obstacles: Buddha says that sometimes the banks, sometimes men around you, sometimes the gods, the philosophies, theologies, sometimes your mind's own whirlpool. And sometimes you yourself can go to decay. If you are not alert and intelligent, you are already decaying, you are already dying. Every day your intelligence becomes more and more dull. Watch a child: how intelligent, how fresh! And watch an old man: how dull, rigid, dead. Every moment, intelligence is slipping by, life is getting out of your hands.

So Buddha says that these things have to be remembered. If these things are remembered and you are not caught by anything, just surrender to the stream and the stream will take you to the ocean.

> *If monks walking on the way are neither tempted by the passions, nor led astray by some evil influences, but steadily pursue their course for nirvana, I assure you that these monks will finally attain enlightenment.*

If monks walking on the way are neither tempted by the passions... The passions are of the body, the passions are of the senses. They are very stupid.

People come to me and they say, "What to do, Osho? I go on eating too much, I go on stuffing myself, I cannot stop. The whole day I am thinking about food." Now the person who is saying this is simply saying that he has lost all intelligence. Food is needed, but food is not the goal. You need food to exist, but there are many people who exist only to eat more and more and more.

Somebody is continuously obsessed with sex. Nothing is wrong with sex, but obsession is always wrong. With what you are obsessed is not the question – obsession is wrong because then it starts draining your energy. Then you are continuously moving in a whirlpool of your own making and you go on round and round and round, and you waste your energy. And one day suddenly you find death has come and you have not lived at all, you have not known even what life is. You have been alive and yet you have not known what life is. You have been here and yet you don't know who you are. What a wastage. And what a disrespectful way of living. I call it sacrilege against existence.

It is good to eat, it is good to love, but if you are eating twenty-four hours a day you are mad. There is a balance. When the balance is lost, then you are falling below human standards.

If monks walking on the way are neither tempted by the passions... Temptation is there, and it will be greater when you start walking on the path. Ordinarily it may not be so, but when you start walking on the path the body will struggle. That's how it happens.

Some people who have come to meditate here were never aware that they were obsessed with food. Meditating, suddenly one day a great obsession arises about food. They feel continuously hungry; they are surprised because it has never been so. What has happened? ...out of meditation? Yes, it can happen out of meditation, because when you are moving in meditation the body starts feeling you are going distant, you are going away. The body starts tempt-ing you. The body will not allow you to become a master.

The body has remained master for many, many lives. You have been a slave. Now, suddenly you are trying to change the whole state, you are trying to make the slave the master, and the master the slave. You are trying to stand on your head – to the body it looks exactly like that, that you are turning things upside down. The body revolts, the body fights, the body resists, the body says, "I will not allow you so easily."

The mind starts fighting. When the body starts fighting you will feel a great obsession for food arising in you. And when the mind starts fighting, you will feel a great obsession with sex arising in you. Sex and food, these two are going to be the problems. These are the two basic passions.

The body lives out of food. When you start moving in meditation the body wants more food to become stronger so it can fight you more. The body wants all strength now so that it can resist the aggression that has come upon it. The effort that you are making to conquer it, to become a master of it, has to be destroyed. The body needs all the energy that is possible. The body becomes mad in eating.

The body survives because of food, and when survival is at stake the body starts eating madly. The mind exists through sex. Why does the mind exist through sex? Because the mind exists by projecting in the future; the mind is a projection in the future. Let me explain it to you.

You are a projection of your mother's and father's sexuality. Your children will be your projection in the future. If you don't eat you will die. If you drop sexuality your children will never be born. So two things are clear: if you drop sexuality, nothing is at stake as far as you are concerned, you will not die by dropping sexuality.

Nobody has ever been heard to die by becoming celibate. You can live perfectly well. Only if you drop food you will die. At the most you can survive three months if you are perfectly healthy, then you will die. Dropping food will be death to you. Dropping sex has nothing to do with you. Maybe your children will never be born; that will be a death to them – death before they are even born – but not death to you.

Through sex the race survives; through food, the individual. So the body is concerned only with food. This body is concerned only with food, but your mind is concerned with sex because only through sex, the mind thinks, will it have a sort of immortality. You will die, that seems certain. You cannot deceive – everybody some day is dying. And every time the bell tolls it tolls for thee. Every time death happens, you become shaken: your own death is coming close. It *will* come. It is only a question of time, but it is to come; there is no way to escape from it. And wherever you escape to, you will find it waiting for you.

I have heard a very famous story, a Sufi story:

A king dreamed. In the night in his dream he saw Death. He became afraid. He asked, "What is the matter? Why are you making me so frightened?"

Death said, "I have come to tell you that tomorrow by sunset I am coming, so get ready. It is just out of compassion so that you can prepare."

The king was so shocked, his sleep was broken. It was the middle of the night; he called his ministers and he said, "Find people who can interpret the dream because time is short. Maybe it is true!"

Then the interpreters came, but as interpreters always have been, they were great scholars. They brought many big books and they started discussing and disputing and arguing. And the sun started rising, and it was morning. And an old man, who was a very trusted servant to the king, he came to the king and he whispered in his ear, "Don't be foolish! These people will quarrel for ever and ever, and they will never come to any conclusion."

Now, everybody was convinced that his interpretation was right, and the king was more confused than ever. So he asked the old man, "Then what am I supposed to do?"

He said, "Let them continue their discussions. They are not going to conclude so soon – and the sun will be setting, because once it has risen the sunset is not very far. Rather, take my advice and escape – at least escape from this palace. Be somewhere else! By the evening reach somewhere as far away as possible."

The logic looked right. The king had a very fast horse, the fastest in the world. He rushed, he escaped. Hundreds of miles he passed. By the time he reached a certain town the sun was just about to set. He was very happy. He patted his horse and he said, "You did well. We have come very far."

And when he was patting his horse, suddenly he felt somebody was standing behind him. He looked back and saw the same shadow of Death. And Death started laughing. The king said, "What is the matter? Why are you laughing?"

Death said, "I was worried because you were destined to die under this tree, and I was worried how you would manage to reach.

"Your horse is really great. It did well. Let me also pat your horse. That's why I came in your dream: I wanted you to escape from the palace because I was very worried how it would happen, how you would be able to reach. The place looked so far away, and only one day was left. But your horse did well, you have come in time."

Wherever you go you will find death waiting for you. In all the directions death is waiting. In all the places death is waiting, so that cannot be avoided. Then mind starts imagining some way to avoid it.

First it spins philosophies: "The soul is immortal. The body will die. I am not going to die." You are even more fragile than the body. This ego that thinks "I will not die" is more flimsy, more dreamlike than the body. The body is at least real; this ego is absolutely unreal. So you spin philosophies: "The soul will never die. I will remain in heaven, in paradise, in *moksha*." But deep down you know that these are just words, they don't satisfy.

Then you find some other way: to earn money, make a great monument, a great palace, do something historical, have a place in history. But that too seems to be meaningless. In such a big history, even if you make all the efforts you will become only a footnote, nothing much. And what is the point of becoming a footnote in a history book? You will be gone all the same; whether people remember you or not does not matter. In fact, who bothers to remember? Ask schoolchildren who have to read history: the great kings who must have made great effort somehow to enter into the history books, and now children are just not bothered at all. They condemn. They are not happy that these great kings existed. They would have been happier if nobody had existed and there was no history to be read and crammed. So what is the point?

Then the mind has a very subtle idea. The idea is: "I will die but my children can live; my child will be my representative. He will live and somehow, deep down in him; I will live, because he will be my extension." It will be your sex cell that will live in your child – in your son, in your daughter. Of course, then sons became more important, because the daughter will move into somebody else's life-stream, and the son will continue your life-stream. The son became very important; he will be your continuity. And the mind starts getting obsessed with sex, goes mad with sex.

Whenever you come closer to meditation, these two things are going to happen: you will start stuffing yourself with food and you will start stuffing yourself with sexuality, and you will start becoming a maniac.

Buddha said: *If monks walking on the way are neither tempted by the passions, nor led astray by some evil influences, but steadily pursue their course for nirvana, I assure you that these monks will finally attain enlightenment.*

You have to be alert not to be distracted by your passions, not to be distracted from the way, not to be distracted from your meditation. Whatsoever the cause of distraction, it has to be avoided. You have to bring your energy again and again to your innermost core. You have to make yourself again and again relaxed, surrendered, non-tense.

> *The Buddha said:*
> *Rely not on your own will. Your own will is not*
> *trustworthy. Guard yourselves against sensualism, for it*
> *surely leads to the path of evil. Your own will becomes*
> *trustworthy only when you have attained arhatship.*

This is a very significant statement. Buddha never said that you need a master, but in a subtle way he has to concede it because a master *is* needed.

Buddha was against masters because the country was so cheated, exploited in the name of guru–disciple relationship. There were so many charlatans and frauds – there have always been and there will always be. And Buddha was very worried that people were being exploited, so he said there is no need for anyone to become anybody's disciple. But how can he avoid a very basic thing? There may be ninety-nine percent frauds, that doesn't matter. Even if one right master exists, he can be of tremendous help.

So in a very indirect way, in a roundabout way, Buddha concedes. He says: *Rely not on your own will...* He says that if you rely upon your own will you will never reach anywhere. Your own will is so weak. Your own will is so unintelligent. Your own will is so divided into itself. You don't have one will; you have many wills in you. You are a crowd.

Gurdjieff used to say you don't have one "I," you have many small "I's," and those "I's" go on changing. For a few minutes, one I becomes the sovereign, and then it is thrown out of power; another I becomes the sovereign. And you can watch it. It is a simple fact. It has nothing to do with any theory.

You love a person, and you are so loving. One I dominates: the I that loves. Then something goes wrong and you hate the person – in a single moment love has turned into hatred. Now you want to destroy the person – at least, you start thinking how to destroy the person. Now the hatred has come in: another I which is totally different is on the throne.

You are happy, you have another I. You are unhappy, again. It goes on changing. Twenty-four hours, day in, day out, your I's go on changing. You don't have one I.

That's why it happens that you can decide tonight: "Tomorrow morning I will get up at three o'clock. Whatsoever happens, I am going to get up." You fix the alarm and at three o'clock you stop the alarm and you are annoyed by the alarm. And you think, "One day – what does it matter? Tomorrow..." and you go to sleep. And again when you get up at eight o'clock in the morning you are angry at yourself. You say, "How could it happen? I had decided to get up. How did I continue to sleep?"

These are two different I's: the one I that decided and the one I that was annoyed with the alarm are different I's. Maybe the first I is again back in the morning and repents. You become angry and then you repent. These are two different I's. They never meet; they don't know what the other is doing. The I that creates anger goes on creating anger, and the I that repents goes on repenting, and you never change.

Gurdjieff used to say that unless you have a permanent, crystallized I, you should not trust yourself. You are not one, you are a crowd: you are polypsychic.

That's what Buddha says: *Rely not upon your own will.* Then on whom to rely? Rely on somebody who has a will, who has an integral I, who has attained, who has become one in his being, is no longer divided, who is really an individual.

Rely not upon your own will. Your own will is not trustworthy. Guard yourselves against sensualism, for it surely leads to the path of evil. Your own will becomes trustworthy only when you have attained arhatship. When you have come to know who you are, when you have become a realized soul, when the enlightenment has happened, then your I becomes trustworthy – never before it. But then there is no point. Then you have come home. It is of no use now. When there was need it was not there. So you need somebody to whom you can surrender, you need somebody with whom trust can arise in you. That is the whole relationship of a master and a disciple.

The disciple has yet no will of his own, and the master has. The disciple is a crowd and the master is one unity. The disciple surrenders. He says, "I cannot trust myself, hence I will trust you." Trusting the master, by and by, the disciple's crowd inside disappears.

That's why I say that when I tell you to do something and you want to do it, and you do it, it is meaningless because it is still according to *your* I, your will. When I say to do something and it is against you, and you surrender and you say yes, then you are moving, then you are growing, then you are becoming mature. Then you are getting out of the mess that you have been up till now.

Only by saying no to your mind do you say yes to the master.

Many times I simply say that which you would like because I don't see that you will be able to do that which I like. I have to persuade you slowly. You are not ready to take a sudden jump. First, I say: change your clothes, then I start changing your body. Then I start changing your mind.

People come to me and they say, "Why should we change clothes? What is the point?" They are not even ready to change their clothes; more cannot be expected of them. They say they are ready to change their souls, but they are not ready to change their clothes – look at the absurdity of it. But with the soul there is one thing: it is invisible, so nobody knows.

But I can see your soul, I can see where you are standing and what you are talking about; I can see through your rationalizations. You say, "What is there in clothes?" but that is not the question. I also know there is nothing in the clothes, but still I say, "change." I would like you to do something according to me, not according to you. That's a beginning.

Then, by and by, first I take hold of your finger, then your hand, then your totality. You say, "Why are you holding my finger? What is the point of holding my finger?" I know what the point is; that is the beginning. I have to go very slowly. If you are ready, then there is no need to go slow, then I can also go in a sudden leap, but people are not ready.

Buddha says: *Rely not upon your own will. Your will is not trustworthy.*

Find a person in whose presence you feel something has happened. Find a person in whose presence you feel a fragrance of the divine, in whose presence you feel a coolness, in whose presence you feel love, compassion, in whose presence you feel a silence – unknown, inexperienced, but it surrounds you, overwhelms you. Then surrender to that person. Then, by and by, he will bring you to the point where surrender will not be needed, you will realize your own innermost core of being, you will become an arhat. The arhat is the final stage of enlightenment.

You become yourself only when all the selves that you have been carrying all along are dissolved. You become yourself only when there is really no self left but a pure nothingness. Then the circle is complete. You have come to the ultimate nothingness, fully aware. You have become a witness of the whole play of life, existence, consciousness.

This state is possible if you don't create obstacles. This state is certainly possible if you avoid obstacles. I can also assure you that if you become driftwood and don't cling to the banks, and don't get attached to whirlpools, and don't start decaying in your unawareness, you are sure, absolutely sure, to reach the ocean.

That ocean is the goal. We come from that ocean and we have to reach to that ocean. The beginning is the end, and when the circle is complete there is perfection, there is wholeness, there is bliss and benediction.

Enough for today.

6

I AM NOT A PERFECTIONIST

The first question:

> *Osho,*
> *What is your view of being successful in ordinary life?*
> *I am afraid you are against success.*

I am neither against anything nor for anything. Whatsoever happens, happens. One need not choose because with choice comes misery. If you want to be successful then you will remain miserable. You may succeed, you may not succeed; but one thing is certain: you will remain miserable.

If you want to succeed, and you succeed by chance, by coincidence, it is not going to fulfill you because this is the way of the mind. Whatsoever you have becomes meaningless, and the mind starts going ahead of you. It desires more and more and more. The mind is nothing but the desire for more. And this desire can never be fulfilled, because whatsoever you have you can always imagine having more. And the distance between that "more" and that which you have will remain constant.

This is one of the most constant things in human experience: everything changes, but the distance between that which you have and that which you would like to have remains constant.

Albert Einstein says, "The speed of time remains constant – that is the only constant." Buddhas say, "The speed of mind remains constant." And the truth is that mind and time are not two things, they are the same; two names for the same thing.

So if you want to succeed, you may succeed but you will not be content. And what is the meaning of a success if you are not content? I say it is only coincidence that you may succeed. The greater possibility is that you will fail because you alone are not chasing success, millions of people are chasing.

In a country of six hundred million people only one person can be the prime minister, and six hundred million people want to be the prime minister or the president. So only one succeeds, and the whole crowd fails. The greater possibility is that you will fail; mathematically that seems to be more certain than success.

If you fail you feel frustrated; your whole life seems to be a sheer wastage. If you succeed, you never succeed; if you fail, you fail – this is the whole game.

You say that you suspect that I am against success. No, I am not. Because if you are against success, then again another idea of being successful will arise: how to drop this nonsense of being successful. Then you have another idea, again the distance, again the desire.

Now, this is what makes people monks, makes people move into monasteries. They are against success. They want to go out of the world where there is competition. They want to escape from it all so that there will be no provocation, no temptation, they can rest in themselves. And they try not to desire success — but this is also a desire Now they have an idea of spiritual success: how to succeed and become a buddha, how to succeed and become a christ, how to succeed and become a Mahavira. Again an idea, again the distance, again the desire, again the whole game starts.

I am not against success, that's why I am in the world, otherwise I would have escaped. I am not for it, I am not against it. I say to be driftwood — whatsoever happens, let it happen. Don't have a choice of your own. Whatsoever comes on your way, welcome it. Sometimes it is day, sometimes it is night; sometimes it is happiness, sometimes it is unhappiness. You be choiceless, you simply accept whatsoever is the case. This is what I call the quality of a spiritual being. This is what I call religious consciousness. It is neither for nor against because if you are for, you will be against; if you are against, you will be for. And when you are for something or against something you have divided existence into two. You have a choice, and choice is hell. To be choiceless is to be free of hell.

Let things be. Just go on moving, enjoying whatsoever becomes available. If success is there, enjoy it. If failure is there, enjoy it. Failure also brings a few enjoyments that no success can ever bring. Success also brings a few joys that no failure can ever bring. A man who has no idea of his own is capable of enjoying everything, whatsoever happens. If he is healthy, he enjoys health; if he is ill, he rests on the bed and enjoys illness.

Have you ever enjoyed illness? If you have not enjoyed it you are missing a lot. Just lying down on the bed doing nothing, no worry of the world and everybody caring about you, and you have suddenly become a monarch — everybody attentive, listening, loving. You have nothing to do, not a single worry in the world. You simply rest. You listen to the birds, you listen to music, or you read a little and doze into sleep. It is beautiful. It has its own beauty. But if you have an idea that you have to be always healthy, then you will be miserable.

Misery comes because we choose. Bliss is when we don't choose.

"What is your view of being successful in ordinary life?" My view is: If you can be ordinary, you are successful.

The patient was complaining to his friends: "After one year and three thousand dollars with that psychiatrist, he tells me I am cured. Some cure! A year ago I was Abraham Lincoln – now I'm a nobody."

This is my idea of being successful: Be a nobody. There is no need for Abraham Lincolns, no need for Adolf Hitlers. Just be ordinary, nobody, and life will be a tremendous joy to you. Just be simple. Don't create complexities around yourself. Don't create demands. Whatsoever comes on its own, receive it as a gift, a grace of existence, and enjoy and delight in it. Millions are the joys that are being showered on you, but because of your demanding mind you cannot see them. Your mind is in such a hurry to be successful, to be somebody special, that you miss all the glory that is just available.

To be ordinary is to be extraordinary. To be simple is to have come home.

But it depends: the very word *ordinary* and you start feeling a bitter taste – ordinary? You and ordinary? Maybe everybody else is ordinary but you are special. This madness, this neurosis exists in everybody's mind.

The Arabs have a special joke for it. They say that when God creates man, he whispers something into each individual's ear and he says: "I never made a man like you or a woman like you; you are simply special. All others are just ordinary." He goes on playing the joke and everybody comes into the world full of this bullshit "I am special. God himself has said that I am unique." You may not say so because you think these ordinary people will not be able to understand it; otherwise, why say? There is no need to say, and why create trouble for yourself? You know, and you are absolutely certain about it.

Everybody is in the same boat. The joke has not been played only upon you, God goes on playing the same joke on everybody. Maybe he has stopped doing it and he has just fixed a computer which goes on repeating the same thing, a mechanical device.

It depends on you how you interpret. The word *ordinary* is of tremendous significance, but it depends. If you can understand... These trees are ordinary. These birds are ordinary. The clouds are ordinary. The stars are ordinary. That's why they are not neurotic. That's why they don't need any psychiatrist's couch. They are healthy, they are full of juice and life. They are simply ordinary. No tree is mad enough to be competitive and no bird is bothered at all about who is the most powerful bird in the world. No bird is interested in that. He simply goes on doing his thing, and enjoys it. But it depends how you interpret.

A father takes his little boy for culture to the Metropolitan Opera. Out comes the conductor with his baton, and out comes the big diva, and she starts to sing an aria. As the conductor is waving his baton, the kid says, "Papa, why is that man hitting that woman?".

The father says, "He isn't hitting her – that's the conductor."

"Well if he ain't hitting her, why is she hollering?" asks the boy.

Whatsoever you see in life is your interpretation. To me, the word *ordinary* is tremendously significant. If you listen to me, if you hear me, if you understand me, you would like just to be ordinary. And, there is no need to struggle to be ordinary. It is already there.

Then all struggle disappears, all conflict. You simply start enjoying life as it comes, as it unfolds. You enjoy the childhood, you enjoy the youth, you enjoy your old age; you enjoy your life and you also enjoy your death. You enjoy all the seasons round the year, and each season has its own beauty, and each season has something to give to you, some ecstasy of its own.

The second question:

> Osho,
> Do you never get tired of talking? Why do you talk
> regularly every morning? Don't you feel like going for
> a holiday sometimes?

I am not a Christian God. The Christian God created the world in six days and the seventh day he rested, hence, the Sunday is the holiday. *Holiday* means the holy day, God's day of rest.

In the East we have never known any god resting. The very idea is stupid: God and resting? Rest is needed if what you are doing is not of your heart, then you get tired. When it is out of your heart and out of your love you don't get tired; in fact you get nourished by it.

Talking to you, I feel nourished. After talking to you I feel more energy than ever because it is my love. I enjoy it. It is not work.

You can get tired if you are working. If you are playing, how can you get tired? Nobody has ever heard that people get tired by playing. In fact, when people are tired by work, they go to play as a rest – they relax. Six days they have been working in the office, in the factory, in the market; the seventh day they go fishing, or they go golfing – they play. They invite friends for a picnic; they go trekking in the hills. That is rest.

To me, every day is a holiday. If you love whatsoever you are doing you are never tired of it; it is nourishing, it is energy-giving, it is vitalizing.

But I can understand the question. The question is from Yoga Chinmaya. His whole concept of work is wrong. He works very reluctantly. He tries hard to avoid work. He finds ways and means to escape from work. He goes on postponing, and he will always be ready with excuses why his work is being postponed. He does not love it; hence the question.

The question is not concerned with me – always remember – the question is yours, not mine. It shows something about you.

Mulla Nasruddin was saying to me one day: "Osho, do you know the difference between a French woman, an English woman and a Jewish woman's reaction when she is kissed in bed by her husband?"

I said, "No, I don't know, you tell me."

He said, "The French woman says, 'Oo la la, Pierre, your kisses are oo la la.'

"The English woman says, 'Jolly well done – I say, Winston your kisses are jolly well done!'

"The Jewish woman says, 'You know, Sam, the ceiling needs painting.'"

It depends how you look at things... Now, Yoga Chinmaya is like a Jewish woman. His outlook toward life is not that of a delighted consciousness. He is simply avoiding, he goes on finding as many excuses as possible. The energy that he puts into finding excuses would be enough to do the work. And then he feels guilty and ashamed.

Work is worship. Work is prayer.

While I am talking to you, it is a prayer to me, it is worship. You are my temples, my gods. Whatsoever I am saying, I am not saying just to teach something. Teaching is a by-product, a consequence. Whatsoever I say to you is a prayer; it is love, it is care. I care about you, I care as much as a painter cares about his canvas.

Have you ever heard about van Gogh being on a holiday? Have you ever heard about Picasso being on holiday? Yes, you must have heard. He used to take many holidays, but always with his canvas and brush. On the holiday also he would be painting. It was not a holiday from painting.

When you love something there is no holiday because then all your days are holidays. Each day to me is a Sunday, full of light – that's why I call it Sunday. Each day to me is a Sunday because it is full of holiness.

Chinmaya's attitude toward work is that of a utilitarian. It is not playful. He is worried about the work, tense about it. That too has a reason: he is a perfectionist, and perfectionism is the root cause of all neurosis. A perfectionist is a neurotic person; sooner or later, he will create more and more neurosis around him.

I am not a perfectionist. I don't bother a bit about being a perfectionist. I am a holistic person. I like things in their wholeness, but I never bother about their perfection. Nothing can be perfect in the world, and in fact nothing should be perfect in the world, because whenever a thing is perfect it is dead.

A poet once lived with me for a few years. He would write, rewrite, again erase, rewrite again. For days on end he would polish his poems. And by the time he would feel it was perfect, I would declare it was dead.

The first glimpse was something alive – it was not perfect, there were flaws in it. Then he went on improving it, removing all flaws, bringing more and more meter, grammar, better language, better words, better sounding words, more music. For months he would polish and change, and by the time he thought it was right to go to the press I would declare, "Now, you send it to the doctor for a postmortem, it is dead. You killed it."

Watch: perfectionist parents always kill their children. Perfectionist saints kill themselves and kill their followers. It is very difficult to live with a perfectionist saint – he is boring, monotonous, and condemning. Whenever you go to him he will be looking from his perfectionist attitude and you will be reduced below your humanity. And he will enjoy condemning you as a sinner. This is wrong, that is wrong, everything is wrong.

I am not a perfectionist. I accept you with all your human frailty, with all your human flaws, with all your human limitations. I love you as you are.

I am not saying be lousy – that is another extreme. That means you don't care at all what you do. A perfectionist cares too much. He is not worried about the work, he is worried about the perfection. He has an ideal to fulfill. And the lousy person does not care at all. With the lousy person the poem will never be written, and with the perfectionist it will be written a thousand and one times, and by the time he declares that he is satisfied, the poem will be dead.

Just between the two somewhere is the holistic approach. Don't be lousy, don't be a perfectionist – be human.

Chinmaya has developed ulcers in the stomach because of his perfectionist attitude. He becomes too worried; he has to do everything as perfectly as possible, it is an obsession. When it is an obsession, then of course you get tired, deadly tired of it. You want to avoid it, because once you take any work in your hands you will go mad, you will become obsessed.

One needs balance. Balance is sanity, and balance is health. I am not tired at all. And if any day I am tired, I will not talk to you because I will never enforce anything on myself. I don't enforce anything on you, how can I enforce anything on myself? If I am tired then it is finished. If I don't feel like speaking, then I can stop in the middle of my talk, or even in the middle of a sentence – I will not complete it, remember. The moment I feel that I am tired it is an indication, a sure indication, that now I have to stop. And I will not wait for a single moment to stop. That's how I live.

I don't enforce anything on myself. Whatsoever is natural is good. Easy is right.

The third question:

> Osho,
> I am losing all meaning, purpose, sense in everything. The world is a scintillating mass of light particles. I am...I am not...I am...I am not...spinning, whirling, a vortex... In that space there is no meaning. I am not happy, I am not sad. There is not even anything to understand, it seems.
> Then, when I return to routine reality, I find I seek a meaning to give life some substance. That meaning is love. Is love something pertaining to the human dimension? Is it something we create, or is it all there is and here for us to discover?
> Thank you for creating a love-space for us.

The ultimate meaning always looks meaningless. The ultimate is certainly empty of all the meanings that you can imagine, all the meanings that you would like it to have. It is empty of all that, it is empty of human ideas. It is empty of human philosophies, theologies. It is empty of human religions, ideologies. It is empty of human language and human theorizing.

So when you start coming closer to the ultimate, to the really real, you start feeling that all meaning is lost. Yes, your meaning is lost. The ultimate has nothing like your meaning, it has nothing to fulfill your ideas of meaning, but that does not mean it has no meaning at all. It has a meaning of its own.

Once you have come to the point where your meaning disappears, then the real meaning appears. In fact, even to call it "meaning" is not right because it does not fulfill any human concept. But still I would like to call it meaning because there is no other word to substitute. It has tremendous meaning, but the meaning is intrinsic; the meaning is not external.

Human meanings are external, never internal. You do something, you earn money, and somebody asks, "What is the meaning of earning money?" And you say, "I would like to have my own house, that's why. That's why I am earning money." The idea of having one's own house gives meaning to the effort that you have to make for earning money. Money in itself seems to be meaningless. The meaning comes from somewhere else. All human activity is like that.

The human activity is divided between means and ends. The end has the meaning, and you go on doing the activity as a means because without it there will be no end. But the ultimate meaning has no division, no split. Existence is not in any way split; existence is not in any way schizophrenic. Existence is one unity, unison. The meaning is intrinsic. Means and ends are not there. The means itself is the end and the journey itself is the goal.

For example, I am talking to you. Now, if I am talking to you to gain something out of it then it is a worldly activity, then it has nothing to do with religion. Listen to it deeply. If I am talking here to gain something from my talking as an end: money, power, prestige, respectability, anything, then my activity is worldly.

If I am talking just out of my love, if I am enjoying talking itself – not that something outside it is waiting for me that will make me happy – if I am happy while talking, if I am happy as I am talking, if my talking is a total activity in itself, means and ends together, then it is a spiritual activity.

That is the difference between a priest and a saint. The priest talks to gain something out of it, the saint talks to share. The saint feels grateful to you that you listened to him, that you became available to him, that you opened your hearts to him, that you allowed him to unburden himself. He has tremendous riches and treasures and he wants to share it. He is like a flower that wants to share its fragrance to the winds, not to gain anything out of it.

The ultimate has a meaning, but the meaning has no connotation of the human idea of meaning, it is intrinsic. That's why Hindus say that it is a playful activity.

You go for a morning walk, and you don't have any idea of a destination; you simply enjoy the morning walk. You go by the same road, in the same direction, to your office also, but then it is not intrinsic – you have to go on the road because you have to reach the office. You are in a hurry, rushing. Then you don't see the trees on the roadside, you don't see the clouds passing in the sky, you don't see the children playing, you don't listen to the dogs barking, you simply rush. Your vision is very narrow. It is focused on the goal: you have to reach your office at eleven o'clock exactly. You are unconcerned about everything that is going on around you. But when you go for a morning walk you are not going anywhere, you are simply enjoying. The very activity of walking is so delightful: the breeze, the morning sun, the birds, the children, the noises, everything. And you are not going anywhere.

God is not going anywhere. He is simply herenow. His activity is not end-oriented. The means and the ends are the same thing. The journey is the goal.

You ask: "I am losing all meaning..." beautiful, fabulous, fantastic. Lose as fast as you can, don't cling, "...purpose, and sense in everything." Beautiful! When all sense, purpose and meaning is lost, the divine sends the divine purpose, the divine meaning is revealed. You are getting ready, ready to receive the gift.

"The world is a scintillating mass of light particles. I am... I am not... I am... I am not."

Good. That's how, if you become aware, you will come to feel: when the breath goes out, you will feel "I am not," when the breath comes in, you will feel "I am." There is a rhythm. This is the rhythm of life and death. Each moment you die and you are reborn. Each moment you disappear and you appear again. Each moment you move into nothingness and you come out of it again. Each moment you become nothing and each moment you materialize. This is the miracle, the magic of existence. This is the mystery.

This is your inner rhythm. If you become aware, you will start feeling it. It is good. Just go on watching it. Don't be afraid and don't try to escape from it because when suddenly you feel "I am not," a fear arises; you start clinging to things. Somehow, you want to feel you are. You don't want to disappear, you don't want to die. If that fear is there, then you will miss this great opportunity – death has become available to you.

When you are not, you are not – then simply be not. And when you are, be again. And don't think there is a contradiction in it. You must be thinking there is a contradiction; that's why you say: "...spinning, whirling, a vortex..." No, it is a simple rhythm, just like day and night, summer and winter. It is a simple rhythm. Enjoy it. Disappear when you disappear; appear when you appear. And don't hanker for the other; just be that which is. And soon you will see a new phenomenon arising in you: the witness – which never disappears and never appears. When you are not, then too the witness is there, otherwise who will know "I am not"? When you are, then too the witness is there; otherwise who will know "I am"?

"I am, I am not" is like breathing: inhalation, exhalation. Allow it, be in deep rest in it, and the spinning and the whirling and the vortex, all those sensations will disappear and a great peace will descend on you as it descended one day on Jesus like a dove. A great peace will descend on you, and in that peace something new will become revealed. That is the witness. You are not that. That witness is what "God" is – the witness of all.

"I am not happy. I am not sad. There is not even anything to understand, it seems." This is a transitory period. Before you really become happy, before you really attain to *anand* – blissfulness – this moment comes when you are neither sad nor happy. A great indifference arises. You simply feel not attached to anything: happiness, unhappiness, you become an onlooker to both.

Sooner or later, when the time is ripe and the season has come for you, suddenly you will see a bliss arising in you. That bliss has nothing to do with your ordinary happiness. Your ordinary happiness is always carrying the seeds of unhappiness in it. Your ordinary happiness always turns into unhappiness, and you know it. You have experienced it a thousand and one times. Your unhappiness carries again the seeds of your happiness. In your laughter there are tears, maybe not visible, but they are there. And in your tears also there is laughter.

I have heard, many times, laughter in your tears, and I have seen tears many times in your laughter. You are a duality.

This transitory period comes when you become a little detached from the duality, when you start understanding that the laughter and the tears are not two separate things. There is nothing to choose: laughter brings tears, tears bring laughter, so what is the point in choosing? You become a little less choosy, then you are neither sad nor happy.

This is what is called silence, peace. If you get in tune with it totally, then will arise bliss, ecstasy. That ecstasy has no seeds of anything. It is pure. It has no duality. It cannot turn into its opposite – it has no opposite to it. That's what we call bliss, *anand*, ecstasy.

It has no opposite; it is simply alone there in its absolute purity, innocence.

First a man has to live in duality – sometimes sad, sometimes happy, again sad, again happy, and he goes on revolving. Then arises peace, if you start becoming watchful. That is the second stage: peace. The duality is losing its hold on you. Then arises ecstasy. Ecstasy is the goal.

God is not only silent. There are a few religions which have stopped at silence; they are not complete religions. For example, Jainism has stopped at peace, silence. I don't think Mahavira stopped there, he was an ecstatic man, tremendously ecstatic, madly ecstatic. But Jainas have stopped at peace. Buddhists have also done that, they have stopped at peace. Buddha was not only a man of peace – certainly he was a man of peace, but he was more, he was plus.

That plus point is missing in Buddhism; it was in Buddha, but it is missing in Buddhism. So whenever a person starts meditating on Buddhist lines he becomes a little indifferent to happiness, unhappiness. He certainly becomes more peaceful, but his peacefulness has a certain quality of sadness in it, a certain quality of unaliveness. He looks a little frozen, he looks a little dead. He is not throbbing, life is not kicking in him. He is not full of juice, he is not juicy. He seems to be dry, desertlike, not blooming. That is the danger of Buddhist meditations. One has to go beyond it.

Always remember that peace is not the goal. The goal is ecstasy. Unless you can dance, unless you can abandon yourself in dance, unless your dance can become a deep orgasm, unless you can bloom, don't stop yourself somewhere in the middle of the journey.

"There is not even anything to understand, it seems." You say "it seems" – in fact, it is so. There is nothing to understand. Life is a mystery which transcends understanding. All understanding is just child's play. You can play around. The really mature person comes to know that there is nothing to understand. In fact, there is nobody to understand and nothing to be understood. Life is a mystery to be lived, not to be understood.

"Then, when I return to routine reality, I find I seek a meaning to give life some substance." That's where you go wrong. You will have to bring your silence and peace back to your routine, normal life. If you again start finding some ways and means to fulfill the zero that is arising in you, to fill that emptiness that is arising in you; if you start finding ways, occupations, methods, relationships to fill the gap that is coming to you, to have "some substance," then you will be in a mess. Because on the one hand a great process is going on, and on the other hand you start destroying that process. Remain insubstantial because that's how reality is.

One of the messages of Buddha is that there is no substance. Matter is immaterial and man has no self. Substance exists not. All desire to have some substance is out of ignorance, is out of fear. You are a nothing, a profound nothing, a bottomless abyss. So don't be afraid, fall into it, go on falling into it. Don't try to hang by some roots somewhere, by some branch of a tree, or with somebody, some occupation, something or other. Don't try to hang anywhere, just drop yourself into this bottomless abyss. Dropping into it you disappear. You disappear like smoke.

The day you have completely disappeared is the day of nirvana – then you know who you really are.

Man is like a zero. The concept of zero was born in India. In fact, the nine digits and zero were invented by Indians. But zero in itself is meaningless. It has meaning only when you join it together with some digit. If you put it behind one, it becomes meaningful – one becomes ten; zero carries the meaning of being equivalent to nine. If you put it behind two, it becomes twenty; the zero carries the meaning of nineteen now. You go on putting bigger figures in front of it and the zero goes on becoming bigger and bigger, and feels very substantial.

That's what we are doing in life. A man is born like a zero. Then put a bank balance in front of him, and he becomes substantial. Then tell him that he has become the president of our country, and he becomes very substantial. The zero carries much meaning now: he has money, power, prestige, name, fame. Then the zero becomes more and more substantial. That's why we hanker after name, fame, money, prestige: to put something so we don't feel empty.

But whatsoever you do is in vain because you are empty.

Emptiness is your nature. You can deceive, but you cannot change the reality.

So this is my suggestion, that even in your ordinary reality, when you descend from your meditative state, bring that zero, and don't try to fill it with anything, because that is very violent. That is like an elephant, that's what Indian scriptures say: The elephant goes to the river, he takes a good bath, showers himself with water, and then comes out of the river and throws dust upon himself. That's how Indian scriptures describe the man who goes into meditation, attains to the purity of nothingness, comes back, and throws dust upon himself. That is foolish, that is suicidal. Avoid it. That is a natural tendency, but avoid it. Don't be an elephant.

"I find I seek a meaning to give life some substance. That meaning is love. Is love something pertaining to the human dimension?" The love that pertains to the human dimension is not really love; it is just a deep urge to fill oneself with the other's being, to put somebody else in front of your zero so you become meaningful. A woman alone feels nothing; moving with the husband, see the woman – she is moving with a figure, the zero is moving with a figure. A man alone feels empty; moving with a woman he feels somebody. A husband is somebody. A bachelor is nobody. We go on finding somehow, with something, to block this experience of nothingness.

No, human love is not really love. It is just a trick to deceive. The real love is something beyond human. And the real love is something which has nothing to do with filling the inner space, just the contrary. It has something to do with sharing the inner space. You don't go like a beggar to the other; you go like an emperor. You don't go to beg; you go to share. And remember these two words.

If you are begging something from somebody, then it is not love. If you are sharing, then it is love. Sharing is in a way beyond human beings, and yet in a way within human capacity. Sharing is the bridge which joins the human to the divine. That's why love is the bridge which joins the human to the divine.

So don't try to find a friend, a girlfriend, somebody to fill your inner space. No. Find someone to share with. Don't find a figure – one, two, three – don't find a figure. Find somebody who is also like a zero. When two zeros meet, there is love. When two emptinesses meet, there is love.

And remember: when two zeros meet, there are not two zeros, there is only one zero. Zero plus zero plus zero – you can go on putting as many zeros as you want, but it always comes to one zero. The total is never more than one zero.

Love is when two persons disappear. Love is when the lover is not and the beloved is not. Even in great love affairs, there are only a few rare moments when love is.

Let me tell you in this way: I have read many great poems, many great epics, but even in a great epic, even in Shakespeare, in Kalidas, in Tulsidas, in Milton, in Dante, only rarely are there a few lines which are poetic. Sometimes just a fragment of a line is poetic, sometimes only a word, just a nuance, is poetic. Even in a great love affair that's how it is: only a few rare moments are of love. But only when you completely disappear and two are not two and a non-duality exists, and the personalities are no longer clashing, personalities have been dropped; then love happens. That love has the quality of timelessness. That love has the quality of prayer. That love is "God."

"Is love something pertaining to the human dimension?" It can pertain to the human dimension if you work for it, if you create opportunities for it, if you become vulnerable to it. Naturally, it is not available. Ordinarily it is not available. Ordinarily, only sex is available, and sex is nothing but a device, an *upaya*, to forget yourself.

Love is a tremendous remembering, a great awareness, a brilliant flame with no smoke. But it exists as a seed in you. You can grow it, you can grow into that reality of love. You have the potentiality, but it has to be made actual.

"Is it something we create, or is it all there is and here for us to discover?" No, we don't create it, love cannot be created. It cannot be manufactured; it is not man-made. Love that is manufactured is false love; it is like plastic flowers. Love that is discovered is real love. You are not to manufacture it, you are to drift into it. You have to relax into it.

Yes, Buddha is right when he says, "Become like a timber floating down the stream, you will reach to the ocean." I assure you, you will reach to the ocean. The ocean is already there: the river has to discover it, not to create it. How can the river create the ocean? Just think of the ridiculous idea. A river? how can it create the ocean? If a river creates an ocean it will be just a small pool of water, it will not be an ocean, it will not be infinite. And if a river creates an ocean it will become dirty, it will become stale, it will be dead.

The river has to seek and discover. The ocean exists already. The ocean exists before the river ever existed. In fact, the river has come out of the ocean, through the clouds. We reach ultimately to the original source, nowhere else. The river falls into the ocean because the river came out of the ocean. We become gods because we come out of existence.

Love has to be discovered — it is already there. And how to discover it? The more you are, the less is the possibility to discover love; the less you are, the more is the possibility to discover it. When the river disappears into the ocean, it discovers the ocean, it becomes the ocean.

The fourth question:

> Osho,
> Is it because of your decision that you don't go out of your residence? Or is it that going out simply doesn't happen?

There is nowhere to go now. All going has stopped because the one who used to go has disappeared. Wherever I am I am here and now. My room is as perfect as any other place anywhere, so what is the point of going anywhere? It is pointless.

You go on searching, you go on going: sometimes to the club, sometimes to the movie, sometimes to the hotel, sometimes here, sometimes there. You go on continuously because wherever you are you are not content. Wherever you are, you feel you must be missing something which must be happening somewhere else.

Of course, you become worried about me also: What does this man go on doing, sitting in his room? Doesn't he get fed up sometimes? Why isn't he going out? Rather than asking me why I am not going out, please start asking why you go on going out.

It happened:

Rabiya al-Adabiya was sitting in her room meditating, praying. Another mystic, Hassan, was staying with her. He came out, it was early morning, the sun was just on the horizon. It was beautiful. It was musical. It was magical. And he called out loudly: "Rabiya, why don't you come out? God has created a beautiful dawn."

And Rabiya laughed and said, "Hassan, when will you become mature? Come in, rather than calling me out. The dawn is beautiful, but here inside I am facing the creator of the dawn."

Right, Rabiya is right: the outside is beautiful, but nothing to be compared with the inside. Once you have an inside view of things who bothers about the outside? The outside is beautiful, nothing is wrong in it, but if you go on moving from one place to another and never come home you will remain in misery.

I don't go, not because it is a decision on my part. For the last twenty-two or three years I have not decided anything. The day I died, 21 March 1953, decision also died. I am not there, so who is to decide? So whatsoever happens, happens – and it is tremendously beautiful. More cannot be expected. It is more than man can ever desire.

Eighty-six year old Harry Hershfield was accosted by a prostitute outside the Lambs Club. Harry told her, "There are three reasons why I can't go with you. First, I have no money..."

The lady interrupted, "Then the other two reasons don't matter.

I have also three reasons why I don't go out. The first is: I am not – and the other two do not matter.

The fifth question:

> Osho,
> For the sake of posterity, your historians and
> chroniclers, and for my sake, would you please be

> *truthful for once in your life – and please cut out a long dissertation on what is truth and what is untruth.*
> *Isn't it the case that the towel has nothing to do with the buffer state of Tibet or with the variety of esoteric meanings emanating from a certain room in Jesus House?*
> *Isn't it simply that you use the towel to chase away an invasion of invisible mosquitoes from Jabalpur?*

The first thing: that which can be said is all untruth; that which cannot be said is the truth. All the scriptures are beautiful lies. And all the sermons of buddhas and christs are beautiful, decorated lies.

You ask me: "...please, be truthful for once in your life..." You ask the impossible. That I cannot do; nobody has ever done it, and nobody can ever do it. Truth cannot be expressed. And by saying it so clearly to you, I come the closest to truth that is possible. It cannot be said. And all that can be said will remain some sort of untruth. Words destroy truth. Expression corrupts truth.

And you ask me about the towel: "Isn't it the case that the towel has nothing to do with the buffer state of Tibet...?"

It has nothing to do with any buffer state or any Tibet. Not at least today does it have anything to do with it. I cannot promise you about tomorrow, and I have forgotten everything about yesterday.

All the esoteric meanings that are being given to it are simply stupid. But there are stupid people who need esoteric fabrications, esoteric theorizations.

Esotericism exists in the world because of the stupid human mind. Otherwise, everything has always been open, in front of you; nothing is hidden from the very beginning. How can truth be hidden? Maybe it cannot be expressed, but that doesn't mean that it is hidden. It is just in front of your eyes. It is all over the place. It is everywhere, within and without.

But it is good to understand how foolish theorizations can arise out of simple things. It was just a joke, but there are people who will not even believe this. They will find some esoteric meaning in it, why I call it a joke. There are difficult people.

It has nothing to do with anything. It is the only thing that I have. Let me tell you one anecdote:

A hippie was walking down the street with a cigar-box under his arm when he met another hippie who asked, "Hey, man, What's cookin'? Where you goin' with that cigar-box?"

"I'm movin'," said the first hippie.

So this is something that whenever I want to move at least I can carry with me. And I was ready to drop it, I had already dropped it, but Maneesha wouldn't allow it. Then she started asking about the robe. I can drop that too, but that will create many difficulties – not for me, for you. Just for your sake, I am not dropping the robe.

A sixty-year-old and an eighty-year-old met. The sixty-year-old said, "I don't know, I just can't seem to satisfy my wife. I try, but... Nothing."

The eighty-year-old answered, "I have no problem whatsoever. Every night I come home and get undressed in front of my wife and I say, 'Take a look. Are you satisfied?' She shrugs yes, and that's it!"

People can go on finding rationalizations – now what type of satisfaction is this? All esoteric explanations are like this, they don't satisfy you, because how can just verbal fabrications of ideas satisfy? Only truth can satisfy. And the truth is that it was just a joke.

I love jokes. And there is no need to find any esoteric meaning in them. They are simple. But it is difficult to accept any simple thing.

Pope Pius XII of Rome is arriving at Heaven's door. St. Peter opens, asks for his name, and shakes his head. "Never heard..."

"So go to God-father, he will recognize me," the Pope demanded.

Off St. Peter went. "Hey boss, do you know a man called Pope Pius XII of Rome?"

"Never heard of him," is God-father's answer.

Peter, back at Heaven's door: "He doesn't know you."

"So go and ask Jesus."

St. Peter, already a little impatient, went off again: "Hey Junior, do you know a man called Pope Pius XII of Rome?"

Junior: "Never heard, never seen him."

Off St. Peter went to tell the desperate Pope the message. "Do me a last favor," said the Pope, "ask the Holy Ghost."

Peter sighed and back in Heaven he called the Holy Ghost: "Hello Smoky, do you know Pope Pius XII of Rome?"

Smoky, murmuring: "Pope Pius, Pope Pius XII of Rome... Send him to Hell! That's the guy who told that dirty story about Mary and me!"

This was the man who invented the story of how Mary became pregnant without ever being in love with any man. There are pundits and scholars, but remember: nobody will recognize you at heaven's gate.

Theories are just futile, but the mind craves and the mind wants to spin around anything. Just see: around the towel. You are creating so much fuss about it. In Chinmaya's room great meetings go on, and people visit him and ask him, and he goes on explaining...

The last question:

Osho,
The towel which landed in front of Maitreya and
which he took into his possession has mysteriously
disappeared. What do you have to say about this?

These towels are very temperamental. I know them: a long love affair. Twenty-five years is too much in this world where even to live with a woman that long has become impossible – three years at the most. Twenty-five years I have lived with that towel. They are very temperamental.

And I have spoilt them also. I have loved them, respected them, worshipped them. Now, Maitreya is a simple man. He must have put the towel somewhere. The towel won't like it that way. It is in his room, I assure you, but he will have to go through a little courtship. He will have to coo and woo. And that particular towel is a lady towel. Today I have a boy towel, so I give it to Maitreya: keep them together. They will feel better and happy.

Enough for today.

7

SEX IS THE BASIC PROBLEM

The Buddha said:
O monks, you should not see women. (If you should have to see them), refrain from talking to them. (If you should have to talk), you should reflect in a right spirit: "I am now a homeless mendicant. In the world of sin I must behave myself like unto the lotus flower whose purity is not defiled by the mud. Old ones I will treat as my mother; elderly ones as elder sisters; younger ones as younger sisters; and little ones as daughters." And in all this you should harbor no evil thoughts, but think of salvation.
The Buddha said:
Those who walk in the way should avoid sensualism as those who carry hay would avoid coming near the fire.

The magnificent temple that Buddha built consists of three floors; his teaching has three dimensions to it, or three layers. And you will have to be very patient to understand those three layers. I say so because they have been misunderstood down the centuries.

The first floor of Buddha's teaching is known as *hinayana*; the second floor is known as *mahayana*, and the third floor is known as *vajrayana*. *Hinayana* means "the small vehicle," "the narrow way." *Mahayana* means "the great vehicle," "the wide way." And *vajrayana* means "the supreme vehicle," "the ultimate way," "the transcendental way." *Hinayana* is the beginning and *vajrayana* is the climax, the crescendo.

Hinayana starts from where you are. *Hinayana* tries to help you to change your mechanical habits; it is just like *hatha* yoga – very body-oriented, believes in great discipline; strict, almost repressive, at least it looks repressive. It is not repressive, but the whole work of *hinayana* consists in changing your centuries-old habits.

Just as a tightrope-walker starts leaning to the left if he feels that he is going to fall toward the right, to balance one has to move to the opposite. By moving to the opposite, a balance arises, but that balance is temporary, momentary. Again one will start falling into the new direction, then again one will need balance and will have to move to the opposite.

Sex is the very basic problem. And all the habits that man has created are basically sex-oriented. That's why no society allows total sexual freedom. All the cultures that have existed – sophisticated, unsophisticated, Eastern, Western, primitive, civilized – all cultures have tried in some way to control the sexual energy of man. It seems to be the greatest power over man. It seems that if man is allowed total freedom about sex, he will simply destroy himself.

Skinner reports about a few experiments he was doing with rats. He has invented a new theory, that electrodes can be put into the human or animal brain, attached to particular centers in the brain, and you just push a button and that center will be stimulated inside you.

There is a sex center in the brain. In fact, you are more controlled by the sex center in the brain than the actual sex center of your body. That's why fantasy works so well. That's why pornography has so much appeal. Pornography cannot appeal to the sex center itself; it stimulates the brain center attached to the sex center. Once the mind is active, immediately the sex center, the physiological sex center, starts being active.

Skinner fixed electrodes in rats' brains and taught them how to push the button whenever they wanted sexual stimulation and an inner orgasm. He was surprised by what happened, he was not expecting this: those rats completely forgot everything – food, sleep, play – they forgot everything. They continuously pushed the button. One rat did it six thousand times and died pushing the button. Six thousand times! He forgot everything, nothing else mattered.

Sooner or later, some Skinner or somebody else is going to also give you a small box to keep in your pocket and, whenever you feel sexual, just push a button and your brain center will become active and will give you beautiful orgasms and nobody will ever know what is happening inside you. But you will almost follow the rat because then what is the point of doing anything else? You will kill yourself.

Sex is such a great attraction that if there were not limitations on it... First there is a limitation that body puts on it. A man cannot have too many orgasms in a day; if you are young, three, four; if you become older, then one; when you become a little older still, then even that becomes difficult – once a week, once a month. And, by and by, your body puts many limitations on it.

Women are freer that way. The body has no limitation. That's why, all over the world, women have been completely repressed. She has not been allowed freedom; she has not been allowed even freedom to have orgasms in the past because she can have multiple orgasms. Within seconds she can have many orgasms – six, twelve. Then no man will be able to satisfy a woman; then no man will be able to satisfy any woman. Then only group sex will be able to satisfy. A woman will need at least twelve husbands, and that will create tremendous complexities.

That's why, down the centuries, for thousands of years, women were brought up in such a way that they have completely forgotten that they can have orgasm. Just within these fifty years women have again started learning what orgasm is, and with their learning, problems have arisen all over the world. Marriage is on the rocks. Marriage cannot exist with women having the capacity of multiple orgasms. And man only has the capacity for one orgasm. There can be no compatibility between the two. Then monogamy cannot exist. It will become difficult.

This society and the pattern that it has evolved up to now is doomed. Man has released some energy that has always been kept under a certain rigid control. But the attraction has always been there, whether you repress, whether you control, discipline, that doesn't make any difference. The attraction is there – twenty-four hours, deep down like a substratum, sexuality goes on like a river flowing. It is a continuum. You may eat, you may earn money, you may work, but you are doing everything for sex.

Somewhere, sex remains the goal, and this pattern has to be changed, otherwise your energy will go on being drained, your energy will go on being dissipated, your energy will go on moving into the earth. It will not rise toward heaven. It will not have an upward surge.

Hinayana works just exactly where you are. You are continuously obsessed with sex? *Hinayana* tries to remove this obsession. It gives you a certain discipline, a very rigid discipline to drop out of it.

Hinayana says that there are four steps to drop out of sex. The first is called purifying. The second is called enriching. The third is called crystallizing. The fourth is called destroying.

First you have to move your total energy against sex, so that sexual habits developed in many lives no longer interfere – that is called purifying. You change your consciousness, you shift. From sexual obsession you move to anti-sexuality.

The second step is called enriching. When you have moved to non-sexuality, then you have to enjoy non-sexuality; you have to celebrate your celibacy. If you don't celebrate your celibacy, again sex will start pulling you backward. Once you start celebrating your celibacy, then the pull of sex will be completely gone, and gone forever.

You are obsessed with sex because you don't know any other

sort of celebration. So the problem is not sex really; the problem is that you don't know any other celebration. Nature allows you only one joy, and that is of sex. Nature allows you only one enjoyment, and that is of sex. Nature allows you only one thrill, and that is of sex.

Hinayana says that there is a greater thrill waiting for you if you move toward celibacy. But the celibacy should not be violently forced. If you violently enforce it you will not be able to enjoy it. One has to be just aware of the sexual habits, and through awareness one has to shift by and by toward celibacy.

Celibacy should be brought very slowly. All that brings you again and again to sexuality has to be dropped slowly, in steps. And once you start enjoying the energy that becomes available, when you are not obsessed with sex, just that pure energy becomes a dance in you — that is called enriching. Now, your energy is not wasted. Your energy goes on showering on yourself.

Remember, there are two types of celibates. One: someone who has simply forced celibacy upon himself — he is a wrong type, he is doing violence to himself. The other: someone who has tried to understand sexuality, what it is, why it is; who has watched, observed, lived through it, and, by and by, has become aware of its futility; by and by, has become aware of a deep frustration that comes after each sexual act.

In the sexual act you have a certain thrill, a moment of forgetfulness, a moment of oblivion. You feel good for a few seconds, only for a few seconds you drop out of this routine world. Sex gives you a door to escape into some other world which is non-tense; there is no worry, you are simply relaxed and melting. But have you observed? After each sexual act you feel frustrated.

Sex has promised much, but it has not been supplied. It is difficult to find a man or a woman who does not feel a little frustrated after the sexual act, who does not feel a little guilty. I am not talking about the guilt that priests have imposed upon you. Even if nobody has ever imposed any guilt upon you, you will feel a little guilt because that is part, a shadow of the sexual act. You have lost energy, you feel depleted, and nothing has been gained. The gain is not very substantial. You have been befooled, you have been tricked by a natural hypnosis; you have been tricked by the body, you have been deceived. Hence, frustration comes.

Hinayana says to watch this frustration more deeply. Watch the sexual act and the way your energy moves into the sexual act, become aware of it and you will see there is nothing in it. As to frustration: the more you become aware, the less will be the enjoyment and the more will be the frustration. Then the shift has started taking place: your consciousness is moving away, and naturally, and spontaneously. You are not forcing it.

The second step becomes available: enriching. Your own energy goes on feeding your being. You no longer throw it into the other's body, you no longer throw it out. It becomes a deep accumulation inside you. You become a pool. And out of that feeling of energy you feel very cool. Sex is very hot. The enriching stage is very cool, calm, collected. There is a celebration, but it is very silent. There is a dance to it, but it is very graceful; there is elegance to it.

Then comes the third step: crystallizing. When this energy inside you has started an inner dance, by and by, slowly, enjoying it more and more, becoming more and more aware of it, a certain chemical crystallization happens in you. Exactly the same word was used by Gurdjieff in his work: crystallization. Your fragments fall together, you become one. A unity arises in you. In fact, for the first time you can say "I have an I." Otherwise there were many I's; now you have one I, a big I which controls everything. You have become your master.

The fourth step is destroying. When you have one I, then it can be destroyed. When you have many I's, they cannot be destroyed. When your energy has become one and is centered, the I can be killed, it can be completely destroyed. When it is a crowd it is difficult to destroy it. You destroy one fragment, there are a thousand other fragments. When you rush after those other fragments, the first one grows again. It is just like the way trees grow branches: you cut one, three branches sprout out of it.

You can destroy sexuality totally only when it has become a crystallized phenomenon. When a person has accumulated too much energy and has become one, is no longer fragmentary, no longer split, no longer schizophrenic, then Buddhists have a special term for it. They call it "Manjushree's sword."

It is said that when Manjushree, a disciple of Buddha, a great disciple of Buddha reached to this third stage, when he reached to this stage of crystallization, in one single moment he took his sword and destroyed it completely, utterly, in a single moment. It is not a gradual process then. That has become known down the centuries as "the sword of Manjushree."

When a person reaches to the third state he can just raise a sword and destroy it completely, in one single attack. Because now the enemy is there, now the enemy is no longer elusive, now there are no longer many enemies, just one enemy confronting you. And the sword is just the sword of perfect awareness, mindfulness, self-remembering. It is a very sharp sword.

When Buddha destroyed his own sexuality, it is said he roared like a lion because for the first time the whole absurdity of it became clear. And so many lives wasted, so many lives of sheer stupidity gone forever. He was so happy he roared like a lion.

These are the four steps, and today's sutras are concerned with these four steps. Before we enter into the sutras, a few more things have to be understood.

The second vehicle is *mahayana*. When your sexual energy is no longer obsessed with the other's body, when you are completely free of the other's body, when your energy has a freedom to it, then *mahayana* becomes possible – the second floor of Buddha's temple.

Mahayana makes it possible for you to be loving. Ordinarily we think sex makes people loving. Sex can never make people loving. In fact, it is sexuality that prevents love from growing because it is the same energy that has to become love. It is being destroyed in sex. To become love, the same energy has to move to the heart center. *Mahayana* belongs to the heart center.

Hinayana works at the sex center – *muladhar*. *Mahayana* works at the heart center – it says that love, prayerfulness, have to be developed now. Energy is there, now you can love. Energy is there, now you can pray.

Mahayana is loving-effort. One has to love unconditionally – the trees and the rocks and the sun and the moon and the people – but now love has no sexuality in it. It is very cool, it is very tranquil.

If you come near a person whose energy is moving in his heart center you will suddenly feel you are moving under a deep cool shade, no hot energy. Suddenly you will feel a breeze surrounding you. The person of love, the person who lives at the heart center, is to a traveler like a shady tree, or cool running water, or a breeze fragrant with many blossoms.

Mahayana is not afraid of sex. *Hinayana* is afraid of sex. *Hinayana* is afraid of sex because you are too obsessed with sex. You have to move to the opposite. *Mahayana* is not afraid of sex – it has attained to the balance, there is no fear of the opposites. *Mahayana* is when the tightrope-walker is balanced; he neither leans to the left nor to the right.

Then the third and the final stage, the third floor of Buddha's temple, is *vajrayana*. *Vajra* means diamond – it is the most precious teaching; certainly very difficult to understand. *Vajrayana* is Buddhist Tantra.

Vajrayana is called *vajra*, the diamond, because the diamond cuts everything. The diamond vehicle, the way of the diamond, *vajrayana*, cuts everything completely, through and through – all materiality, all desire, all attachment. Even the desire to be born in heaven, the desire to be in a peaceful state, the desire to become a buddha, the desire to have nirvana, enlightenment, even these beautiful desires are cut completely.

Vajrayana knows no difference between the world and nirvana, knows no difference between ignorance and knowledge, knows no difference, no distinctions – all distinctions are dropped. It knows no distinction between man and woman.

Now let me explain that to you:

On the stage of *hinayana*, man is man, woman is woman. And man is attracted toward woman, and the woman is attracted toward man – they are out-going; their attraction is somewhere outside them. Of course, they will be slaves. When your attraction is somewhere outside you, you cannot be independent of it.

That's why lovers never forgive each other, they cannot. They are annoyed. You love a person and you are irritated by the person at the same time. There is a reason for it. There is constant fight between lovers. The reason is: you cannot forgive the lover, because you know you are dependent on him or on her. How can you forgive your slavery? You know your woman makes you happy, but if she decides not to make you happy, then suddenly you are unhappy. Your happiness is in her hands. Her happiness is in your hands. Whenever somebody else controls your happiness, you cannot forgive the other.

Jean-Paul Sartre says, "The other is hell," and he is right. He has a great insight into it. The other is hell because you have to depend on the other. Sex cannot make you free. Somehow it takes you away from yourself; it takes you farther and farther away from yourself. The goal is the other.

Gurdjieff used to say sex is one-arrowed – the arrow is moving toward the other. Exactly the same metaphor has been used by *vajrayana*: sex is one-arrowed – it goes toward the other. Love is double-arrowed – it goes to the other and to you also. In love there is balance.

One arrow going toward the other, then you have to work with *hinayana*. Two-arrowed: one arrow going toward the other, one arrow coming toward you – you have attained to balance; that lopsidedness is no longer there.

A man of love is never angry with the other because he is not really dependent on the other. He can be happy alone too, his arrow is double-arrowed. He can be happy alone, of course, he still shares his happiness with the other, but he is no longer dependent on the other. Now it is no longer a relationship of dependence, it is a relationship of interdependence. It is a mutual friendship. They share energies, but nobody is anybody's slave.

In *vajrayana* the arrow completely disappears. There is no you and no other; I and thou, both are dropped. The mechanism has to be understood.

When you are looking for a woman or for a man, you don't know one very important factor: that your woman is within you and your man too. Each man is both man and woman, and each woman is both woman and man. It has to be so because you are born out of two parents. One was man, one was woman; they have contributed to your being fifty percent each. You have something of your father and you have something of your mother. Half of you belongs to the male energy; half of you belongs to the female energy, you are both.

In *hinayana* you have to work hard to bring your energy to the inner woman or the inner man; that is its whole work.

Just recently, in this century, Carl Gustav Jung became aware of this fact, of this fact of bisexuality, that no man is pure man and no woman is pure woman. In each man a woman exists, and in fact every man is searching for that woman somewhere outside.

That's why suddenly one day you come across a woman and you feel, "Yes, this is the right woman for me." How do you feel it? What is the criterion? How do you judge? It is not rational, you don't reason it out. It happens so suddenly, like a flash. You were not thinking about it, you have not reasoned it out. Suddenly, if somebody asks you, "Why have you fallen in love with this woman?" you will shrug your shoulders. You will say, "I don't know, but I have fallen in love. Something has happened."

What has happened? Jung says that you have an image of woman inside you; that image somehow fits with this woman. This woman seems to be similar to that image in some way or other. Of course, no woman can be absolutely similar to the inner woman, that's why no lover can ever be absolutely satisfied. A little similar, maybe the way she walks, maybe her sound, her voice, maybe the way she looks, maybe her blue eyes, maybe her nose, maybe the color of her hair.

You have an image inside you that has come from your mother, from your mother's mother, from your mother's mother's mother – all the women that have preceded you, they have contributed to that image. It is not exactly like your mother, otherwise things would have been simple. Your mother is involved in it, your mother's mother is also involved, and so on and so forth. They all have contributed little bits.

It is the same with your man: your father has contributed, your father's father, and so on and so forth. From your father to Adam, and from your mother to Eve, the whole continuum has contributed to it. Nobody exactly knows, there is no way really to know whom you are seeking. A man is searching for a woman, a woman is searching for a man – the search is very vague. There is no clear-cut image, but somewhere in your heart you carry it; in the dark corner of your soul you keep it, it is there.

So often many women and many men will appear to fulfill something of it, but only something. So each lover will give you a little satisfaction and much dissatisfaction. A part that fits will satisfy, and all other parts which don't fit will never satisfy.

Have you seen that whenever you fall in love with a man or a woman you immediately start changing the man and the woman according to something that you also don't know what? Wives go on changing their husbands their whole lives: "Don't do this. Be like this, behave like this."

Just the other day, Mulla Nasruddin's wife was saying to me, "Finally, Osho, I succeeded."

I asked, "About what?"

She said, "I have stopped Mulla Nasruddin biting his nails."

I said, "Biting his nails? Fifty years you have been married together – Mulla is seventy – now you have been able after fifty years?"

She said, "Yes!"

I asked, "But how did you succeed, tell me?"

She said, "Now I simply hide his teeth so he cannot bite."

People go on trying to change. Nobody ever changes. I have never seen it, I have never come across it. People even pretend: "Yes, we have changed," but nobody can change. Everybody remains himself. The whole effort is futile, but the urge to change is there. Why is the urge to change there?

The urge to change is for a real necessity. The woman is trying to make her husband fit with some vague image inside her, then she will be happy: if he does not drink, if he does not smoke, if he does not go after other women, if he always goes to the temple, if he listens to the saints, and a thousand and one things. She has a certain image: she wants her husband to be a hero, a saint, a great man. The ordinary human being does not satisfy her.

And the husband is also trying in a thousand and one ways: brings beautiful clothes, diamonds, rubies and pearls, and goes on decorating his wife. He is trying to find a Cleopatra. Somewhere he has some image of a beautiful woman, the most beautiful woman. Now he tries – even from his very childhood.

I have heard...

The old man asked his precocious six-year-old how he liked the new little girl next door.

"W-e-l-l," said the kid, "she's no Elizabeth Taylor, but she's nice."

Now even small children think about Hema Malini and think about Elizabeth Taylor. And he says, "She's no Elizabeth Taylor, but she's nice." And this conflict continues. The reason is that we are always looking for someone who is not outside.

Hinayana turns you from looking outside. It says: "Close your eyes to the outside." *Mahayana* makes you more alert and aware, fills your inner chamber with more light so that you can see the inner woman. And *vajrayana* makes it possible for you so that you can have an inner orgasm with your man inside or your woman inside. That *inner* orgasm will satisfy you, nothing else. These three steps are of tremendous meaning.

So don't be worried about these sutras that we will be discussing today.

Just two days ago, one woman sannyasin wrote to me, "Osho, what is happening to me? When you were talking about Hasids I was so flowering, so floating with it. After each talk I would leave happy and dancing and joyous. Now you are talking about Buddha, and I am very depressed. I love my man and he is a very beautiful man, and the Buddha says, 'Nothing is there in the body, it is just a bag full of filth.' I don't want to hear things like that."

I know nobody wants to hear, but they are true. And unless you pass through the Buddha you will never reach to the Hasids. Hasidism is *vajrayana*, it is the ultimate flowering. Listening to Hasidism you feel very happy, when I talk about Tantra you feel very happy; you think you are all Tantrikas. It is not so simple, it is not so cheap. To be a Tantrika is the ultimate flowering of religion. Don't deceive yourselves. It is hard, arduous, to reach to that point.

Vajrayana is Tantra, Buddhist Tantra, pure Tantra. But just look at the arrangement of things. *Hinayana* is the first step, and *hinayana* seems to be absolutely repressive. But Buddha says: "Unless you change your old patterns you can go on rationalizing and you can go on living in your unconscious, robotlike life, and you can go on repeating it again and again. You have done it many times."

How many times have you fallen in love with a beautiful man or a beautiful woman, and how long does it last? One day Buddha proves to be right: your beautiful woman, your Elizabeth Taylor, suddenly one day you find she is a bag full of filth, and he is saying it from the very beginning. But, of course, when you are on your honeymoon these sutras will not appeal to you.

Never take Buddhist sutras when you are going on a honeymoon. But when you are approaching the divorce court these sutras will be very relevant. You will immediately see what he is saying. One day comes the ultimate divorce. The ultimate divorce is the day when you simply understand the whole absurdity of searching for the other.

Divorces have happened many times to you, but you again and again forget. One divorce is finished, even if it is not finished, the court proceedings may still be on, you are again falling into another love affair. It may be, in fact, that you are asking for the divorce because you have fallen in another love affair. Before you are out of the first prison you have already entered the other. You have become so accustomed to living in chains that freedom tastes bitter.

To that woman sannyasin who is feeling very depressed I would like to say this: that depression shows something is hitting deep in the heart. Buddha has some truth, you cannot avoid it. You would like to avoid it. Who wants truth? People like lies, lies are very comfortable. Truth is always destructive, shattering.

But don't make any judgment too soon. This is Buddha's first layer of teaching. The second layer is more relaxed. The first layer is of great struggle. *Hinayana* is struggle, sheer force of will, because that is the only way you can get out of the mess you have been for so long – a sheer struggle to get out of it. The second step is perfectly relaxed. *Mahayana* is very relaxed and graceful. The third step is of tremendous celebration. On the third step you transcend all discipline.

This is the beauty of the Buddha's path; it is very scientific. Each step is a must. If you lose one step, the whole building will collapse, the whole temple will disappear.

Hinayana is very great discipline. *Mahayana* is relaxed

discipline. And *vajrayana* is no discipline – one has come to such a point where he can have total freedom. But you have to earn that total freedom.

Hinayana is based in the body, the material part of your being. When you are in your body you can enjoy life only in drops. In fact, in the East, semen is called *bindu* – *bindu* means a drop. You can enjoy sex only drop by drop. And you are so vast that this enjoyment drop by drop is more frustrating than fulfilling.

I have heard...

The oversized elephants were picketing the zoo. A lion happened to be strolling by and asked, "Why are you picketing?" and one of the elephants answered, "We're tired of working for peanuts."

This is what sex is – just working for peanuts.

In Tibet they have a metaphor for it, they call it *preta*. *Preta* means a hungry ghost. They depict a hungry ghost in a certain way: he has a belly like an elephant, and a neck as thin as thread, and a mouth as small as the eye of a needle. Of course, he has to remain hungry for ever and ever, because of that small mouth like an eye of a needle. He goes on eating twenty-four hours, but he has a belly like an elephant, so he goes on eating and eating and eating and always is hungry.

That's how sexuality is. You are vast, you have no boundaries, no limits. Unless your bliss also is as vast as your being it is not going to give you any contentment. And sex is just drip, drip, drop, drop. You can just entertain yourself, you can go on hoping against hope, but it is not going to fulfill you.

Sex creates neurosis, it is neurotic because it can never satisfy you. Now go to the madhouses of the world and just watch the mad people and you will always find that somewhere or other there is a sexual problem. That's what Freud says, that all pathology is somehow connected with sex. Too much sex obsession becomes neurotic. If you live in the body, you are bound to become neurotic. You have to go a little deeper and higher than the body.

The second layer Buddhists call the heart. You can call it mind, but the heart is a better word. The heart includes the mind; it is bigger, more satisfying, more space is available. You feel freer.

Love is freer than sex. In love there is less conflict than there is in sex. Then still higher there is the vast open sky of *vajrayana*. Buddha gives it the name of compassion. You live in passion and you have to reach to compassion.

Passion is obsession, neurosis. Compassion is when your energy has flowered. You are so contented within yourself, you are so enough unto yourself, now you can share, you can shower your bliss. Now you *have* to give. Neurosis is when you go on demanding and nobody is ready to give to you, and you are a hungry ghost. Your demands are great, and all that the world provides is just peanuts.

When, at the stage of *vajrayana*, you are vast, full of energy, a great reservoir of energy, a pool, a tremendous pool, then you can give. In sex you ask. Passion means demand, passion means begging.

Have you not seen it? Whenever you are sexually attracted to a woman you go around her and wag your tail – you are a beggar. In compassion you are an emperor – you share, you give; you give because you have. In sex you ask because you don't have. And this sex continues from the childhood to the very end. Children are getting ready for it, for this absurd journey. Old people are tired, sitting by the roadside, very jealous of those who are still not tired and are young; feeling very jealous. Out of their jealousy they start preaching, out of their jealousy they start condemning.

Remember, a saint never condemns. If he condemns, then he is not a saint, he is still interested in the same things. It is just that now he is jealous. Have you seen this jealousy? A young boy climbing up a tree and you immediately say, "Get down. You may get hurt or you may fall down." Have you seen that in your voice there is something of jealousy? You cannot climb the tree now, you are old. Your limbs are more rigid, they have lost their flexibility. You are jealous, but you cannot say you are jealous. You hide your jealousy.

Whenever a person starts condemning sex, somewhere he must be carrying a jealousy. Buddha is not condemning. He is simply factual. He simply says whatsoever is the case. And he wants you to come out of it because your destiny is bigger, higher is the potentiality.

A woman, an old woman, reached the insurance company's office. "But lady, you can't collect the life insurance on your husband, he isn't dead yet," said the insurance man.

"I know that – but there's no life left in him."

She has come to collect the insurance...

When no life is left in you, you start hiding the fact, you start becoming religious. Your religion may be just a garb. Buddha is not saying that you have to become religious when you are old. Buddha is saying you have to become religious when the passion is alive, when the fire is alive, because only when the fire is alive can it be transformed, you can ride on the energy.

Buddha introduced something absolutely new into the Indian consciousness. In India, sannyas was for old people – old, almost dead, one foot in the grave – then people used to take sannyas. The Hindu sannyas was like that: only for old people. When you have nothing left in you, then try sannyas – that was the last item. Buddha introduced a new element. He said that is foolish, only a young person can be really religious because when the energy is there you can ride on it. He introduced sannyas to young people.

And, of course, when you introduce sannyas to young people you have to make sure that they don't go on moving toward sex. For old people you need not bother too much. So in Hindu *shastras*, in Hindu scriptures, there exists nothing like *hinayana* because there is no need. Old people become sannyasins; what is the point? There is no need to be worried about them. They can live as they want. But when a young person becomes a sannyasin, then much care has to be taken. He has energy, he has fire, and that fire can misfire too, it can lead him into wrong directions. And he is very fresh, inexperienced. For him these sutras are very helpful.

Mulla Nasruddin tells this:

My mother-in-law is a widow; she is eighty-two years old. One night, just to get her out of the house, I arranged a date for her with a man who is eighty-five years old. She returned home from the date very late that evening and more than a little upset.

"What happened?" I asked.

"Are you kidding?" she snapped. "I had to slap his face three times."

"You mean," I answered, "he got fresh?"

"No," she replied, "I thought he was dead!"

Now if you initiate such dead people into sannyas, then there is no need for these sutras.

Buddha had to make it certain because he did a very dangerous thing. He was very courageous: he introduced thousands of young people into sannyas. He had to make absolutely certain that their energy moved from body to heart, from heart to soul. And every care had to be taken.

The first sutra:

> *The Buddha said:*
> *O monks, you should not see women. (If you should have to see them), refrain from talking to them. (If you should have to talk), you should reflect in a right spirit: "I am now a homeless mendicant. In the world of sin I must behave myself like unto the lotus flower whose purity is not defiled by the mud. Old ones I will treat as my mother; elderly ones as elder sisters; younger ones as younger sisters; and little ones as daughters." and in all this you should harbor no evil thoughts, but think of salvation.*
> *The Buddha said:*
> *Those who walk in the way should avoid sensualism as those who carry hay would avoid coming near the fire.*

To initiate a young man is to initiate somebody who is carrying hay – he should avoid fire.

Now, try to understand. These simple words are not so simple, they have many depths and layers.

First: they are addressed to monks, not to ordinary people. "O monks," Buddha says that the word *monk* is very beautiful, it means one who has decided to live alone. *Monk*, the very word, means solitary. Words like *monopoly*, *monogamy*, come from the same root. *Monogamy* means one husband; *monopoly* means one man's power; *monastery* means where monks live, those who have decided to live alone.

Ordinarily, one is seeking the other. The monk is one who has decided that the search for the other is futile. One who has decided to be alone. He has searched enough into relationship, but that which he was searching for he could not find there, frustration was the only gain. He has failed; he has tried, but in vain. Now he decides, "Let me try alone. If I cannot be happy with others, let me try to be happy alone. If I cannot be happy in relationship, then let me be out of relationship, let me drop out of the social structure. I will try now to be alone. I have tried outside, now let me try inside. Maybe that which I am desiring is there."

To be a monk means a decision: "Love has failed, relationship has failed, society has failed, now I will try meditation, now I will try my innermost core. Now I am going to be my only world, the only world there is. I will close my eyes and remain into myself." To be a monk is a great decision. The path of the monk is the path of the lonely, the solitary.

One day or other, everybody comes to feel that relationship has failed. You may not be courageous enough to drop out of it, that is another thing. Or you may be not intelligent enough, that's another matter. Great courage is needed; even a little *chutzpah*, what Jews call *chutzpah*, is needed. Not only a little courage but a little dare-devilishness, otherwise one cannot get out of the old pattern; the familiar is so familiar. And the familiar may be uncomfortable, but still it is familiar; one has become accustomed to it.

People go on smoking knowing well that emphysema is there, knowing well that cancer is approaching, they go on coughing, go on suffering, and go on asking how to drop it. Now there is no pleasure in it, but still they cannot drop it, just an old habit, just a mechanical habit. They are not intelligent people. When you ask how to stop smoking, you are declaring you are stupid. You don't have any intelligence, and you don't have any courage to move into some new pattern of life. Yes, a little *chutzpah* will be good. Let me explain it to you, what *chutzpah* is.

A man entered into a bank with a gun. He forced the cashier to give him $50,000. Of course, there was no choice for the cashier because the man was standing there and he was saying, "Give it to me immediately, otherwise get ready to die!"

He delivered him $50,000.

The man went to the next window and tried to open an account with the money.

This is *chutzpah*!

Or there is an even better story.

A man killed his mother and father, was caught red-handed, and appealed for mercy. And when the magistrate said, "Mercy, for you? What are your reasons?"

He said, "Now I am an orphan."

This is *chutzpah*!

Courage is needed, great courage is needed. And to be religious is to be almost madly courageous. Otherwise there are millions of habits; one is entangled completely. It is not that you have one chain on your body, you have millions of chains. And things become more complicated because you have decorated the chains and you think they are ornamental. In fact, you have made them golden and they seem valuable. You don't think they are chains. You have decorated the prison so long and so beautifully that you have forgotten that it is a prison, you think it is your home.

A day is bound to come in everybody's life when a person realizes: "All that I have tried has failed." Courage is needed to recognize: "I have failed utterly." Let me repeat it: only a courageous person can accept: "I have failed completely." Cowards always go on rationalizing. They say, "Maybe we have failed in this, but we will try another. Once more," they say, "then we are finished. One marriage more, then we are finished."

That's what psychologists call the gambler's psychology. He goes on losing but he thinks, "One more time, maybe this time I am going to win." If he starts winning, then too he cannot leave because he thinks, "Now I am winning. Now I am fortunate, now God is with me, fate is with me – I should not lose this opportunity. One stake more..."

If he is losing, he goes on playing. If he is winning, he goes on playing. And the final result is always failure. Whether you win or lose in the middle makes no sense. Ultimately failure comes into your hands.

Courage is needed to recognize: "I have failed." The monk is one who has recognized the fact that all his ways of life have failed, all his ideas have failed and his mind has proved impotent: "Now I am going to make a drastic change in my life. I am going to bring a radical transformation. I will turn inward." This turning inward makes a man a monk.

A monk is a rebellious person. He completely drops out of the society, out of relationship.

Buddha says that you can come back to the society at the third stage when you are a *vajrayanist*, when you have come to the third stage of flowering, but not before it.

So remember, these words are not uttered for householders. These words are not uttered for those who are still in the world and still dreaming. These words are uttered to a specific group of people who have dropped out of the world and who have decided to search within, to explore their own souls. They have explored others' bodies because as far as others are concerned you can explore only the body, you cannot get deeper than that. These people have turned away from that. Now they are trying to explore their heart, they are trying to explore their transcendental witnessing self.

O monks, you should not see women.

Don't see women! You will be surprised. Buddha used to say to his monks that even in dreams this sutra has to be followed, even in dreams you have to remain so alert.

This sutra is a sutra of awareness. The actual thing happened in this way: one of Buddha's great disciples, Ananda, was going to another town to preach. He asked Buddha, "Bhagwan, if I meet a woman on the way, how am I supposed to behave?" This is the story of this sutra being born.

Buddha said, "You should not see women. You close your eyes. You avoid" – because the eye is the first contact with the other. When you see a woman or when you see a man you touch the other's body with your eyes. The eye has its own touch. That's why you are not expected to stare at somebody. If you stare that shows you are uncivilized, unmannerly. There is a certain time limit: three seconds you can look; that is allowed. But more than that means you are uncivil, unmannerly, ungentlemanly. If you look at a woman for three seconds it is okay; beyond that the woman will start feeling uncomfortable. And if you go on staring, she will report to the police, or she will start screaming or shouting or she will do something.

Seeing is not just seeing: eyes touch; not only touch, there are ways to penetrate the other's body with the eye. The eyes can function like knives. And the eyes can be lustful, then the other feels you have reduced her or him to an object of lust, and who are you to reduce somebody? This is offensive.

In Hindi we have a very beautiful word for such a person, we call him *luchcha*. *Luchcha* means one who goes on looking at you – exactly this. Literally, *luchcha* means one who goes on staring. *Luchcha* comes from a Sanskrit root *lochan*, *lochan* means the eye. *Luchcha* means one who goes on eyeing you, staring at you, and whose stare becomes like a knife, whose stare becomes lustful, whose stare becomes violent; who uses his eyes as if eyes are sexual organs. That man is a *luchcha*.

...you should not see women. When Buddha is saying this, he is saying you should not stare. Of course, when you are walking on a road in a town, sometimes you may have to see a woman, but that is not the point. You should not see: you should not try to look; there should not be any deliberate effort to look at a woman; it should not be deliberate. You simply pass on.

Buddha used to say to his disciples: You should not look, really, more than four feet ahead. The eyes should remain just four feet ahead, more is useless, more is unnecessary, a wastage of energy. Just walk silently, looking four feet ahead; that's enough.

Don't stare because the stare simply shows that deep down lust is boiling. And once you see something, immediately desire arises. If you don't see, desire does not arise. You are walking on the road; you were not thinking of diamonds, for years you may not have thought, and suddenly you find a diamond there by the side just waiting for you. Suddenly it catches your eyes, and desire arises. You look all around: is anybody watching or not? You have become a thief. And you had not been thinking about a diamond; there was no desire at all. Just the eye contact and the desire has arisen from the unconscious. It must have been in the unconscious, otherwise it cannot arise.

Buddha says, "You know well your unconscious is full of sexuality, so better not to stare otherwise that which is in the unconscious will be stirred again and again." And that which is stirred again and again is strengthened. That which is stirred again and again and never allowed to rest and disappear becomes stronger. And a monk is one who has decided to drop out of relationship.

...you should not see women. It is said Ananda asked, "But if a situation arises in which one has to see a woman, then what?" So Buddha said:

> *(If you should have to see them), refrain from talking to them.*

If you don't talk to a woman, you cannot relate to her. Relationship arises with talking. Communication arises with talking. You can sit by the side of a woman for hours and if you have not talked there is no bridge; you are as distant as stars. You can sit by the side, even your bodies touching, but if you have not talked there exists no bridge, your personalities remain far away.

You can see in a commuter train so many people crowding the compartment, everybody touching everybody's body, but nobody talking. They are far away from each other. Once you talk, distance disappears; words bring you together.

The shy character noticed a blonde in a low-cut dress sitting alone next to him at the bar. He gathered all his courage and sent a drink to her. She silently nodded her thanks. He repeated the same gesture six times. Finally, the drinks in him spoke up and he got up all the courage he could muster and mumbled, "Do you ever make love to strange men?"

"Well," she smiled, "I never have before, but I think you've talked me into it you clever, silver-tongued devil you."

Now, he has not talked much, only one sentence. Even a single gesture of communication can create relationship. If you don't talk you remain separate. That's why if you are sitting silently with people that shows something has gone wrong. If the husband is silent and the wife is silent, then it seems that something has gone wrong. That means communication has broken, the bridge is broken. When they are laughing and talking then there is a bridge, there is communication.

Animals have sex but no sexuality. Man has sex plus sexuality. Sex is physical, sexuality is mental, and when you talk, your talk can be sexual. Animals have sex; that's a physiological act. They don't talk, they don't have any language; but man has language and language is one of the most powerful instruments in the hands of man. You communicate through it, you relate through it. You seduce through words, you insult through words, you show your love through words, you show your hate through words. You repel or attract through your words.

Buddha knows that the word is very potential.

In the Bible they say: "In the beginning was the Word" – maybe it is so or not – but in the very beginning of every relationship there is a word. Maybe in the beginning of the world it was so, maybe not, but every relationship starts with a word. Can you start any relationship without a word? It will be difficult, very, very difficult. Silence will surround you like a citadel.

So Buddha says: (*If you should have to see them*)... If some situation is there, for example, a monk is passing and there is an accident and a bullock-cart has fallen by the side in a ditch and a woman is there, hurt, broken, what is the monk supposed to do? Should he go without helping? No, compassion is needed. Buddha says: Help but don't talk, see but don't talk.

Ananda asked, "But there can be certain situations in which one has to speak."

(*If you should have to talk*)...

says Buddha,

> ...*then you should reflect in a right spirit: "I am now a homeless mendicant."*

Never forget that you have fallen out of relationship. The old habits are strong. The pull of the past is strong. So remember that you are a mendicant, that you are a monk, that you are a *bhikkhu*.

> *"In the world of sin I must behave myself like unto the lotus flower whose purity is not defiled by the mud."*

So Buddha says, "If you have to see, if you have to talk, if you have to touch, okay, but remember one thing: you should remain like a lotus-flower, transcendental to the mud." You should remain aware; your awareness is your only shelter.

Have you seen? Whenever you are aware, you are alone. Whenever you are aware you are cut away from the whole world. You may be in the marketplace, but the marketplace disappears. You may be in the shop, in the factory, in the office – if you are aware, suddenly you are alone.

When I entered my high school I had a very eccentric teacher, a Mohammedan teacher whom I loved. I loved him because he was very eccentric; he had a few whimsical ideas. For example, he would not allow any student to say, "Yes sir," when the attendance was to be taken. He would insist: "Say, 'Present sir.'" We used to annoy him by saying "Yes sir," but he would not allow it. Unless you said "Present sir," he would not allow you inside the class. He would force you to stand outside.

Now, this was just whimsical. It doesn't matter whether you say "Yes sir," or you say "Present sir." But I started feeling that he had some point in it, and I started meditating on it. And whenever he would call my name I would say "Present sir," and I would not only say it, I would feel: "I am simply present, aware, alert." And I had beautiful moments. Just for half a minute, I would become so present that the class would disappear, that the teacher would disappear. He also became aware of it.

One day he called me; he said, "What do you do? What are you doing? Because when you say 'Present sir' I see a sudden change on your face, your eyes go blank. Are you playing some trick upon me?" It was known in the school that before I entered the school, if some boy was to be called to the principal's office, then the boy was in trouble. When I entered the school the dictum had to be changed. Whenever I was called to the principal's office, the whole school would know: "The principal is in trouble!"

So he said, "What! You are creating some trouble? And I feel very awkward when you say 'Present sir.' And you change so tremendously, as if you are transported into another world. What exactly do you do? You embarrass me. If you continue doing this, then I will allow you to say 'Yes sir.'"

I said, "Now it will not make much difference – I have learned it. And I am going to use it my whole life. And I am thankful to you that you insisted. The word *present* opened a door."

You try it. Walking on the road, suddenly become present. Just say to some unknown god "Present sir," and be really present. Just become a flame of awareness. And suddenly you will see you are not in the world, you have become a lotus-flower, the mud cannot touch you. You become untouchable, you become something of the beyond, incorruptible.

Buddha said: If you have to see, if you have to talk, even if you have to touch, then be present. Remember, be mindful that you are a mendicant, that you are pure awareness.

And he says:

"Old ones I will treat as my mother..."

Have you looked at the psychology of man? Can you ever think of making love to your mother? Even thinking is impossible. Something suddenly cuts the whole idea. The whole thing seems ugly – making love to your mother? or making love to your sister? The whole thing seems to be impossible, inconceivable. But your sister is as much a woman as anybody else's sister. Somebody else will fall in love with your sister – bound to – but you never fall in love with your sister. Who loves his own sister? The moment you say "sister," some distance arises. Then sexual approach becomes impossible. The very word functions like a conditioning, you have been conditioned from the very childhood. You have been so conditioned, it has been repeated so often that the relationship between a sister and a brother is a holy relationship, that to think of sex is unimaginable.

Buddha says, "One who has become a monk has to create, at

least in the beginning, these barriers, so he does not slip into old habits." And Buddha must have been a great psychologist, he must have known the laws of conditioning. He must have known whatsoever is known by Pavlov in the modern times; he must have known everything about conditioned reflex. It is a conditioned reflex: the moment you say "sister" something simply disappears. Sex becomes irrelevant. You call somebody "mother" and sex becomes non-existential.

Buddha says:

> "Old ones I will treat as my mother; elderly ones as elder sisters; younger ones as younger sisters; and little ones as daughters." and in all this you should harbor no evil thoughts, but think of salvation.

Take each situation as a challenge for your awareness, as a challenge you have to work through toward your salvation.

> The Buddha said:
> Those who walk in the way should avoid sensualism as those who carry hay would avoid coming near the fire.

This is the first step. The second step: you are allowed to be loving because old habits are broken, now there is no fear. In the third step you are allowed to be completely free of all discipline, because now your awareness has become a permanent phenomenon in you, now there is no need to think that "this woman is my mother," or "this woman is my sister."

In the third step, *vajrayana*, you have come in contact with your inner woman. Your attraction for the outer woman has disappeared. The very moment you have come in contact with your inner woman, you have met the perfect woman you have been always seeking and seeking and never finding. You have met your inner man, you have found the perfect man. Yin and yang, they have become a circle, they have joined together.

That is the theory of Ardhanarishwar in Hindu mythology. In Shiva, half is man and half is woman. And Shiva is said to be the greatest god – *mahadeva*. All other gods are small gods; Shiva is the great god. Why is he called the great god? Because he has come to meet the inner woman, he has become ultimate unity; the woman and the man have disappeared.

The same phenomenon has happened in a buddha. You see what grace surrounds a buddha, what feminine beauty, and what strength, what power. Power comes from the man and the grace comes from the woman. Buddha is both: tremendously powerful and yet tremendously fragile, like a flower; can face the storm, is ready to face the whole world, and yet so open, so vulnerable, so soft, so delicate, almost feminine.

Look at Buddha's face – so feminine. In India we have not even put a mustache and beard on him, just to show that the face has become absolutely feminine. Not that he was not growing a beard, not that he was lacking in some hormones, but we have not put a beard on him. We have not put a beard on Mahavira, on the twenty-four *tirthankaras*, on Ram, on Krishna, we have not put it there. Not that they all were lacking in hormones; one or two maybe were lacking, but they all could not have been lacking. They must have grown beards, and they must have grown beautiful beards, but it is a symbol that the man has come to meet the woman inside, the man and the woman have mingled and merged and become one.

This is the meaning of the name that I have given to these talks on these forty-two chapters: *The Discipline of Transcendence.* It starts with the discipline of *hinayana*, then with the relaxation of *mahayana*, then the no-discipline of *vajrayana*. But one has to begin from the beginning, one has to start by sowing the seeds, then comes the tree, and then the flowering.

Enough for today.

8

THE FORBIDDEN PATH

The first question:

> Osho,
> I am yearning for the snake to become alive in me,
> setting me aflame...
> Am I on a forbidden path? I am scared.

The forbidden path is the path. There is no other path. There is a certain rule to evolution, a certain principle to it. The principle is: before you can become really innocent you have to lose all innocence. Before you can really become pure you have to move in all sorts of impurities. Before you can come home, you have to wander, go astray.

That's the whole meaning of the Christian parable of Adam being expelled from God's paradise. He had to be expelled. It is not that Adam is responsible for his expulsions, it is a certain basic rule of life.

God told Adam: "The Tree of Knowledge is the forbidden tree, you are not supposed to eat from it." Only one commandment was given to him: he was not to eat from the Tree of Knowledge. But this functioned as a provocation.

If God really wanted him not to eat from the Tree of Knowledge, the better course would have been that Adam was never told about it. Paradise is infinite with millions and millions of trees. Even by now, Adam would not have been able to discover one Tree of Knowledge. But the moment God said: "Don't touch that tree, don't go near it, don't eat it," that tree became the most important tree. Certainly, obviously.

Adam must have started dreaming about it. A temptation – going into the forest, into the garden, again and again the tree would call him. He must have gone close to it, looked, waited, brooded; many times he must have been just close to it, at the very brink of committing the sin, of disobeying, of being rebellious.

There is a fundamental law to it. Adam has to be expelled. Unless Adam is expelled, Adam will never become a christ. He has to go astray to come home. Very contradictory. But unless you move into sin, you don't know what sainthood is.

Every child is a saint, but that sainthood is very cheap. You have not earned it; it is just a natural gift, and who bothers about a natural gift? You have to lose it. When you lose it you become aware of what you have lost. When you lose it then you start suffering, then you feel a great hunger for it. When you lose it, then by contrast it becomes clear what it was.

If you want to see the beautiful dawn you have to wander into the dark night. Only after the dark night is the morning beautiful. If you really want to be rich, you have to become poor. Only after poverty do you start feeling the beauty of riches.

The contradiction is only apparent; they are complementary.

Christians have a theory; they call it *felix culpa* – a happy fault. Adam's sin has been known to Christian theology as *felix culpa* – a happy fault – since it brings about the need of Christ the Redeemer. If there had been no disobedience on the part of Adam then there would have been no Christ.

Adam is human consciousness going away from God. Christ is the same human consciousness returning back home. Adam and Christ are not two persons. Adam is the going away, Christ is the coming back. It is the same energy.

Disobedience is needed to become obedient. Rebellion is needed to know what surrender is. Ego is needed to become egoless. Every saint has a past and every sinner has a future. Remember it, and never be afraid of the forbidden.

The forbidden is the path. Go into it. Go courageously. Go totally, so that you can finish the attraction. And you are not going to find anything in it. You will come out of it empty, and that will be a great experience, a great maturity. Sin can never be fulfilling, so why be afraid?

If there were any possibility that sin might fulfill somebody, then there would have been danger. But sin has never fulfilled anybody. The more you go in it, the more frustrated you are. The more you go in it, the more you know it is just stupid, it is just unintelligent, it is just an old, routine rut, a vicious circle. You are not moving anywhere. You are not going anywhere, you are not growing.

The more deeply you understand it, the greater is the possibility that you will start on the backward journey, you will start coming to the original source. Of course, when I say coming back to the original source I don't mean that you will really regress backward. You will still go onward, but the journey will turn toward the source. There is no going back. A second childhood comes. In India, when a person moves through that second childhood we call him twice-born – *dwij* – again born. He has attained to a new birth. He has again become a child, again innocent.

So don't be afraid. The world is a temptation you have to go through, a temptation that has to be suffered. And the Devil is a partner with God; he is not the enemy, he is the partner. He tempts you, he takes you into the forbidden, he helps you to disobey. He provokes you, he allures you, he seduces you. If you go wholeheartedly with him, sooner or later you will understand that he is the deceiver. Immediately he disappears.

The moment you realize the Devil is a deceiver, the Devil disappears. That realization is death for him. Suddenly you start laughing. A great laughter arises in you. You start roaring like a lion, a great uproar. Now you have seen the truth, why God had told you not to eat the fruit of a certain tree. He wanted you to eat it.

Of course, God cannot be so foolish. If he did not want it, then he would have kept quiet. He could have removed the tree as any ordinary gardener could do. He did not remove the tree, he simply gave the commandment. And this is very psychological. The parable is really one of the most beautiful psychological parables.

Wherever you are not allowed to go, you want to go. If some film is running in the town and there is an advertisement "only for adults," all the children will rush – then there must be something for them. If it is only for adults, then it is a provocation.

Say to people: "Don't do this," and they will do it. You can be certain about it. And God made it absolutely certain. He must have been a little suspicious about Adam, so he created Eve. Man is a coward unless a woman tempts him. He may hesitate, but when a woman is there to tempt him, man becomes very brave. When the wife is there, the husband becomes very brave. Never fight with a husband when the wife is present, he will kill you. He has to prove himself because the wife is there. When he is alone you can fight; he will not bother, he will say it is okay.

When you have a woman with you, you become a daredevil. You have to prove to the woman that you are a hero, a great, courageous man, brave. Then you can be mad, you can do anything.

But even then God was suspicious: maybe the woman is not enough. He created a snake: the snake seduced the woman, the woman seduced Adam. Of course it was very well planned, it was a beautiful drama, well planned. All the characters are there. Adam can always say, "I am not responsible. Eve is responsible." She can always say, "I am not responsible, it was the snake." And of course the snake cannot speak, so the story ends there. If the snake could speak he would have said, "God is responsible." Nobody has asked the snake, "Who is responsible?" The snake is completely silent.

Look: whenever you say somebody else is responsible, what are you doing? You are simply shifting the responsibility. The husband says that the wife is responsible; the wife says the children are responsible, and children, of course, are dumb, they cannot say anything. So there it stops. We go on throwing responsibility on each other.

You become religious the day you recognize "I am responsible." Be courageous. Feel your responsibility, and go into all that tempts you, and go fully aware, go conscious. Go deliberately into it.

I would like to tell you another law of life: if you go deliberately into something, it can never become a bondage to you. Don't go as if you are being pulled. Don't go like a slave, go like a master. Even if you are going into something which is forbidden, which is a declared sin by all the religions, go courageously and go with responsibility. Say: "I want to go and I want to explore this dimension. And I am going." Don't feel guilty because if you feel guilty you will go halfheartedly. When you go halfheartedly you are stuck, then you will never be able to come back. If you go wholeheartedly you will immediately see the falsity of it, the foolishness of it. Go wholeheartedly, and explore it completely, utterly completely. Explore all the corners of it so it is finished. Once you have seen the whole game, you are out of it.

You ask: "I am yearning for the snake to become alive in me..." The snake is there. God never creates a man without the snake already there: it is built in, it is there. Call it sex or call it kundalini – it is the snake. Sex is the snake moving downward. Kundalini is the same snake, the same serpent-power, moving upward.

Ordinarily, when a child is born, the snake is there coiled near the sex center – what yogis call *muladhar* – the basic, root center: it is coiled there, sleeping energy. At the time when the child becomes mature, sexually mature, at the age of fourteen or about then, the snake uncoils and starts going downward, toward the valley. That's what sexuality is.

One day, when you have explored sexuality and have found nothing of worth, except trouble, anxiety, anguish, suffering – the snake starts moving upward. It is the same snake. Now it starts moving toward the peak, toward the mountain.

When it starts moving upward, a great transformation is happening. From Adam you are becoming a Christ. And when the snake has hit the ultimate in you, *sahasrar*, the seventh chakra of your being, the highest peak, the Everest, the Gourishankar – when it has hit that chakra, suddenly you are neither Adam nor Christ, you are God himself.

To feel oneself as an Adam is a dream, nightmarish. To feel oneself as Christ is still a dream – better than the first, not nightmarish at all, very sweet and beautiful, tremendously beautiful, but still a dream. To come to know oneself as God is to come to reality, is to come home.

The snake is there, and it is very much alive. You may have become afraid about the snake. The society is working against you. The society does not want you to be an individual aflame with energy; the society wants you to remain controlled. The society is afraid. Even a single individual can become very explosive.

That's what happened when a Christ moved on the earth, or a Buddha – just as a small atom can explode and can destroy a whole big city like Hiroshima. Just a tiny atom, invisible to the eyes. Nobody has ever seen it, it is not even visible to instruments – an invisible particle can explode and can generate so much energy. What to say about a human consciousness?

If a human consciousness explodes, society does not know how to control it. So society keeps you plugged to the lowest rung. It does not allow you to move. It keeps you just on the earth; it never gives you wings. You have wings, but it does not even make you aware that you have wings. It teaches you everything, but the most basic is not taught.

In the university your head is stuffed with rubbish. In schools, colleges, in universities, your head is used as a dustbin: people go on throwing things in it. They are taking revenge on their own teachers. They have filled their heads with straw, now they are doing the same with others – and religiously, very seriously. Have you seen professors, chancellors, vice-chancellors? So serious, as if they are doing a great service to humanity. They are simply destroying.

When the head becomes too heavy you lose contact with your heart. When the head becomes too important you tend to forget about the heart. And the heart is the source of your life energies. From the heart you are connected to the sex center, and from the heart you are connected to *sahasrar*. The heart is the bridge between the sex and *sahasrar;* the heart is the bridge between the valley and the peak. And they go on stuffing your head. They train your head so much you become so clever, you become so efficient with the head that you simply bypass the route that goes through the heart.

Life moves through the heart. The snake is alive, but your heart is closed. The snake is alive and ready to jump on its journey, you will just have to open the doors of your heart. That's what I mean when I say dance, sing, be ecstatic, celebrate, love, feel.

The real university of the future will be a training center for the heart, not for the head. These universities that exist today are just out of date; they are just ruins of the past. They can exist in the museums, but they should no longer be allowed to exist in reality. The real university has to be a great training for the heart, for the feeling.

Your snake is alive. Just open your heart – your snake is groping. When I see into you when you come to me and I personally encounter you, I see the snake groping for the heart. It cannot go toward the head without moving from the heart, there is no way. It can only go to the head through the heart. When it goes through the heart it does not reach to your reason, it reaches to your intuition. When it goes through the heart it hits the *sahasrar*. The *sahasrar* is also in the head, but it is not the head that you are aware of.

Even biologists, physiologists, say that half of the head simply seems to be useless – what is the function of it? Only half seems to work. The other half which seems useless and nonfunctioning is the seed of the *sahasrar*. When your energy moves through the heart, it reaches to the other half of the head which is ordinarily not functioning. It functions only when a man becomes a buddha.

And I will repeat again: the forbidden path is the only path. Be courageous. Remember: sin is a *felix culpa* – a happy fault – because that is the only way one comes to become a saint.

The second question:

> Osho,
> This drama has occupied me since the transference of the towel. You passed your towel to sannyasins saying that it would descend like god – but it landed on the floor. Then yesterday again you have taken it back. Buddha transferred the flower to Mahakashyapa which is still with him.
> Osho, is there no one out of all your sannyasins who can receive your towel? Please say something and clear it clearly.

But the question is unsigned... It must be from a coward. My whole feeling is not to answer it. Because if you cannot even declare your name you are afraid – even to ask a question you are afraid – you don't want to expose yourself, even in front of me.

My feeling is not to answer it, but the question is good even though the person may be a coward. So I am not answering the questioner, I will answer the question.

The mind can look at things always in two ways, remember it. The mind can look in a negative way, the mind can look in a positive way. And the religious person is one who tries to find the positive door because through the negative you never reach to the real.

The real is always positive. The positive person uses even the negative to find the positive, but the goal remains the positive.

For example, this happened. I told you: Wait for the towel. It will descend like a god on somebody's head. But it descended onto the floor. Now there are two possibilities: one, either nobody is ready to receive it, or, so many are ready that the towel is in a difficulty. But the negative mind always looks from the negative.

That's what I would like to say to you: I have many more Mahakashyapas than Buddha had and the towel was in a difficulty. Worried, it hit the beam – where to descend? On whom? It would have been unjust to choose one and not to choose the other.

In the whole history of humanity there has never been such laughter as there is around me. When Buddha was holding the flower in his hand only one sannyasin, Mahakashyapa, smiled. Hence, the flower was transferred to him. All were long-faced people, sad. They must have been thinking esoterically "What does it mean?" It means nothing. It is simply a meaningless gesture.

Mahakashyapa laughed, looking at the whole ridiculousness of it. He laughed, not at the flower; he laughed, not at Buddha; he laughed at all those fools who had surrounded him there. They were just thinking, "What is it?" And they must have been going round about in their heads and spinning theories and looking into scriptures and into memories in the past: "Has there been any precedent?" And they must have been trying to find some hidden meaning in it. There is nothing hidden in it.

A buddha is as open as a flower. There is nothing hidden in it. Buddhists have a saying from Buddha that there is nothing hidden in existence; from the very beginning there is nothing hidden. Everything is just in front of you. You just need to open your eyes.

Seeing the whole absurdity of the so-called great scholars who surrounded Buddha – great pundits, logicians – Mahakashyapa laughed. Buddha called him and gave him his flower. And he said to his disciples: "Whatsoever can be said I have told to you. That which cannot be said I transfer to Mahakashyapa."

Now, for two thousand five hundred years those foolish scholars and pundits are again thinking: "What happened?" They are again thinking: "What transpired between Buddha and Mahakashyapa? What was delivered?"

In Zen the masters give this as a koan. They say to their disciples: "Sit silently and find the answer why Buddha chose Mahakashyapa, why Mahakashyapa laughed, why the flower was given to him, and what Buddha means when he says, 'That which cannot be said, I am delivering to Mahakashyapa. And that which can be said I have told to you.'"

Of course truth cannot be said, so Buddha is delivering truth to Mahakashyapa. And all that can be said about truth is again a beautiful lie. So Buddha has told lies to others and truth has been given to Mahakashyapa. And Mahakashyapa was not one of the most prominent disciples, not at all. In fact, nobody hears his name except in this story.

Sariputta was a great scholar; Maudgalyan was a great scholar; Ananda was the chief disciple – and there were many. Mahakashyapa? Nobody had ever heard about him. Must have lived a very silent life, unobtrusive, unpretending; must have been a nobody. But only a nobody can laugh. He must have seen through the whole stupidity of the scholars.

Zen masters say to their disciples: "Think about it, meditate over it, contemplate, and bring the answer." And disciples go and meditate and bring answers, and all answers are wrong. One day, after years it happens, sometimes after twenty years.

There are stories on record that a disciple meditated for twenty years, came again and again. Every month he came, then twice a year then once a year. He would find a great answer, would create a philosophy around it and bring it to the master and the master would say – from the very beginning, just seeing the disciple – "Wrong!" And he had not said anything yet. It is not a question that you can bring an answer to – your face shows it, that you are serious. So the master would say, "Wrong."

The disciple became very worried and he said, "But what does this mean? I have not even said anything."

And the master would say "It is not a question of saying or not saying. It is the way you come, the way you hold your head, the way your face looks: the question is still there. You cannot deceive me."

Then twenty years pass, and one day he came, giggling, and the master said, "So you have got it!"

Now the seriousness had disappeared. Now he understood the point: it is not a question of philosophy. He understood the point that for these nineteen years he had been following not Mahakashyapa, but Sariputta, Maudgalyan, Ananda – those serious faces. Now he understood that it is nothing, just a joke. Buddha played a game. Only a buddha can play such a beautiful game.

Now you ask why the towel did not descend on somebody's head. I have so many laughing Mahakashyapas and very few Sariputtas, very few scholars and pundits. My whole effort is to bring laughter to religion. I would like you to laugh your way to God. Unless you reach laughing, you will not be allowed, you will not be welcomed, you will not be accepted.

I would suggest one thing to you: if you go to God, rather than taking a prayer with you, take a joke. He always waits for people who can tell a good joke to him, then he laughs, and in his laughter is grace, and in his laughter is benediction.

But for the next time, I would like the questioner to sign his name. People would have enjoyed your name, they would have laughed. At least don't deceive here; you deceive everywhere.

A man threw a rupee to a blind beggar, who expertly retrieved it. The man was astonished. "I thought you were blind." And there was a sign in front of the beggar: I am blind.

"No, sir, I am not that blind beggar who usually sits here. Today is his day off and he has gone to see a movie. In fact, I am his friend; I am just tending his shop. Really, I am deaf and dumb."

This is how things are. You go on deceiving. You go on pretending that you are somebody else. You have many faces, and your original face is lost in your many masks. Unless you recognize your original face, you will not be able to reach anywhere. You will not have any meaning to your life. You will miss this opportunity.

This life is only for those who are real. Your facade, your mask, has to be dropped. My whole effort is to go on hammering so that it becomes a little loose and your real face starts coming up. You will be surprised yourself because your real face is the face of God himself.

The mask is yours, the falsity is yours. Ordinarily you don't exist as a real person; you are a mythology, you are a myth, not reality. This word *mythology* is beautiful; it comes from a Latin root *myth*; and *myth* comes from a Sanskrit root *mithya*. *Mithya* means the false, the unreal, the fictitious. From *mithya* comes *myth*; from *myth* comes mythology.

You are a myth, you are a mythology. You are just a fiction, you are not real. And how can the fiction meet the ultimate? The fiction can meet only another fiction. Only the real can meet the real, the similar can meet the similar. So drop your masks, come into the open.

When I ask that your question should be signed, that simply means that you accept that the question is yours, that you accept the responsibility of asking it. And if I ridicule the question, I prove that the question is stupid, you accept it, that it is your question, and you accept the ridicule. And you are not hurt about it because this is a surgical operation. If you start crying and weeping and you don't allow me to operate, then take your fee back because then it is meaningless. Why are you lying down on the operation table?

The day you become a sannyasin you will remain on the operation table until I have succeeded in cutting off your head completely.

But you are very clever, you are very political. But remember that the politician is the most stupid man.

Let me tell you one anecdote:

Mulla Nasruddin decides he needs a new brain, so he goes to the brain bank. The caretaker shows him the bottled brain of a great mathematician, for 6,000 rupees only. "Too expensive," Mulla says. The caretaker leads him to the brain of a nuclear physicist, for 9,000 rupees. "Much too expensive," Mulla replies. Finally the caretaker offers him the brain of a politician, for 20,000 rupees. "Why should I pay that kind of money for the brain of a politician?" Mulla protests.

"But, sir," the caretaker explains, "this brain has never been used."

The politician never uses his brain. To deceive, much brain is not needed. To be true, much brain is needed. To cheat, not much brain is needed, very ordinary, very low IQ. But to be honest, to be true, to be totally nude, in the open, great intelligence is needed.

The third question:

> Osho,
> Why do you appear to give more attention to
> Westerners and, on the whole, to almost ignore
> Indians? I am thinking especially of when you give
> sannyas.

This question is very important and has to be understood both by Indians and non-Indians.

When a Westerner comes to me I have to approach him through his head because there is no other entry possible. When an Indian comes to me a simpler approach is possible – through the heart. When an Indian comes to me he comes for *satsang*; he wants just to be in my presence. He has no questions.

Those Indians who have questions never come to me. I have created too many barriers for them to come. Those Indians whose minds are too much stuffed don't come to me, and I don't want them here. I have made every possible effort to prevent them from coming to me. I am not interested in them.

The Indians who come to me, come to be with me silently. They can understand the language of silence. But when a Westerner comes, he cannot understand the language of silence, he can understand only the language of logic. So I have to talk; I have to talk too much to the Westerners. By and by, I persuade them to become silent. By and by, they also become Indians. But it takes time.

For a spectator it may appear as if I am not paying attention to the Indians. And the question is from a Westerner. You may see that when an Indian comes to take sannyas, I simply give him sannyas. Even if I ask him whether he has something to ask, he says no. Sometimes I don't even ask him, I can see that he has not come to ask any question, he has come to be with me. That is far more significant, far deeper. He has come just to see me, just to be with me. He wants a bridge in silence.

But to a watcher it will seem that I am not paying much attention, because when I talk then you think I am paying attention. When I talk for half an hour to one person, of course, you think I have been too attentive to him. That simply shows that the person is too much in the head and I have to persuade him.

The Western mind is only mind; it has forgotten the heart. The Eastern mind is not only mind – the heart is still predominant, fortunately, and the mind is secondary. So there is no need to talk much. He touches my feet and he is happy, he is tremendously happy – he has touched something real, he has touched something from the unknown. To a Westerner it seems just meaningless: Then why have you come? Just to touch the feet? Just to sit silently? You can sit silently at your home. Then why did you travel so far?

The Westerner knows only one way of communication and that is through language, through logic, reason. I have to convince him. The Indian needs no conviction. He is convinced about the fact of sannyas. If he has not taken sannyas, it is not that he is not convinced, it is only that he is not courageous enough. He wants a little courage.

He is convinced! He is convinced for many lives that sannyas is the only way to be, to be rightly in existence. Sannyas is the only way to reach the ultimate, to reach truth, he is convinced. That is in the blood and in the bones. An Indian is born with the desire to be a sannyasin. He may not be able to dare – that's another thing. So when he comes to me, he has not come for any conviction – conviction is already there – he has come to me just to feel my vibe, so that he can gather a little more courage and take the jump.

When a Westerner comes, he is not convinced at all. Sannyas? Seems just outlandish, bizarre, eccentric. For the Westerner, sannyas simply has no appeal. He has never thought about it.

So many Western sannyasins are here: have you ever had any dream in your life that you would become a sannyasin? Even now that you have become a sannyasin, you are puzzled. What has happened to you? What are you doing here? What is such an intelligent person doing here?

Ask Heeren: he is continuously thinking, such an intelligent person, almost a Jew – what is he doing here? He should be somewhere in the London market earning more and more money, having bigger and bigger houses. What is he doing here jumping and dancing like a fool?

The Westerner comes to me without any conviction, without any idea of what sannyas is. I have to talk him into it. I have to pull him into it. And I have to be very logical. I use logic only for Westerners. For Indians I use magic. And these are two different approaches.

The fourth question:

> *Osho,*
> *Lately I feel you have been throwing us back on*
> *ourselves more and more.*

Where else should I throw you? That is the only place. That's where you belong.

The whole effort of a master is to bring you back home, to throw you back to yourself, to make you that which you are meant to be, to help you to be yourself. If there is some teacher who pretends to make you somebody else, beware. Escape from him, he is like poison, he will destroy you.

I am not trying to make you into something else that you are not. I am simply helping you to be yourself – whosoever you are, whosoever Allah wills you to be. I can only cooperate with the will of Allah; I am not here to interfere. Whatsoever you are going to be, whatsoever your destiny is, I simply help you toward that destiny. I don't interfere.

One day, suddenly, you will see you have become absolutely independent, absolutely your own authentic being. That will be the day for my happiness, and that will be the day for your gratitude. You will feel grateful. That day you will understand why I continue to throw you back to yourself. I don't want to become a crutch to you. I would like your own limbs to be strong enough. I don't want to be a crutch, I don't want to become your eyes because that will be impossible. You will be deceived.

I don't want to give you what I know. In the first place, it cannot be given. In the second place, if it is given it is immediately corrupted. The moment it reaches you, it mixes with you, it is corrupt.

Knowledge is possible only when your eyes open, when it is your own vision, when you have the clarity. I am not giving you answers – I am simply trying to take away the questions. Remember it. I am not giving you any answers; that's why my answers are so elusive, so roundabout. I simply want to take away the thorn of question from your heart.

My answer is just a trick. Once the questions have disappeared, you are the answer. And there are not many answers, remember – there is only one answer because there is only one life and there is only one question. Because you don't know the one answer you go on asking a thousand and one questions.

I am not supplying you with any answers. In fact, I am pulling away the very earth beneath you. I will leave you hanging in the abyss, the bottomless abyss. You will be scared.

My whole work is to help you not to get scared, to help you to keep courage because once you allow yourself to fall into the abyss... The questionless mind, the thoughtless mind is an abyss because it is a no-mind. When the question is not, where is the mind? Then the mind has disappeared. And with the mind disappears the ego. And with the mind disappear I and you. With the mind disappear the master and the disciple. With the mind disappear all distinctions. You start falling.

If you allow me and if you cooperate with me, I would help you to fall like a feather, slowly, slowly into the empty abyss of being. That is the answer.

The answer is your being. The questions come from your mind. The mind is not your being. Be mindless. Be beyond mind.

You would like to cling to me because that is very cheap and easy. You can throw all your responsibility on me. You can say, "Now you take care." And you can go on living your life the way you were living. That's what people do in the world: they choose a master, they surrender, and they say, "Now I am finished, now you take care of me." And they go on living the same way. The same dishonesty, the same distrust, the same falsity, the same myth – they continue as if they have done all that they were needed to do. This won't help.

Surrender is not throwing away responsibility. Surrender is simply an indication of trust, that you trust this man. Now whatsoever he is going to say, you are going to do. Surrender is the beginning of a great effort. Surrender is the beginning of a great journey. Surrender is getting into the stream.

When you surrender to me, you simply surrender to me so that I can make you yourself. You have tried in your own way and you have failed. You have tried and followed many people and you have failed because those people were not interested really in you, they were interested in their own idea. Somebody was trying to make you become a Christian. Somebody was trying to make you a Hindu. Somebody was trying to change you into a Mohammedan. They were interested in their own ways. They had their own ideas to impose on you. You were victims. With me, I am not trying to make you a Christian or a Hindu or a Jaina or a Buddhist, I am simply trying to make you just the one that you are, that you are meant to be, that existence wants you to be.

That's why I go on answering different people in different ways.

Later on you will not be able to figure out what type of man this was, what manner of man this was. If you look through all of my books you will not be able to sort it out – what system? There is no system because my approach is individual. I say one thing to one person, and immediately just the opposite to another person.

Just last night, to one I said, "You become a Buddhist monk, be completely out of your sexuality, forget about it." And immediately after him, to another person I said, "You indulge, you move into relationship." Now, it will be difficult for anybody to sort out what type of system this is.

My approach is individual. I talk to one person, then I forget the whole world. And when I talk to the person I am not important, that person is important. When I talk to a person, I don't talk out of an ideology, I don't have a ready-made system; I don't try to fix that person in that system because that will be inhuman, that is violence.

Whenever you find a saint trying to fix you into some system, trying to force you into some system, remember, he is a murderer, he is very violent. His violence may have a sugarcoating to it – all your so-called mahatmas are like that, very violent, tremendously violent people; trying to fix you into a mold. The mold is prefabricated. The mold was already there when you were not there; when you come, the mold is there – you have to fit with the mold.

When you come to me, I have no mold. I don't fit you into something. I simply look into you and I try to see where your innermost energy is moving and I help it to move in that direction. That is your way. That's where you should be. You are not courageous enough to move into it; I help you, I give you courage. I give you a promise: "I am with you, you go, don't be worried." But I help you to be yourself.

To me religion means freedom to each individual, absolute freedom to each individual. Of course, in that freedom a great discipline is implied, but that discipline has to arise out of your own consciousness; it has not to be imposed by anybody else. But right now, when you are in the process, you will not be able to understand it totally. The day you arrive, then you will understand what this man was doing to you. You will feel grateful.

There is a story about a Chinese monk who was celebrating. Somebody asked, "Why are you celebrating? What has happened?"

He said, "This is my master's birthday."

The master had died, but the questioner was worried. He said, "But as far as I remember, you approached that master many times and he always refused to become your master, so why are you celebrating? This ceremony is to be done only by a disciple who has been accepted by the master. So why are you bothering? In fact, he rejected you so many times."

The man started laughing. He said, "Because he rejected me, I fell upon myself. And the day I realized my being, I felt grateful to him. He is my master. If he had not rejected me I might not have arrived, because in fact I was trying to find some support, somebody to lean on. I was not really interested in becoming absolutely individual and free.

"I was talking about liberation, but I was not really trying to be liberated. I was trying to find a beautiful cage, a beautiful prison, some holy prison, some religious pattern. But this man was simply incredible. How many times I approached him and he would just throw me out and he would say, 'Go home! I am not your master.' And now I know he was my master and this was his teaching. His rejection was his acceptance, because he could see through me that this was the only way I could grow. That's why he rejected me. But by rejecting me he accepted me."

Can you see the point of it? I will go on throwing you upon yourself. Sometimes you will feel hurt. Sometimes a great pain will arise in you. But one day, finally when you come home, you will be thankful that I never became a crutch to you.

The fifth question:

> Osho,
> You made me realize I was a coward and I accepted it and was happy. Now I am getting a feeling that I am becoming brave, and I am scared.

It is from Raj Bharti. He is an army man, and of course he used to believe that he was a brave man. But he may have entered the army only to have this feeling of being a brave man. He is a colonel, so he has credentials; he can prove that he is brave. But I looked into him and I saw that he was a coward, and he was brave enough to accept it. He accepted it without any complaint, without any grudge. He accepted it totally. That was beautiful.

When he accepted it, that very moment I knew that now he would become brave because this is the beginning of bravery. Only a brave man can accept that he is a coward. Cowards can never accept it. Cowards try to prove that they are brave.

I had one teacher who continuously tried to prove that he was a very brave man. I approached him and I said, "You stop this nonsense. You talk so much about bravery that I have a suspicion that you are a coward, and if you don't stop it, I will create trouble."

He said, "What do you mean?"

I said, "That you leave to me – but you stop immediately because I know you are a coward. I have seen you trembling in the class. When you enter the class you perspire, and you talk about bravery! You immediately stop it, otherwise you will have to prove that you are a brave man, and it is going to be difficult."

Not only did he stop, he simply disappeared. He resigned from his post. After a few years, when I was in the university, I came across him at a railway station. I said, "Where have you been?"

He said, "You are dangerous. I am really a coward, but when you said that I would have to prove my bravery and I started thinking about it, I said I better get out from here."

Colonel Raj accepted it so simply, so innocently that in that very moment he started becoming brave. This is the logic of life. It is a very absurd logic. A coward goes on trying to prove that he is brave; a brave man accepts even his cowardice. A violent man tries to become nonviolent; a really nonviolent man accepts all violence that is inside him.

A very sexual man goes on trying to become celibate; a real celibate accepts all the sexuality that is in him. A sinner goes on pretending to be a saint. A real saint is one who knows how many possibilities of getting into sin are still alive in him.

Now he says: "Now I am getting a feeling that I am becoming brave, and I am scared."

Again you are getting into the old rut. When you were a coward you accepted that you were a coward and you started becoming brave. Now you have started feeling that you are brave and you are becoming cowardly, you are scared. See the logic of it.

Never claim that you are brave and you will remain brave. Never claim that you are beautiful and you will remain beautiful. Never claim that you are wise and you will remain wise. The moment you claim, you have fallen into the trap again.

The Upanishads say: The one who knows never says that he knows. The one who says he knows does not know.

So see the game of the mind. Just watch. Don't start believing that you are brave, otherwise you will become a coward again. But if you can watch this whole game and you can remain just a witness, then cowardice, bravery, all disappear, and that which is left is the real you. It is neither. It is transcendental.

The sixth question:

> Osho,
> You tell us every day to surrender, yet it still doesn't happen – why not? I really want to let go, yet trying doesn't work, nor does not trying. What to do and when, if ever, will it happen?

It is not a question of your doing or your not-doing, because not-doing is also your doing. It is not a question of doing at all, positively or negatively. When you are neither doing nor not-doing, then it happens.

You move from one polarity to the other. First you try to do; when it doesn't happen you say, "Okay, so I will not do now – let us see whether it happens or not." But the expectation is the same. It was behind doing, now it is behind non-doing. You are expecting it to happen. You are desiring it to happen. You are hoping for it to happen.

Unless the desire disappears, unless the hope is abandoned, it will not happen. Surrender happens only when the desire, the hope, disappears. In total abandon it happens.

So neither your doing nor your non-doing is needed because they are not different basically. Behind both is the same desire.

Let me tell you one anecdote:

Mulla Nasruddin had to drive his wife and mother-in-law from Mumbai to Pune, and all along the way the two women in his life were giving advice on how to drive.

Finally Nasruddin couldn't take it anymore and pulled the car to the side of the road, furiously turned to his wife in the back seat and whined, "Alright. Now let's get this straight once and for all. Who's driving this car? You or your mother?"

But whether the mother decides or the wife decides it is all the same: somebody else is deciding. Whether you try to let it happen by doing, or you allow it to happen by not doing, you don't allow existence any chance.

Surrender is a gift from existence. When you are completely absent, neither doing nor not doing, it happens. But it has nothing to do with you, so you can completely forget about it. You simply do your ordinary things: eat, sleep, walk, dance, sing, love – you do your ordinary things and you just forget all about surrender. One day, suddenly, it is there.

Doing the ordinary things of life, not waiting for any extraordinary happening, not waiting for some miracle, one day it is there. It is simply there. One morning you rise and it is there – your whole room is full of a benediction. And after that, you cannot lose it; there is no way to lose it. Because, really, in surrender what actually happens is that your own nature comes to a flowering. But it is a gift from existence. Don't even pray for it because in your prayer also there will be desire.

The seventh question:

> Osho,
> I went in search of Mulla Nasruddin and could not
> find him. So, upon your suggestion, I looked up Yoga
> Chinmaya and asked him why you threw your towel.
> He gave a half-hour-long discourse on the deeply
> symbolic and highly esoteric reasons. I came away
> laughing.
> Osho, you tricked us again! Yoga Chinmaya is Mulla
> Nasruddin.

He is trying hard but he is not yet. It is a very difficult thing to be Mulla Nasruddin.

To be Mulla Nasruddin means two things: Be foolish in your wisdom and be wise in your foolishness. It is a very great contradiction. Be wise in your foolishness and be foolish in your wisdom. Yoga Chinmaya is trying hard; but he has only been able to do the second part up to now. The first part is more difficult. If he goes on working hard at it, he may succeed.

You should be aware of the fact that Mulla Nasruddin is a Sufi device. It is to make you clear that life is wise in its foolishness. And when you try to be wise you become a fool. The greatest wise people are like fools, and the greatest foolish people are those who pretend that they are wise.

Socrates has said, "When I was not aware, when I was ignorant, I used to think that I knew. When I was ignorant I used to think that I knew. Now that I know, I know only one thing – that I know not."

In the tremendous flowering of wisdom, one becomes a fool. Jesus is a fool. Saint Francis is a fool. Buddha is a fool. Their ignorance is profound, their ignorance is ultimate. In their ignorance they declare that life is a mystery – immeasurable, infinite. There is nobody to solve it. It is not a problem to be solved: it is a mystery to be lived. In their ignorance they have become absolutely innocent. That is their wisdom.

Then you go to the great philosophers – Hegel, Kant, Aristotle, Plato – they prove that they are very wise. That is their foolishness.

If you have to choose, choose the fool and you will become wise. Don't choose to pretend wisdom, otherwise you will become a fool.

One day I was walking with Mulla Nasruddin on the road. It suddenly started raining. I told Mulla Nasruddin, "Mulla, it is raining. Open your umbrella."

He said, "Wouldn't do any good, it is full of holes."

I was surprised. I said, "So why are you carrying it? Why did you bring it in the first place?"

He said, "I didn't think it would rain."

There's this busy hospital clinic where patients can come for free medical treatment. Lots of elderly people who have nothing to do come just to tell the doctor their troubles. Mulla Nasruddin went every day. There was nothing wrong with him. But the doctors humored him, listened patiently, and actually looked forward to his visits. One day he didn't show up. Next day, his doctor asked, "Where were you yesterday? – we missed you."

"I'll tell you the truth," he replied. "I was sick."

Mulla Nasruddin is so content and so happy, I asked one day, "What is your philosophy, Nasruddin? How do you avoid worries?"

He said, "This is my philosophy in short. Life is very simple. The first thing to remember about life is: don't worry about it. Really, there are only two things to worry about. Either you're successful or you're not successful. If you're successful, there's nothing to worry about. If you're not successful, there are only two things to worry about. Either you're healthy or you're unhealthy. If your health is good, there's nothing to worry about. If your health is bad, there are only two things to worry about. Either you're going to live or you're not going to live. If you live, there's nothing to worry about; and if you don't live, you have only two things to worry about. Either you are going to heaven or you're not going to heaven. If you go to heaven, there's nothing to worry about, and if you go to the other place, you'll be so doggone busy shaking hands with all your old friends, you won't have time to worry."

I bless Yoga Chinmaya and hope that one day he will become Mulla Nasruddin. The day one becomes Mulla Nasruddin, one has arrived home.

The drunk Mulla Nasruddin was stopped by a policeman as he staggered about the street at three o'clock in the morning.

"Can you explain why you are out at this time?" asked the policeman.

"If I could," said the Mulla, "I would be home by now."

If you knew what life is, you would be home by now. All esoteric explanations, all explanations as such, are foolish.

Chinmaya is doing well as far as fifty percent of Mulla Nasruddin is concerned. All explanations are foolish because all so-called wisdom is foolish. But this is how one grows. The other fifty percent will also be coming – when foolishness becomes wisdom.

The last question:

> Osho,
> Very mysterious things are happening. A towel has been found in the question box and we don't know from where it has come!
> Could you please enlighten us.

Certainly, mysterious things are happening. That's what Yoga Chinmaya said to his chief disciple, Priya, just two days ago – that many mysterious things are happening. And he said the day before yesterday, "The day after tomorrow many more mysterious things are going to happen." Today is that day after tomorrow, and now this has happened.

Now it is absolutely difficult to use logic, I will have to use magic. Let me give myself a little moment, a little time, to use my magic...

The towel is from a woman – Indian not Western; married not unmarried; a sannyasin. Her name starts with *U*. And if you want more information about her, you can inquire care of Colonel Raj Bharti.

Enough for today.

9

THE WORLD HAS NEVER LACKED BUDDHAS

The Buddha said:
There was once a man who, being in despair over his inability to control his passions, wished to mutilate himself. The Buddha said to him, "Better destroy your own evil thoughts than do harm to your own person. The mind is lord. When the lord himself is calmed, the servants will of themselves be yielding. If your mind is not cleansed of evil passions, what avails it to mutilate yourself?" Thereupon, the Buddha recited the gatha: Passions grow from the will, the will grows from thought and imagination: when both are calmed, there is neither sensualism nor transmigration. The Buddha said, this gatha was taught before by Kashyapabuddha.
The Buddha said:
From the passions arises worry, and from worry arises fear. Away with the passions, and no fear, no worry.

Man is in misery, and man has remained in misery down the centuries. Rarely can you find a human being who is not miserable. It is so rare that it almost seems unbelievable. That's why buddhas are never believed. People don't believe that they ever existed. People can't believe it. They can't believe it because of their own misery. The misery is such, and they are entangled into it so deeply, that they don't see that any escape is possible.

People think the buddhas must have been imagined and that they are the dreams of humanity. That's what Sigmund Freud says, "Buddhas are wish fulfillments." Man wants to be that way, man desires to be out of misery, man would like to have that silence, that peace, that benediction, but it has not happened. Freud says that there is no hope, it cannot happen. By the very nature of things man cannot become happy.

Freud has to be listened to very keenly and very deeply. He cannot be simply rejected outright; he is one of the most penetrating minds ever. When he says that happiness is not possible, and when he says that hoping for happiness is hoping for the impossible, he means it. His own observation of human misery led him to this conclusion. This conclusion is not that of a philosopher. Freud is not a pessimist. But observing thousands of human beings, getting deeper into their beings, he realized that man is made in such a way that he has a built-in process of being miserable. At the most he can be in comfort, but never in ecstasy. At the most we can make life a little more convenient – through scientific technology, through social change, through better economy, and through other things – but man will remain miserable all the same.

How can Freud believe that a buddha has ever existed? Such serenity seems to be just a dream. Humanity has been dreaming about Buddha.

This idea arises because Buddha is so rare, so exceptional. He is not the rule. Why has man remained in so much misery? And the miracle is that everybody wants to be happy. You cannot find a man who wants to be miserable, and yet everybody is in misery. Everybody wants to be happy, blissful, peaceful, silent, everybody wants to be in joy, everybody wants to celebrate but it seems impossible. Now, there must be some very deep cause, so deep that Freudian analysis could not reach it, so deep that logic cannot penetrate it.

Before we enter into the sutras, a basic thing has to be understood: Man wants happiness, that's why he is miserable. The more you want to be happy, the more miserable you will be. Now this is very absurd, but this is the root cause. And when you understand the process of how the human mind functions you will be able to realize it.

Man wants to be happy, hence he creates misery. If you want to get out of misery, you will have to get out of your desire for happiness. Then nobody can make you miserable. Here is where Freud missed. He could not understand that the very desire for happiness can be the cause of misery. How does it happen? Why in the first place do you desire happiness? And what does it do to you, the desire for happiness?

The moment you desire happiness you have moved away from the present, you have moved away from the existential, you have already moved into the future which is nowhere, which has not come yet. You have moved in a dream. Now, dreams can never be fulfilling. Your desire for happiness is a dream. The dream is unreal. Through the unreal, nobody has ever been able to reach to the real. You have taken a wrong train.

The desire for happiness simply shows that you are not happy right at this moment. The desire for happiness simply shows that you are a miserable being. And a miserable being projects in the future that some time, some day, some way, he will be happy. Out of misery comes your projection. It carries the very seeds of misery. It comes out of you – it cannot be different from you. It is your child: its face will be like you; in its body your blood will be circulating. It will be your continuity.

You are unhappy today; you project tomorrow to be happy, but tomorrow is a projection of you, of your today, of whatsoever you are. You are unhappy — tomorrow will come out of this unhappiness and you will be more unhappy. Of course, out of more unhappiness you will desire more happiness in the future. And then you are in a vicious circle: the more unhappy you become, the more you desire happiness; the more you desire happiness, the more unhappy you become. Now it is like a dog chasing its own tail.

In Zen they have a certain phrase for it. They say: Whipping the cart. If your horses are not moving and you go on whipping the cart, it is not going to help. You are miserable, then anything that you can dream and anything that you can project is going to bring more misery.

So the first thing is not to dream, not to project. The first thing is to be herenow. Whatsoever it is, just be herenow, and a tremendous revelation is waiting for you. The revelation is that nobody can be unhappy in the herenow.

Have you ever been unhappy herenow? Right this moment you are facing me: is there any possibility of being unhappy right now? You can think about yesterday and you can become unhappy. You can think about tomorrow and you can become unhappy. But right this very moment, this throbbing, beating, real moment, can you be unhappy right now without any past, without any future?

You can bring misery from the past, from memory. Somebody insulted you yesterday and you can still carry the wound, you can still carry the hurt, and you can still feel unhappy about it: Why? Why did it happen to you? Why did the man insult you when you have been doing so much good for him, and you have been always a help, always a friend — and he insulted you. You are playing with something that is no more. The yesterday is gone.

Or you can be unhappy for tomorrow. Tomorrow your money will be finished, then where are you going to stay? Where are you going to eat? Tomorrow your money will be finished — then unhappiness enters in.

Either it comes from yesterday, or it comes from tomorrow, but it is never herenow. Right this moment, in the now, unhappiness is impossible. If you have learned this much, you can become a buddha. Then nobody is hindering your path. Then you can forget all of Freud. Then happiness is not only possible, it has already happened, it is just in front of you. And you are missing it because you go on looking sideways.

Happiness is where you are; wherever you are, happiness is there. It surrounds you. It is a natural phenomenon. It is just like air, just like sky. Happiness is not to be sought: it is the very stuff the universe is made of. Joy is the very stuff the universe is made of. But you have to look direct, you have to look in the immediate. If you look sideways then you miss. You miss because of you. You miss because you have a wrong approach.

This is the most fundamental truth Buddha brought to the world. This is his contribution. He says to go on dying to the past and never think of the future – and then try to be miserable. You will fail. You cannot be miserable. Your failure is absolutely certain; it can be predicted. You cannot manage, howsoever efficient you are in being miserable, howsoever trained, but you cannot create misery this very moment.

Desiring for happiness helps you look somewhere else, and then you go on missing. Happiness is not to be created, happiness is just to be seen. It is already present. This very moment, you can become happy, tremendously happy.

This is how it happened to Buddha. He was the son of a king. He had everything, but was not happy. He became more and more unhappy because the more you have, the more unhappy you become. That is the misery of a rich man. That's what is happening in America today: the richer people are getting, the more unhappy they are becoming; the richer they are getting, the more they are completely at a loss what to do.

Poor people are always certain about what to do: they have to earn money, they have to make a good house, they have to buy a car; they have to send their children to the university. They always have a program waiting for them. They are occupied. They have a future. They have hope: some day or other... They remain in misery, but the hope is there.

The rich man is in misery and the hope has also disappeared. His misery is double. You cannot find a poorer man than a rich man; he is doubly poor. He remains projected in the future, and now he knows the future is not going to supply anything because whatsoever he needs, he has. He becomes troubled, his mind becomes more and more anxious, apprehensive. He becomes anguish. That's what happened to Buddha.

He was rich, he had everything that it was possible to have. He became very unhappy. One day he escaped from his palace, left all the riches, his beautiful wife, his newly born child, and escaped. He became a beggar. He started seeking happiness. He went to this guru, to that guru; he asked everybody what to do to be happy, and of course there were a thousand and one people ready to advise him and he followed everybody's advice. And the more he followed their advice, the more confused he became.

Buddha tried whatsoever was said to him. Somebody said: "Do *Hatha* yoga" so he became a *Hatha* yogi. He did yoga postures and he did them to the very extreme. Nothing came out of it. Maybe you can have a better body with *Hatha* yoga, but you cannot become happy. Just a better body, a more healthy body, makes no difference. With more energy you will have more energy at your disposal to become unhappy, and you will become unhappy. What will you do with it? If you have more money, what are you going to do with it? – you will do that which you can do. And if a little money makes you so miserable, more money will make you more miserable. It is simple arithmetic.

Buddha dropped all yoga. He went to other teachers, the *Raja* yogis, who teach no body postures, who teach only mantras, chanting, meditations. He did that too, but nothing came out of it. He was really in search. When you are really in search then nothing can help, then there is no remedy.

Mediocre people stop somewhere on the way; they are not real seekers. A real seeker is one who goes to the very end of the search and comes to realize that all search is nonsense. Searching itself is a way of desire, and that is what Buddha recognized one day. One day he had left his palace, he had left his worldly possessions; after six years of spiritual search, he dropped all search. The material search was dropped before, now he dropped the spiritual search. This world was dropped before, now he dropped the other world too.

He was completely rid of desire, and that very moment it happened. That very moment there was benediction. When he was completely rid of desire, when he had lost all hope, the future disappeared because the future exists because of your hope. Future is not part of time, remember. Future is part of your hope, desire; future is part of your greed. Future is not part of time.

Time is always the present. Time is never past, never future. Time is always here. The now is infinite. The time never goes anywhere and never comes from anywhere. It is already here and always here. It is your greed, it is your desire, it is your hope that some way, in some situation, you are going to be happy.

All desire dropped, all hope dropped, all hope abandoned, suddenly Gautama Siddhartha became a buddha. It was always there but he was looking somewhere else. It was there, inside, outside. It is how the universe is made. It is blissful, it is truth, it is divine.

Man remains miserable because man goes on missing this fundamental truth about his desiring. This has to be understood, then these sutras will be very simple.

> *The Buddha said:*
> *There was once a man who, being in despair over his inability to control his passions, wished to mutilate himself. The Buddha said to him, "Better destroy your own evil thoughts than do harm to your own person. The mind is lord. When the lord himself is calmed, the servants will of themselves be yielding. If your mind is not cleansed of evil passions, what avails it to mutilate yourself?"*

There are many things to be understood. First: a great misunderstanding exists that Buddha was anti-body. That is absolutely wrong. He was never anti-body. He was not for the body, that's true; but he was never anti-body. This sutra will make it clear. He says: *There was once a man who, being in despair over his inability to control his passions, wished to mutilate himself.*

There have been many persons like that, not only one person. Millions of people have destroyed their bodies in the search for truth, God, ecstasy, or whatsoever you call it. Millions of people have concluded that the body is the enemy. There is a certain logic in it.

People think it is because of the body that you are in misery.

People think it is because of the body that you have sexuality; it is because of the body that you have greed; it is because of the body that you need money; it is because of the body that you need relationship. People think it is because of the body that the whole trouble arises, so why not destroy the body? Why not commit suicide?

There have been many religious sects which are suicidal, which really teach suicide, which say, "This body has to be dropped. If you are courageous enough, then in one leap, drop this body. If you are not courageous, then slowly, in parts, cut the body, drop the body."

There was a very popular sect in Russia before the revolution – it was very popular – that used to teach people to cut off their sexual organs. And there were thousands and thousands of people who followed it – just to mutilate the sexual organs. The idea is that by cutting off the sexual organ you will go beyond sex. This is simply foolish because the sex does not exist in the sexual organ, it exists in the mind. You can cut off the sexual organ and sex will still exist. In fact, now it will become more neurotic because there will be no way to fulfill it.

There have been sects all over the world which teach fasting. Once in a while, once a month, fasting can be of help, can be very healthy, can be a cleansing process. But to go on long fasts is destroying the body. But there have been sects: in Buddha's time there was this sect of the Jainas which was obsessed with the idea of fasting. "Go on fasting – one month, two months, three months – and if you die while you are on a fast, you will reach to the highest heaven."

Why did this idea of fasting become so deep-rooted? Food and sex seem to be the two obsessions of man. And the people who think, "How to get out of the misery?" think these two things are the reasons why they are miserable. In fact, just the opposite is the case.

I have heard...

One airline received this letter: "Gentlemen, may I please suggest that your pilots do not turn on the little light that says 'Fasten Seat Belts,' because every time they do, the ride gets bumpy."

Now you can misunderstand the effect for the cause and the cause for the effect, and it seems logical. The man who wrote the letter must have seen again and again: whenever it is announced that you should fasten your seat belts, suddenly the ride gets jumpy, bumpy, rough. He had seen it many times. He must have been a professor of logic. Watching it again and again: whenever the light comes on and the announcement, immediately something goes wrong. His suggestion is very logical – and yet absurd. The announcement comes only because the ride is going to be bumpy. The announcement is not the cause; the announcement does not create it. It is going to be bumpy; the announcement tries to help you.

But it happens in ordinary life too. Your mind is sexual. The cause is there. The body simply follows it. But when the body follows then you become aware. You are not yet so aware that you can see it when it is in the mind. When it enters into the body it becomes very solid, then you become aware. Your awareness is not sharp. You cannot catch it in the cause. When it has already moved into the effect, then you catch it. You catch it when it is already beyond control. You catch it, you become alert about it only when it has already become solidified.

There are three states of any idea arising in you. First, the idea is wordless; it is not formulated in thoughts. That is the subtlest thing. If you can catch hold of it there, you will become free of it. The second stage is when it has entered into words; it is formulated – there is a thought arising in you. People are so sleepy that they don't become aware even at the second stage. When the thought has become a thing, when it has already entered into the gross body and the body has become possessed by it, then you become aware. It simply shows your unawareness.

Hence, Buddha says that if you really want to get rid of the misery, the pain, the life that is almost like hell, you have to become more and more aware. The more aware you become, the deeper you can see into the cause. The deeper the cause is known, the more capable you become to get out of it. If you can catch some desire when it has not even entered into your conscious mind and it is still just a feeling with no words, just in the unconscious striving to get to the conscious, there it is very simple to stop it.

For example: you can throw a small seed very easily. There is no trouble about it. But when it has taken root and has become a great tree, it will be difficult to uproot it.

First the idea arises in the innermost core. Then it enters into the mind. Then it enters into the body. You feel it only when it has entered into the body. There are even more sleepy people who don't even feel it there. When it has entered into the world, then they feel it.

For example, anger arises first in your deepest core, wordless, undefined. Then it comes to be a thought. Then it enters in your body; adrenaline and other poisons are released in the bloodstream – you are ready to kill somebody or beat somebody, bite somebody. You are getting mad. But you may not even become aware. When you hit somebody it has entered into the world. That is the fourth stage. Then you become aware: "What have I done?"

Haven't you observed it many times? When you have hit somebody – your child, your friend, your wife – then suddenly you become aware: "What have I done? I never wanted to do it. It has happened in spite of me," you say. This simply shows your unawareness.

Go deeper, and catch hold of anything arising in the first step. And then it is so easy – just like you can destroy a seed very easily, but to destroy a tree will be difficult. And when the tree has sent its millions of seeds into the air, then it is almost beyond your control. The winds have taken the seeds to faraway fields; now it is impossible to find where they have fallen. Now the tree is not one; it has created many possibilities of its own being. It will be imitated in many fields.

Buddha says that destroying the body is not going to help. If your eyes make you desirous of beautiful women or beautiful men, it is not going to help if you destroy your eyes.

There is a story in India about a saint, Surdas. I don't think it is true. If it is true, then Surdas is not a saint. Surdas can only be a saint if the story is untrue. I am ready to say that the story is untrue; I cannot say Surdas is untrue. He is so authentic, his insight is so pure that the story must be wrong.

The story is: Surdas left the world. He was moving in a town. He saw a beautiful woman, and he followed almost as if a magnet were pulling him. He started feeling guilty too. He is a sannyasin, renounced the world – what is he doing? But he was incapable of controlling himself, so the story goes.

He went to the woman, he asked for food, but that was just an excuse. Then he started to go to the same woman every day just to have a look at her face, just to have a look into her eyes, just to have a little contact. He started dreaming about her. The whole day he was continuously thinking and fantasizing, and was waiting for the next day when he would be able to go to the woman again.

Then, by and by, he became aware that he was getting into a trap. And the story says that because it was his eyes that made him aware of the beauty of the woman, he destroyed his eyes and became a blind man.

I say, and I say it categorically, this story is simply invented because this is so foolish. Surdas cannot do it. It must have been invented by other blind people; it must have been invented by other stupid people who always go on inventing stupid things. It is stupid because eyes cannot do anything – it is the mind. It is the mind that approaches through the eyes. It is the mind that approaches through the hand.

When you hit somebody or you kill somebody, it is not the hand that is the murderer, it is you. And it is not going to help if you cut off your hand. And you cannot go to the court and say to the magistrate, "It was my hand."

It happened once in a court that a man argued this way. He said, "It is my hand which has killed." The magistrate was also very clever and cunning – they have to be clever and cunning because they have to deal with clever and cunning people. They have the same logic.

The magistrate said, "You are right, you are absolutely logical: you have not killed – your hands have killed. So your hands will remain in the prison. You can go home, but the hands cannot go." So the hands were chained and the magistrate said, "Why don't you go now?"

He said, "How can I go without the hands?"

And the magistrate said, "If you cannot go without the hands, how can the hands do something without you? You are both partners. And in fact the hand is simply a servant, you are the master."

There was once a man who, being in despair over his inability to control his passions wished to mutilate himself.

Buddha is not against the body; he is not anti-body. He cannot be, because the body is so innocent. It has never done anything wrong. It is so pure; you cannot find a purer thing in existence.

Yes, one thing is certain, that whatsoever you want to do, the body follows you. It is a servant and very obedient. Even if you are going to murder somebody, the body follows; it never says no. If you are going to the temple to pray, the body follows. It never says no. Whether you are going to commit a crime or going to pray in the temple, the body follows you so obediently, like a shadow.

No, the body is never responsible. One thing has to be understood about the body. The body is a unique thing in the world; nothing can be compared to it. It has one unique situation and that is: it is the only object in the world that you can look at from both the sides, from without and from within. If you look at a rock, you look from the without. If you look at the moon, you look from the without. Except for the body, your body, everything else you look at from the without. Your body is the only object in the world you can look at from the without and you can look at from within.

Hence, the body is the door for the within, the body is the door for the inner journey, how can Buddha be against it? And you can see Buddha's body – so beautiful, so graceful – how can he be against it? Watch Buddha's statues: he must have loved his body, he must have had tremendous compassion for his body. His body is flowerlike, it is a roseflower or a lotus. No, he cannot be against the body. And if people interpret that Buddha is against the body, those people are putting their own interpretations on him.

The Buddha said to him, "Better destroy your own evil thoughts than do harm to your own person. The mind is lord. When the lord himself is calmed, the servants will of themselves be yielding."

Buddha's whole effort is to make you aware that, whatsoever you are, the cause is your mind. If you are miserable, the mind is functioning in a wrong pattern. If you are happy, the mind is functioning in the right pattern.

Happiness is nothing but the humming of the mechanism of mind when it functions perfectly. When the mind is simply in tune with the universe, you are happy. When the mind goes against nature, against the natural law – what Buddha calls *dhamma* – when the mind goes against Tao, when the mind goes against the current, when the mind tries to swim upstream, then there are problems, there is misery. When the mind simply follows the stream like driftwood, just goes with the stream wherever it is going, it is happy. And one day it reaches to the ultimate, the oceanic bliss. There is no need to reach to it, there is no need to make any effort – effortlessly it happens.

So Buddha says that the basic question is not of the body, and it is not of the soul. The soul has no problems, and the body also has no problems. The problem is just in between the two. This mind which links the body and the soul is the problem; this mind that bridges the unknown to the known, the invisible to the visible, the formless to the form – this bridge is the only problem. If you can solve the mind, suddenly you are at home.

The mind is the problem. What can we do to change the mind? What can we do to have a better functioning mind? Again a desire arises, and again you are in the trap of the mind.

If I teach to you that you should become desireless and you will be happy, immediately a desire arises in the mind to become desireless. Immediately you start looking for clues, methods, techniques to become desireless. Now, to become desireless is again a desire. If I say mind is the problem, you immediately ask how to solve it, how to dissolve it, how to get rid of it, but the one who is asking the question is mind itself. And the one who is going to try is mind itself. So whatsoever you do you will never get out of the mind by doing anything. Still your question is relevant: Then what should we do?

We should look into the nature of the mind and not try to do anything. Just a great insight into the nature of your mind is all that is needed. Let me try to explain it to you.

Buddha says, "Desire and you will be miserable." Suddenly a desire arises to be desireless because we want to be happy and we don't want to be miserable. And desire arises and new misery arises. When Buddha says that desire creates misery, he means simply to watch how desire arises, how it creates misery. Just go on watching. Each desire brings its own misery.

You are passing down the road, you see a beautiful car just pass by – a flash – and a desire arises to possess this car. Now you become miserable. Just a moment before you were perfectly okay, there was no misery, and here passes this car and misery arises. Buddha says: "Watch."

Just a moment ago you were humming a song and going for a morning walk and everything was beautiful: the birds were singing, and the trees were green, and the morning breeze was cool, and the sun was fantastic, everything was beautiful. You were in a poetic world full of joy and verve and gusto, and you were juicy and you were part of this beautiful morning. Everything was simply just as it should be. And then a car passes.

It is not that the owner of the car has come to disturb you; he may not even be aware of you. He is not trying to create any misery for you – don't be angry at him. It is not that the car is creating misery in you, because how can the car create misery in you? It is your desire.

Seeing the car a desire arises: "I should become the possessor of the car; this car has to be in my garage." And suddenly, trees are no longer green, birds are no longer singing, the sun is no longer shining, it is already sunset. From morning the sunrise has disappeared; everything is dismal and dark. You are full of desire, you are surrounded by smoke. You have lost contact with life immediately. Just a flicker of desire and you are millions of miles away from beauty, from truth, from joy.

Just watch. Buddha says to simply watch. Stand by the side of the road, watch: what has happened? Just a small desire arising and you are thrown into hell, and you were almost in heaven. You change from heaven to hell so many times in twenty-four hours; you don't watch.

People come to me and they ask, "Is there any heaven? Is there any hell?" And I am surprised because they go on continuously shunting like a goods train between heaven and hell. Just a second is needed, a split second – in no time they are in hell and in no time they are in heaven.

Just watch how desire brings hell, how desire is hell. And then don't ask how to attain to desirelessness, there is no need. If you have looked into the nature of desire and you have felt it brings misery, that very understanding will be the dropping of desire. Just go on watching. If it is not dropping that simply shows that your insight is still not deep enough, so make your insight deep.

It is not a question that somebody else can enlighten you about; it is your desire and only you can watch. I cannot watch your desire. You cannot watch anybody else's desire. It is your private world. Hell or heaven are private things. And within a split second you can shift from one to another.

Just watch...

Buddha's word is, "Watch." Be watchful. Don't create any desire for desirelessness, otherwise you are simply behaving in a very stupid way. Now you are creating a new desire and this will create misery. You simply go into the nature of the desire, look deep into it. Watch how it creates darkness, how it brings misery, how suddenly it takes you, overpowers you. Just go on watching.

One day it is going to happen: a car will pass by and, before the desire has arisen, you will become watchful, and suddenly laughter will come to you. You have become watchful; the desire has not arisen. It was just going to be, it was just ready to jump upon you and take you to hell. But you were watchful, and you will feel so happy. For the first time you will have a key. You will know now that just being watchful, the desire has not arisen, the car has passed. The car has nothing to do with desire. Desire arises because you are unconscious, unaware, sleepy; you are living the life of a somnambulist, drunk.

Awareness is desirelessness. Awareness of the desire brings desirelessness. And this key has to be used to open many locks.

If you are greedy, don't ask how to get rid of it because that is greed again, under another name, in another form. You have heard saints, mahatmas, you have read scriptures, and they say if you are greedy you will go to hell. Now greed arises to go to heaven. Those scriptures say that in heaven everything is just beautiful, fabulous. They create greed. And now you ask how to get rid of greed because a new greed has arisen in you: how to achieve heaven? How to enter paradise? How to live there for ever and ever, eternally, ecstatically, blissfully? Now this is a new greed.

This is not the way. The Buddha's way is really the best that has ever been brought to earth. The Buddha's way is the most penetrating and the most revolutionary way possible. He says to watch greed. Just watch greed and see what it is and how it creates misery for you. In that watching a light will start arising in you, your inner flame will burn bright, and the darkness of greed will disappear.

It is the same with violence, the same with anger, the same with possessiveness, and the same with all that makes you miserable.

A maidservant happened to belch in front of her master – of course, the master must have been Western because in India nobody takes any notice of belching. The master became very angry and was going to strike her, but seeing her young and beautiful body his anger suddenly abated, and he took his pleasure with her.

The next day when he was in his study there was a knock on the door. It was the maidservant. "What is it? What do you want?"

"Please, sir, I belched again a little while ago."

Once you taste something, whatsoever it is, the desire arises again and again to repeat it. Whatsoever you have known in your past, you go on asking for again and again in the future. Your future is nothing but your modified past. Your future is nothing but the desire to repeat your past.

If you live a bored life, nobody else is responsible for it but you. You ask for boredom, and boredom is misery. You ask for boredom because you ask for repetition. Something happened... For example, you were sitting and the first star of the evening was becoming visible, and you watched. It was a quiet evening and it was cool and birds were returning to their nests. It was silent and it was very musical and you were in tune. Just watching the star becoming visible you felt beautiful. Now, you have tasted something – you will gather it like a treasure. This treasure will make you miserable.

First, you will hanker for it again and again. That hankering will create misery. And it cannot be repeated by your hankering, remember, because it happened only because there was no hankering in you. You were simply sitting there not knowing what was going to happen. It happened in a state of innocence. It happened in a state of non-expectation. It happened because you were not looking for it. That is a basic ingredient in it. You were not looking, you were not asking. In fact, you were not desiring, you were simply there. Suddenly you became aware: the first star. And in that moment when you became aware of the first star, you were not thinking that it was happiness, remember that too. That comes later on; that is a recapitulation.

In that moment you were simply there – not happy, not unhappy, nothing. These words don't mean anything. Existence is so vast that no word is meaningful about it. But then it is gone and there remains a memory. And you say again and again, "It was beautiful – how beautiful, how divine." Now a desire arises to repeat it every evening. Next day you are waiting again, but now the whole situation has changed: you are waiting for it, you are looking for it, you want to repeat the old experience. Now, this is something new which was not present in the previous experience. So this won't allow you. You are looking too much. You are not relaxed; you are tense, afraid you may miss the first star. You are apprehensive. You are worried whether it is going to be again or not. It is not going to be.

First, it is not possible now because you have lost that innocence, that inexperienced state where no memory existed, where past was not, where future was not. Secondly, if some day it is repeated it will be boring because it will be a repetition. You have already known it. The beauty is in the new, it is never in the old. The beauty is in the fresh, it is never in the dead. The beauty belongs to the original, never to the carbon copy. The beauty is when an experience is firsthand, not secondhand. Now, if it happens at all, it will not make you happy, it will be a secondhand experience. And remember: existence is never secondhand. Existence is always fresh.

To know that godliness in the beauty of the evening, or in the beauty of a bird on the wing, means you have to be absolutely innocent. The past has to be completely dropped and the future is not to be allowed to interfere. Then, and only then, there is beauty and there is benediction, there is blessing, there is happiness and bliss.

Once you experience something you start asking for it, you become a beggar. Then it will never happen. And you will carry the memory like a wound.

Have you seen it? Watch it: whenever you are happy, in that moment you don't know it is happiness. It is only afterward when the experience is gone, faded away, is no more, then mind comes in and starts looking for it, starts comparing, evaluating, judging, and says, "Yes, it was beautiful, so beautiful." When the experience itself was present, mind was not present.

Happiness is when mind is not.

When mind comes in, happiness is no longer there. Now there is only a memory, a dead memory. Your lover is gone; you are just carrying a letter written by your lover. The flower has faded; just an image in your mind. This image will not allow happiness to enter again in your being; this image will be the barrier, will be the rock.

Buddha says: "Don't carry the past and don't ask for the future – just be herenow. Then there is no-mind, and the body simply follows that no-mindness."

Right now the body follows the mind. The mind is the culprit and you go on punishing the body. It is almost like a small child: he comes running into the room, gets hit by the door, becomes angry at the door, starts beating the door as if the door is the culprit.

Not only children but even grown-up people do such things. You are writing and your fountain pen is not flowing well; you become angry and you throw it on the floor – you punish the fountain pen. And still you think man is rational? Still you believe man is a rational being?

When you come home angry, have you seen? You open the door in such anger, you bang it. Now, the door has not done anything to you.

It happened once:

A man came to see a Zen master; he banged the door, he threw off his shoes. He came to the master, bowed down, touched his feet. The master said, "I cannot accept your greeting. You first go and ask the door to forgive you, and the shoes."

The man said, "What are you talking about? Do you want me to become a laughingstock?" And there were so many people sitting around.

The master said, "If you don't do this then I am not going to allow you to be here, you simply get out. If you can insult the door and if you can insult the shoes, then you have to ask for their forgiveness. When you insulted them, then you never felt that you were doing something ridiculous? Now you feel ridiculous? Go and do it!"

The man went. He asked – first he looked a little foolish, felt a little foolish, and people were watching, but he asked to be forgiven. He said, "Sir, please, I was not conscious and I have done something wrong unconsciously, forgive me." And he was talking to the shoes and to the door, and when he came back he was a totally different man.

The master took him close and hugged him. And the man said, "It is tremendous. When I was asking to be forgiven, first I looked foolish, then suddenly I felt so good, have never felt like that. I actually felt they have forgiven me. I felt their compassion and their sympathy and their love."

You go on behaving in such unconscious manners. That unconscious mannerism of your behavior is all that Buddha means by the word *mind*. Mind is your sleep. Mind is your absence. And if the body follows this mind, this sleepy, drunk mind, don't get angry at the body.

"The mind is lord. When the lord himself is calmed, the servants will of themselves be yielding." When the mind is calm it becomes no-mind. No-mind and a calm mind mean exactly the same thing; they don't mean two different things. A calm mind, a cool mind, is a no-mind because mind is the fever. Mind is the continuous anxiety, tension, the disease – yes, the disease is the mind. When the disease has disappeared you function from a state which is of no mind, and then the body follows it.

The body is a follower. If you have mind, the body follows the mind; if you have no-mind, the body follows the no-mind. But don't start fighting with the body. Don't be stupid.

> *"If your mind is not cleansed of evil passions, what avails it to mutilate yourself?"* Thereupon the Buddha recited the gatha: *Passions grow from the will, the will grows from thought and imagination: when both are calmed, there is*

neither sensualism nor transmigration. The Buddha said, this gatha was taught before by Kashyapabuddha.

Buddha says, "There have been millions of buddhas before me and there will be millions of buddhas after me."

This is something very new in the world of religions.

Mahavira says, "There have been only twenty-three *tirthankaras* before me, and there will be no *tirthankara* anymore."

Mohammed says, "There have been only four prophets before me and there will be no prophet after me."

Jesus says, "I am the only begotten son of God."

Buddha is rare. He says, "There have been millions of buddhas before me, and millions of buddhas will be after me." And this seems to be truer because only twenty-three *tirthankaras* in the whole of infinity? Then what about Ram, then what about Krishna? They are not included in the Jaina *tirthankaras*.

Mohammed says, "There have been only four prophets before me" – then what about Mahavira? And what about Krishna? And what about Buddha? They are not included in it.

Jesus says, "I am the only begotten son." This looks absurd, that God should have only one son. And what has he been doing afterward? Following birth control? This looks absurd, and creates fanaticism. Then the Christians think they are superior because they are the followers of the only son that God has. Others are prophets, at the most, if they recognize them at all. But theirs is the only son of God. That creates ego, superiority.

Hindus say they have only twenty-four avataras. A few centuries ago they had the idea of ten avatars. Then they expanded it a little because Jainas were claiming twenty-four *tirthankaras* so there was great competition. So they said, "Okay, we will also have twenty-four." The number twenty-four became very standard; even Buddhists started saying that there are only twenty-four buddhas. And when *tirthankaras* are twenty-four and buddhas are twenty-four, then to have only ten avataras looks a little poor. So Hindus extended the idea; they dropped the idea of ten avatars; they also claimed they have twenty-four avatars. But what about Mahavira? What about Adinatha? They are not included.

Buddha includes all. He is tremendously inclusive. And he

creates no superiority; he says that millions of buddhas have been before and millions will be afterward. The world has never lacked buddhas. That is how it should be because to be a buddha is just to be aware of your nature. It is nothing special. It looks special because you have not tried it; otherwise it is your own treasure, it has only to be claimed.

Look at the beauty of it: Buddha claims nothing special for himself. He says that many buddhas have been, millions and millions will be afterward. Look at the beauty of his declaration: about himself he is saying, "I am just one in millions – nothing special about me." This is how a really religious person should be: nothing special, very ordinary. When there are millions of buddhas, then how can you be special? You can be special if there is a limited number.

There was much conflict, because when Mahavira claimed that he was the twenty-fourth, there were eight others who were claiming that they were the twenty-fourth. There was trouble! Nobody was ready to believe in the other, and there are no ways to prove it really. How can you prove who is the real *tirthankara*?

A few chose Goshalak and followed him; a few chose Mahavira and followed him. A few chose others – Ajit Keshkambal, Sanjay Vilethiputta, and there were other claimers – how do you decide? Christians say that Jesus is the only son of God and Jews crucified him. How do you decide? Jews thought he was a cheat.

Jews are also waiting for a messiah. They have been waiting for centuries, but they never allow anybody to become that messiah because then for whom will they wait? They are hoping and hoping and hoping, and they have waited so long that now it has become habitual for Jews – they don't allow anybody. Jesus claimed; many others have claimed after Jesus, but whosoever claims: "I am the messiah" has to be destroyed, has to be rejected, has to be proved a cheat.

The messiah is certainly to come, but they don't allow anybody to claim it. Centuries of waiting, and they have become addicted. Now they will wait – even if God comes they will crucify him because they will say, "Who wants you? We love waiting, we exist in our hope." Jews go on hoping.

But everybody tries – Jews think they are the chosen race, that

God has chosen them specially; Hindus think they are the chosen race; Jainas think they are the chosen ones. Buddha is rare. Buddha says that there were millions of buddhas before, countless. In fact, he has said that if you count the grains of sand in the Ganges, there have been more than that many buddhas before, and there will be more later on. This makes his own stature very ordinary, but this is his beauty. Not to claim for any extraordinariness is what extraordinariness is. And when you claim, when you claim you are superior, you are simply showing that you suffer from an inferiority complex.

Now, Mohammed says that there will be no more prophets. Why are you closing the door? Now if somebody claims "I am the prophet," Mohammedans will kill him because Mohammed has closed the door. But who is he to close the door? The door belongs to nobody, or it belongs to all. How can he close it?

Why this idea in the first place? Mahavira thinks he is the last, Mohammed thinks he is the last, Jesus thinks he is the last – then what do you mean by this? You simply don't allow evolution, you don't allow any new idea to evolve. You close the door, you make a closed dogma, so that nobody can disturb the dogma.

Buddha keeps all doors open: he says millions... He remembers this *gatha* from some past buddha, Kashyapabuddha was his name. He says, "This *gatha* was told by Kashyapabuddha."

Passions grow from the will, the will grows from thought and imagination: when both are calmed, there is neither sensualism nor transmigration.

The will means the ego. The will means to fight against existence. Whenever you see somebody fighting upstream, you say, "He is the man of willpower." What do you mean by willpower? All will is against existence. You fight with it. You try to do something which is not in the nature of things. You try to force something. If you are violent with nature, then you have will.

Many people come to me and they say, "Osho, somehow help us to have more willpower." Why? Am I your enemy? Should I help you to become more mad? Willpower? But in the West, willpower is very important; because the whole West thinks that to have a strong ego is a must, you should have willpower, you should develop willpower. Thousands of books exist in the market on how to develop willpower. And they are sold because people want to be more and more refined in their egos.

Buddha says: *Passions grow from the will...* Desires grow from the will. The I, the ego, is the root of your mind. Your whole mind is centered around the I. *...the will grows from thought and imagination...* Thought comes from the past; imagination means movement in the future. Whatsoever you have experienced, thought, learned, is your ego. And whatsoever you want to experience in your future, would like to have in your future, is your will. These are two aspects of the same phenomenon. *...When both are calmed...* When thought is no longer there, when past is no longer there, and when imagination, projection, dreaming, future is no longer there: *...when both are calmed, there is neither sensualism nor transmigration.* Buddha says that then all sensualism disappears; then one is no longer greedy for senses and the experience of the senses.

Remember: by the disappearance of sensualism he does not mean that your sensitivity disappears; you become tremendously sensitive. A sensual person is not a sensitive person; a sensual person is very gross, very rough, very primitive. A sensitive person is very developed, highly developed; he is very receptive. A sensual person is after pleasure, and the sensitive person is one who knows bliss is here and he is open to it, and he goes on being showered by the divine bliss. He soaks it up like a sponge. He is sensitive.

The sensual person is always after something, trying to achieve money, power, prestige. The sensitive person is simply alive herenow, enjoying the beauty that is available. When tomorrow comes then tomorrow will take care of itself.

That's what Jesus means when he says, "Think not of the morrow." That's what Jesus says when he shows to his disciples the lilies in the field and says, "Look, how beautiful they are. And they toil not. They are simply here; they don't worry about what is going to happen tomorrow. Even Solomon, in all his glory, was not so beautiful," says Jesus, "as these poor flowers of lilies."

A sensitive person is a flowerlike person, open to existence, enjoying it – enjoying it tremendously – but not seeking anything. His search has dissolved. He is not chasing anything.

I have heard...

A man lost everything at the casinos in Vegas. He tried every one in town and each was a disaster. All he had left now was a Kennedy fifty-cent piece. He kept tossing it in the air – a la George Raft – as he walked along the street trying to figure out a way to get another stake, when his coin slipped out of his fingers and fell into a grating in the middle of the street.

Our hero was after it like a shot, but before he could grab it he was hit by a taxi and carried off to the hospital with a broken leg.

He was out in a couple of months, and with the settlement from the insurance company he started back to the casinos. On the way, he limped past the same grating where he had lost his coin. He started to look down to see if he could find it when he was hit by another taxi, and he was back in the hospital with his other leg broken.

"How could you get knocked twice in exactly the same place?" the nurse asked him. "I mean, what in the world made you go back to that stupid grating?"

"That was my good luck charm," he explained, "and I didn't want to lose it."

People go on chasing, go on being hit every time. Their whole life becomes just wounds and wounds and wounds, but again and again they go on chasing the same things, as if they don't see what is happening to them.

A man of sensitivity remains wherever he is, and life seeks him. A man of sensuality rushes from here to there, from there to somewhere else, chasing and chasing. And this is the beauty of the whole process: if you are chasing God you will never meet him, because you don't know where he is. If you are chasing happiness you will never meet it, because you don't know the whereabouts, you don't even know the face of happiness. Even if you come across her, you will not be able to recognize her. The person who is sensitive simply sits wherever he is and happiness comes to him, and bliss comes to him, and God comes to him.

This is to be remembered: It is not only you who are seeking God – God is also seeking you. And the case is such that he comes and knocks at your door, but you are never there. You are somewhere else. He goes on knocking at your door but you are never found there because the door is in the present and you are in the future or in the past.

The Buddha said:

> *From the passions arises worry, and from worry arises fear. Away with the passions, and no fear, no worry.*

Observe it. These are not theories. These are facts of life. Buddha is not a theoretician, not a metaphysician – not at all. He is just a scientist of the basic facts of life. He talks only about a fact. You need not believe in it, you have simply to watch and you will find the truth of it.

He says: *From the passions arises worry...* Whenever desire arises, worry arises: How to get it? How to reach it? How to achieve? You are worried. When you are worried there are a thousand and one alternatives. Then more worry arises: Which will be the right alternative to reach to it? Which will be the right path? And then fear arises whether you will be able to reach it. There are so many competitors in the world, and so many people have tried and failed. Look at Alexander and Genghis Khan and Nadir Shah – so many people have tried, and tried so powerfully, tried so hard, and still they have failed. What is the guarantee that you will succeed? Then fear arises. These are simple facts.

A man comes into a store to buy a suit. The salesman tries one jacket on him after another. He says to the customer, "Turn around, let's see it in this light; now let's look at it in the rear-view mirror; now from this angle, now this angle." Still the man asks to try on other jackets.

Finally the boss comes up to them and picks out a jacket. The customer puts it on and buys it immediately. Says the boss, "See how easy it is to make a sale?"

"Okay," says the salesman, "you made the sale, but who made him dizzy?"

Once a passion is there it will make you dizzy – worries, apprehensions – what to choose, what not to choose, where to go, how to go, what will be the right technique, the right method, the right approach? And then the fear: whether you will be able to make it? A constant fear. One becomes dizzy.

Passion is the salesman. And then comes the Devil: the boss. Then you are thrown into hell. Desire makes you dizzy. And nobody can be certain, nobody.

I was reading a beautiful anecdote:

Father O'Malley and Rabbi Cohen were playing golf. On the third hole, Father O'Malley hit one into the rough, and he hollered, "Oh, shit!" And he looked up to heaven and said, "Dear Lord, I'm terribly sorry. It was an oversight."

On the fifth hole he made another terrible shot into the rough. Again he shouted, "Oh, shit!" Again he looked up to heaven and said, "Dear Lord, again please excuse me. I'm terribly sorry."

On the ninth hole, same thing again, into the rough. He hollered "Oh, shit!"

Just then there was a bolt of lightning and Rabbi Cohen was struck and killed. A loud rumbling was heard in heaven and a voice saying, "Oh, shit!"

Even a God can miss, so what is the guarantee of your ever being successful? One goes on being afraid, trembling, shaking with fear.

Passions create worry; worry creates fear. *Away with the passions, and no fear, no worry.*

But people have only passions in their lives, that's why they have only worries and fear and nothing else. So many people come to me who want to get some peace of mind, want a way to get out of their worries. But if you tell them, "Get out of your passions," then they are not ready to follow you. They want some mantra, some cheap thing, so they can go on desiring, they can go on chasing their passions and still remain unworried.

A politician used to come to me, and he would always say, "Somehow, Osho, help me to have some peace of mind."

I said, "Being a politician you should not ask for it – it never comes to a politician. Peace of mind? If it can happen to a politician, then are the saints fools? What are they doing? Then why should they leave ambition? It can never come. Ambition creates tension, worry. You get out of your politics."

And he would say, "You may be right, but right now I cannot get out of it."

Then I told him, "Then you be at ease with your tensions, accept them. You are trying to do something which is not possible. You want to eat your cake and have it too."

Then he started going to Maharishi Mahesh Yogi. For many days he didn't turn up. One day, suddenly we met in a train. I asked him, "You have not been coming to me for many days."

He said, "What is the point of coming to you? You say get out of politics. Mahesh Yogi is better. He says, 'Wherever you are, I will make you more efficient. You are a politician? You will become a better politician – just do TM.'"

Now that fits, that completely fits. You are not to change anything; just repeating some foolish thing – blah, blah, blah – and that's all. Twenty minutes you repeat it and, wherever you are, all success is guaranteed to you, all efficiency is guaranteed to you. Even thieves are doing TM, smugglers are doing TM, politicians are doing TM. The smuggler thinks that if he does TM he will never be caught, he will become more efficient.

Meditation is not so cheap. Meditation is a total transformation of your being. And a great understanding is needed and a great intelligence.

Buddha's sutras are only for those who are really intelligent people and who really want to get out of the misery that they have created around themselves. It is only for those who are really fed up with misery and are ready to get out of the trap.

It is up to you, it depends on you. You have created it. Once you understand how you have created it, it will disappear because then you will not be able to create it anymore.

Enough for today.

10

RELIGION IS THE ULTIMATE LUXURY

The first question:

> Osho,
> It is a sight for gods to see that so many men and women, mostly young and intelligent, from all over the globe, have gathered at this place to seek truth and true religion. But aren't you at the same time laying the foundation of another organized religion, a global one this time, which will again turn into an impediment in the way of truth and religion itself, or do organized religions too play a positive role?

The first and the most important thing to remember is to never think of the future, and never be entangled with the past. While I am here, enjoy me. While I am here, don't miss this opportunity.

This is mind playing games. You are not enjoying me, you are not delighted; you are creating a worry for yourself. Now the worry is about the future. Who are you to be worried about the future? How can you manage to control it? There is no way. The future will take its own course. We cannot manage the future in a certain way that it should be so or should not be so. All efforts have always failed.

Buddha tried to prevent any organized religion in his name. He tried to prevent any image ever to be made of him, but there are more images of Buddha than anybody else in the world. There are a few temples which are called "thousand Buddha temples" – one thousand images. There is one temple in China, a cave temple, which has ten thousand Buddha images.

Even Buddha couldn't manage it. There is no way to manage it. The only way is to use the present, and leave the future for the future. There will be people when we will not be here, and it is their freedom to do whatever they are going to do with my words. If they want to make chains out of them, that is their freedom. If they want to be liberated by these words, that is their freedom. If they want to make a prison out of the temple that we are creating, then it is their freedom, and it is their choice. Who are we to interfere?

Now, Krishnamurti tries to interfere with the future. He thinks continuously about what will happen in the future – so no clue should be left for the future, so the religion cannot be organized. But to be constantly concerned so much about the future is wrong. Who are we? The future belongs to the future and will belong to future generations who will do whatsoever they like to do.

One thing I can say: it is their freedom whatsoever they do, and I have nothing against them. If they want to live in prisons, they will live in prisons. They will find a way to make a prison out of anything; they have always done so.

I am not concerned with the future at all. I am totally here now. This is what I would like you to be also, here and now. Whatsoever is transpiring between me and you, don't allow any interference. This idea is just a trap of the mind. This is the first thing I would like to say.

The second thing: even organized religions play a positive role. The positive role consists in provocation, in challenge. Even the prison plays a positive role: it provokes the spirit of the courageous, it becomes a challenge for freedom, it has its role, its function.

I am not saying to live in the prison. In fact, the prison itself forces you to get out of it. The prison itself can be used in a positive way. If you are thrown in a prison your spirit will continuously meditate and think about how to get out of it, how to find ways and means to escape. In a prison the courageous soul will start brooding and dreaming about freedom. The bigger the prison, the greater the enforced structure of it, the more the challenge will be. Only cowards will accept it.

But cowards, even if they are out of prison, will remain in prison because they are not going anywhere – they are imprisoned in their cowardice. The courageous, even in a prison, will try to break through, they will try to get out. And in that very effort to get out, a strength is born. In that very struggle to get out, a new being is born; they have a new sense of urgency, a new force and power.

Nothing is wrong. But remember, when I say nothing is wrong I am not saying to relax and go to sleep in a prison. I am saying the prison can be used in a positive way. Even your home can become a prison if you use it in a negative way – that's what it has become for millions of people. They live in their homes, but they live in a prison. They call it their home, but it is their cowardice. They have lost the adventure of the soul, they are no longer adventurous, they are no longer wanderers. They are no longer interested in the unknown, in the unfamiliar. They always carry their maps wherever they go. They always have their guides wherever they go. They live a borrowed life. They don't have any passion to live fresh, to live young. They don't have any passion to move into the uncharted territory, to go to the ocean, to go into danger, and to face life.

When you are in danger and you are facing life you are for the first time in contact with your soul. The soul is not cheap. You have to put everything at stake. That's why I say even an organized religion can be a positive thing.

Buddha was born as a Hindu. Hinduism became the prison. He tried hard to get out of it, and he succeeded. Krishnamurti was trained in a certain discipline, was an inmate of a prison called theosophy, but he tried hard, broke out of it, became free of it. If you ask me I will say one thing: if there had been no theosophical imprisonment for him in his childhood, it would have been difficult for him to become a free man. Annie Besant and Leadbeater and other theosophists created the whole situation – unknowingly, of course, they were not meaning it. They were trying to do something else. They were creating a dogma around him, a cult around him. And they were so hard upon him that it became really impossible to live in it. He had to get out of it. The credit goes to those people – Leadbeater and Annie Besant.

If the prison had been a little more comfortable. If the prison had not been so hard and if the discipline imposed had not been so arduous. If the ideals had not been so superhuman and he had not been asked to play a role so unnatural to him, he might have relaxed, he might have accepted it. That's what has happened to you.

A Christian remains a Christian because Christianity is no longer a great pressure. On Sunday you can go to the church – it is a formality. It remains the life of a non-Christian. You go on fulfilling the formalities of being a Christian. Your Christianity is not even skin deep, and the church does not demand much. The church says, "You just come on particular days to the church: when your child is born come to the church for the baptism; when somebody dies, come to the church; when there is marriage, come to the church. Just do these three things and you will remain a Christian. Sometimes on Sundays come and participate in the ritual."

Nothing much is asked. The prison is not much of a prison. It is almost as if you are free, only on Sundays you go to the jail and sit there for one hour and come home and you are again free. Who bothers? Who will fight against it? It is so convenient and comfortable.

That's why so many people are Hindus and Mohammedans

and Jainas. Nobody is asking anything of them. These religions are just formal rituals; they don't challenge you. Nothing is at stake. It is very difficult to get out of them because the prison is very lukewarm. You have become adjusted to it. It is so convenient and comfortable that you have become adjusted to it. It looks almost like a good policy, a good compromise.

Krishnamurti fell into the hands of a very fanatical group – theosophists. It was a new religion. Whenever a religion is new, it is very fanatical. By and by, it relaxes and compromises and becomes just a social phenomenon; then it is no longer religion. Theosophy was just in its beginning, and Krishnamurti was only nine years old when he fell into the hands of those fanatics. They tried hard. They wouldn't allow Krishnamurti to meet and mix with ordinary children, no, because they had a goal that he had to become the world teacher, *jagatguru*. He had to become the coming Buddha; he had to become the incarnation of Maitreya.

He was not allowed to move with any girl, because he might have fallen in love and the whole dream of the theosophists would have been shattered. He was constantly guarded. He was not allowed to move alone; somebody was always with him, watching him. He was forced to follow very strict rules: three o'clock in the morning he had to get up and take a cold bath; and then he had to learn Sanskrit, and he had to learn French, and he had to learn English, and he had to learn Latin and Greek because a world teacher should be well cultured, sophisticated. And he was just a nine-year-old child.

When he was twelve years old they started forcing him to write a book. Now what can a twelve-year-old child write? In fact, the teacher, Leadbeater was writing in his name. Krishnamurti would write and Leadbeater would correct it and make it perfect. The book still exists. A beautiful book, but you cannot expect it of a boy just twelve years old. It is not from him. Even Krishnamurti cannot remember it. When he has been asked he has said, "I don't remember when I wrote it, I don't remember at all how it came into being."

They were talking nonsense – esoteric nonsense: "In his dreams he goes to the seventh heaven, and there God himself is teaching him." And just a twelve-year-old child – very vulnerable, soft, receptive; he would trust. These people were world-famous, they had great names, and the movement was really big and worldwide; thousands and thousands of lodges were opened all over the world.

Just a twelve-year-old boy had become a world-famous personality. Wherever he was going, thousands of people would gather just to see him. If you look at those pictures you feel pity for him, compassion. He was continuously in a cage. It was natural for him to renounce, I think it would have happened to anybody – it had nothing to do with Krishnamurti. Anybody in his place, if he had any spirit left, would have renounced this whole nonsense and would have come out of it. It was too much of a prison.

He could not write letters to anybody because he might have made some relationship through the letters. A world teacher needs to be completely unattached. He started feeling a little love for a woman who was old enough to be his mother, but even that was stopped. It was nothing to do with sexuality or anything, he just started feeling love from the woman. The woman was already a mother of three children, but the theosophists wouldn't allow it. They stopped it.

He was completely in seclusion, never allowed to move into the outside world. He was not allowed to enter in any school, in any college, because there he would meet ordinary people and he would become ordinary. Special teachers were appointed; he was taught specially. And all around him, just a nine-year-old boy, all around him was such big talk of masters. Master K.H. sending messages, letters falling from the roof. The messages were all managed, and the theosophists were caught later on. Everything had been managed. The roof was specially made and a letter would drop suddenly, and it was for Krishnamurti – a message had come from the unknown.

Just think of a small boy... No freedom allowed, a great urge came to be free. One day – nobody was expecting that he would renounce it – the theosophists had gathered from all over the world for the first declaration in which Krishnamurti was expected to declare that he was the world teacher and that God had entered into him.

Suddenly, without saying anything to anybody... He could not sleep the whole night. He brooded over it: he had become a slave, and they are all do-gooders. They have made him a slave because they want to do good to him and they love him, and their love became nauseating; and their well-wishing became poisonous. The whole night he brooded: what is he to do? Whether he was to continue and become part of this nonsense, or get out of it?

And blessed he is that in the morning when they had gathered and they were waiting for God to descend in him and to declare that he is now no longer Krishnamurti but Lord Maitreya – Buddha has entered in him – he suddenly declined and he said, "It is all nonsense. Nobody is descending in me. I am simply Krishnamurti and I am nobody's master. And I am not a *jagatguru*, not a world teacher. And I dissolve this nonsense and this organization and the whole thing that has been made around me."

They were shocked. They could not believe it: "Has he gone mad, crazy?" They had put much hope in him, much money; it was a great investment, years of training. But it was going to be so. If he had been absolutely a dead man, then only would he have accepted it. He was alive. They could not kill his life, and that aliveness exploded.

If he had been a dull, mediocre mind, maybe he would have accepted, but he has an intelligence, a tremendous awareness. He got out of it. That whole movement and the whole organized thing functioned as a positive challenge.

As far as I see, nothing can hold you. If you are alert, you will use organized religion as a challenge. If you are not alert, then organized religion or no organized religion, wherever you are you will create an imprisonment around you. You carry it around you – in your cowardice, in your fear, in your urge to be secure and comfortable.

The second question:

> Osho,
> For the last twenty-five years I belonged to the
> organization of the Seventh Day Adventist church,
> (Saturday Sabbath). Though I am concentrating in
> listening to you, I have not passed the stage of

> *conflicts. One of the conflicts has been whether Ellen G. White, the founder of the church, was the messenger of God or not.*
> *Please explain it to me.*

Either everybody is a messenger of God, or nobody. The whole idea that somebody is a prophet and somebody is a *tirthankara* and somebody is a messenger or a christ is absurd. You all come from the same source. We all come from the same root. Nobody is special. And this is what a religious man tries to live.

A religious man is one who sees that he is ordinary. A religious man is one who sees that he is exactly the same as others and he does not pretend to be special, because the very idea: "I am special" is foolish, the very idea: "I am the chosen one" is egoistic. A religious man cannot claim that. A religious man has no claim. He simply accepts and he realizes that he is a part of this cosmos as you are a part of this cosmos. He never puts himself above you. This is his superiority, that he never puts himself above you. This is his "aboveness," that he never thinks that he is extraordinary or special in some way. He never carries the attitude of "holier than thou." He knows that you are also gods and goddesses. Maybe you don't recognize it – that's the only difference.

The difference between me and you is only one: I recognize who I am; you don't recognize who you are. There is no other difference. You are exactly the same as I am. You are a buddha asleep, but there is no question about any difference. A buddha is a buddha, whether asleep or awake. You may not have come across your divineness, you may not have tried, you may not have opened the door of your inner treasures, but the treasure exists. You may think that you are not special and I am special, but how can I think the same way? You may think that; it is natural for you to think that.

People may have thought that Christ was special – that is natural, because Christ looks special. He is special in a way because he has recognized his godhood, and in that very recognition he has become luminous, a clear light without any smoke, a pure flame. People recognize that he is special. But how can Jesus say he is special? In recognizing his own inner flame, in recognizing his own inner godhood, he has recognized everybody's godhood, and not only about human beings but about trees and birds and animals, even rocks. Even rocks he knows now are gods – fast asleep, snoring. Some day or other rocks will awaken and will become gods.

You may not see who you are, but I see who you are. The day I recognized who I am, I recognized everybody's innermost core. A religious person cannot think he is special. And a religious person cannot think that you are condemned, that you are sinners. A religious person starts laughing. He laughs at you because you are a saint and think yourself a sinner. He laughs at you because you are God and think yourself somebody else. The whole thing seems to be absurd – what a drama. Everybody has a mask and has completely forgotten his own original face. Your original face is God's face.

So whosoever tries to prove that he is special, whosoever – Ellen G. White or Reverend Moon or Satya Sai Baba – says that he is special is simply asserting that he has not yet known.

Satya Sai Baba said, "How can ants know the depth of the ocean?" Now this is foolish, this is stupid, because ants are as much gods as Satya Sai Baba. If you ask me whether Satya Sai Baba is a god or not, I will say yes, he is a god – he is a fraud god, but a god all the same. He is a magician god, he is lost in magic. Somebody may be a fool, then he is a foolish god, but I cannot deny that he is a god, I cannot say that. Everybody is a god playing different roles.

You cannot say that somebody else is just like an ant – even ants are not ants. That's what a religious person recognizes. He said, "Dogs can go on barking, but the stars will not fall down." Now you are looking at the dog in a very condemnatory way. And "dog" is nothing but "god" read backward. And who is dog? About whom are you talking? Dogs exist not, because a dog is also a god – pretending to be a dog, playing the game of being a dog.

A religious person, one who has come home, recognizes that the whole existence is divine, unconditionally divine. There are not "gods" and "not gods." The whole existence is made of one fiber and that fiber is divine.

But there are people who go on searching for new trips for the ego. Sometimes it is money, sometimes it is politics, sometimes it is religion, but the search is the same – the ego. And religion happens only when there is an ego-loss; when the ego is lost, when the ego is shattered and you are suddenly there with no idea of any "I." You are, but there is no "I" in it.

I am not saying become humble because the ego can even try that. It does try. It can become humble, it can pretend to be humble, but then look in the humble man's eyes: he says, "I am nobody," but he is waiting for you to say, "You are the greatest man." He says, "I am humble, I am just dust on your feet," but don't accept him. Don't say, "Yes, we know – we have always known. You are not saying anything new to us," otherwise he will never be able to forgive you. He will take revenge. He's not saying that you have to accept it. In fact, he is saying, "Look, how humble I am. Look, here is the most humble man in the world." But the game is the same: "I am the most humble man in the world, but "I am."

Somebody says, "I am the richest man in the world." Somebody says, "I am the most powerful man in the world." Somebody says, "I am the most humble man in the world." Where is the difference?

I am not saying become humble. Ego can become humble. I am talking about ego-loss. You have to see into the ego: its complexity, its subtle games. You have to become aware of all its games. One day, when you have looked into all its games, it simply disappears. Just by looking into them, just a clarity, just an awareness, and it disappears. It disappears as darkness disappears when you bring light into the dark room. Just bring awareness.

I am not saying practice humility, and I am not saying become a humble man, I am saying whosoever you are, just bring light to your life, bring a little more awareness, and you will see that ego is like darkness disappearing. One day when there is no ego, there is no humbleness either.

A really religious person is neither humble nor egoistic, he is simple. A humble person is very complex: he has practiced humility. Anything practiced is always complex, and anything practiced is always false. Anything practiced means simply a pseudo thing.

Practice means you are imposing something upon yourself which is not there inside you in the first place. Otherwise, what is the need of practicing it? If you have understood, you have understood – there is no need for practice. Practice simply means you are trying to substitute understanding with practice. But nothing else is going to help except understanding, awareness.

I have heard...

Jesus is about to walk on the waters of the Dead Sea. He begins walking on the sea, and he turns to his disciples and says, "Trust in me, come follow me, and walk on the sea." Eleven of his disciples begin to follow him. Only Thomas remains behind on the shore.

When the others inquire of him, Thomas explains that he had better stay dry as the cold waters are liable to affect his rheumatism.

Jesus turns his head and says to Thomas, "Thomas, trust in me. Come follow me and walk on the sea."

So Thomas begins to walk and is quickly in water up to his knees. Thomas cries, "Jesus! Jesus!"

And Jesus once again says, "Trust in me, come follow me and walk on the sea."

This goes on with Thomas calling for Jesus' help as Thomas continues to walk on.

When the water has reached to the chin of Thomas, Peter turns to him and says, "Thomas, why must you always be different? Why can't you walk on the stones like everyone else?"

There are people who can't allow themselves to be like everyone else, they have to be special in some way or other. This is a disease, a neurosis.

You cannot be different. Basically, we all belong to one consciousness. All differences are superficial, just on the surface. Of course, you have a different skin and I have a different skin. Somebody has a white skin and somebody has a black skin and somebody has a different nose, and somebody has a different color to his eyes, and somebody has a different color to his hair, but deep down, the deeper you go, the more we are the same.

The English word *self* is very beautiful. Its original meaning is "same" – self means "the same." You use the words *myself, himself, herself, themselves.*

Myself, yourself: "my" is different, "your" is different, but the "self" is the same. The word *self* means "the same." "Self" is neither mine nor yours. When it becomes mine, it is "myself"; then the "self" has something added to it, plus to it. When the "my" is dropped, there is only "self" left; when the "you" is dropped, there is only "self" left. When the body and mind and the superficial distinctions are no longer there, deep in the innermost core we are one – we are just the self, the same.

Don't try in any way to be special because all those trips are ego trips and lead you into frustration and worry and fear.

But when somebody comes and claims he is special, he can always find a few disciples. The reason is not that his claim is true, the reason is that people are in very deep uncertainty, people are in confusion. They want somebody to cling to. They want somebody to make them certain. When somebody comes and says, "I am coming as a special messenger from God"... These people are almost mad people, and they will speak with such power, with such force, with such fire, that you will start feeling that there must be something in it. You start feeling because you are confused. You always wanted somebody to tell you how to live your life. You always wanted somebody to lead you. You always wanted somebody who is certain, so you can get rid of your uncertainties. You always wanted somebody who knows, so you need not be worried about your ignorance.

Now here comes a man and when he declares forcibly, fire in his eyes and magic in his words, a few people are bound to become victims of him. They will trust him, and if you say to these people, "You are fools," they will not listen to you. Because it is not a question of whether their prophet is wrong or right; the moment you say their prophet is wrong, you are again bringing their uncertainty back, you are again making them confused. They were confused; now they are no longer confused, they are following somebody.

Even a Muktananda can have followers, can get followers. Seeing it I am simply surprised. I cannot see how it is possible. Muktananda getting followers? If it is possible, then you are unnecessarily waiting – you can become a great leader. If Muktananda can become, then anybody can become.

I knew a man in Jabalpur who was a follower of Muktananda and I told him, "You are simply foolish. You yourself can become a leader."

He said, "How can I become? I don't know anything about religion."

I said, "You come with me." I was going to Calcutta. I said, "You just come with me and keep quiet."

He said, "What do you mean?"

I said, "We are going to play a game just to make you clear about how things happen."

He followed me. I said, "Just one thing: you are not to say anything; you just keep quiet. When people ask some question, you close your eyes, you start swaying, and I will see that things happen."

So he came with me. The host where we were staying asked me immediately, "Who is this man?"

I said, "He is a *paramahansa*. He keeps quiet – he is a great soul."

The man said, "But we never heard about him, so how did you hear?"

"He never publicizes, he is not a Mahesh Yogi, he does not believe in advertisement. He is very, very esoteric."

The man fell at his feet. The garland that he had brought for me... He forgot me completely. And that man, I had trained him in the train as to what to do, so he started swaying. The host also started swaying. I said, "Look, your kundalini is rising!"

He said, "I can feel something; in my spine, there is some sensation. I have never felt it and I have been to so many saints, but this man is a miracle. Can't he say anything?"

I said, "He never speaks."

Within three days there was a great crowd – people coming and bringing money and flowers. And in the night the man would say to me, "This is incredible! You must be doing something," he said to me, "because how can I raise their kundalini? I don't know anything about kundalini – my own has not risen yet! You must be doing something, you are playing a trick, otherwise, how can it happen? And one person can be a fool, but so many persons!" And rich people coming in their Cadillacs and Lincolns and Impalas, such.... And this man was an ordinary businessman.

Three days after when we came back I told him, "Now what do you want? Do you want to continue your old business?"

People need somebody to guide them. People need somebody to befool them. People need somebody to give them certainty. People are so shaky, uncertain of everything. Just claim, just your claim is enough, but it has to be very, very absolute. If you hesitate you are gone – then in the spiritual world, in the spiritual supermarket, you are nobody. Claim absolutely, unconditionally, never hesitate. And that is one of the qualities of fools: they never hesitate. To hesitate you need some intelligence. A very intelligent person is always hesitant.

Lao Tzu says: "I hesitate on every step. I must be confused. My whole town, everybody that I know, is so absolute; people are so clever – I must be muddleheaded, because I feel so shaky. Alternatives are there: what to choose, what not to choose?"

He is being ironical, he is joking. It has always been so. An intelligent person is hesitant; an idiot, never hesitant. Have you ever seen buffaloes hesitant? They simply go on. On the road they don't bother about the traffic rules. You go on honking your horn – they don't bother about you. They simply go like spiritual saints.

People are insecure, uncertain. They need somebody to claim. And when you need, somebody is bound to claim and exploit you.

The third question:

> Osho,
> When I laugh at your jokes in the lecture I feel it is just
> a reflex, that my laughter is happening on the surface
> and not penetrating into my being. I am laughing less
> and less. Now even your towel madness does not
> move me.
> Is this a question?

It is a question and a very serious one because to me laughter is one of the greatest spiritual qualities.

Try to understand: only man, *only* man, can laugh, no other animal can laugh. It is possible only at the stage of man that laughter happens. If you come across a donkey laughing, you will go mad. Or a horse laughing – then you will not be able to sleep again. Animals don't laugh. They don't have that much intelligence. For laughter, intelligence is needed – the greater the intelligence, the deeper the laughter.

Laughter is a symbol that you are really human. If you cannot laugh, then you are below human. If you can laugh, you have become human. Laughter is a sure indication of humanity.

Aristotle says that man is a rational animal. I don't believe it because I have watched man and I don't see any rationality in him. My definition is: man is a laughing animal. Laughter means you can become aware of the ridiculousness of things.

And also: man is the only animal who can get bored. Boredom and humor are two aspects of the same coin, two sides of the same coin. Only man can get bored and only man can laugh. These are the two specific qualities that exist in man. They are the definition of humanity. Animals are never bored. They go on doing the same routine every day, year in, year out, from birth to death – they are never bored. You cannot see boredom on their faces because for boredom also intelligence is needed.

The more intelligent a person, the more bored he is in the world. Buddha became bored with the whole nonsense that is called life. He became bored with birth, he became bored with love, he became bored with death. In the East, religion is nothing but a search to get out of this boring existence, how to get out of *avagaman* – this constant coming and going, this continuous birth and death. It is boring, it has nothing new in it. And the idea of many lives makes it even more boring.

Christians are less bored, Mohammedans are less bored, Jews are less bored because they have only one life. You cannot be very bored in one life. Once you are born, and then you die after seventy years. In seventy years, thirty years you sleep, fifteen, twenty years you work – continuously you are working – three years you waste in eating. First you eat and then you defecate, so man is just like a pipe: in one end you go on pouring things, from another end you go on throwing out.

If you count all the activities of man then shaving, standing before the mirror... I was just reading an article: a man stands before the mirror – and it is about men, it is not about women – seventy days continuously, if we take it continuously, in his whole life. Seventy days he has been just standing before the mirror. Now look at the absurdity of it. And this is about men – I think they have given the data about men and not about women because it cannot be counted. Women go on standing before the mirror, just looking at themselves. Once you have looked, finished. Now what are you looking for? Is something missing? Or can't you believe that it is you?

If you see the whole activity of life, it is boring. But if life is only one, it is not so boring. That's why Christians, Mohammedans and Jews cannot be very religious. Hinduism, Jainism, Buddhism, have brought another quality to religion. They say it has been so millions of times: rebirth, again and again; reincarnation, again and again. It is not one life; one life is only one movement of the wheel. The wheel has been moving since a beginningless beginning. And you have done the same thing millions of times, and still you are not bored? Then you must be absolutely stupid. An intelligent person is bound to become bored.

Boredom is human, and because man can become bored, man can laugh also. Laughter is another extreme of the same energy. The whole spectrum is between boredom and laughter.

That's why I use so many jokes – because I know religious truths are very boring. So first I take you toward boredom, I go into delicate matters, I take you into boredom. When I see now it is too much and you will not be able to tolerate any more, then I tell you a joke. The pendulum swings back. You are happy again. Again I can bore you. You are fresh, you are ready. You can still tolerate again ten, fifteen minutes. When I see that now you are coming to your limit, that you will get mad at me – I don't want to be killed – again, immediately, I talk about something so you can laugh and you can forgive me.

Boredom and laughter are the most important qualities of human consciousness, but people are not ordinarily aware of either. When you get bored, before you become aware, you simply get occupied into some other activity which gives a new thrill, sensation. You go to the movie, you sit in front of the TV, you go to a friend, start talking to somebody, the neighbor. You don't have anything to say, he has nothing to say – you have talked about these things millions of times. Again about the climate, again about the weather, again about how your children are and how your wife is – and you are not a bit concerned. But you are bored. Something you have to do to forget it. You have to talk.

A person, in the usual daily routine, uses five thousand words. You may be thinking I am talking too much – you are wrong. Once I have talked, I keep quiet – but I never go beyond the limit of five thousand words. You spread it out over the whole day. I am finished in the morning. But I never go beyond the limit. I go on looking at the clock.

People go on talking just to avoid their being, avoid their boredom. The husband is bored with the wife, the wife is bored with the husband, the mother is bored with the children, the children are bored with parents – everybody is simply bored. But we keep it below consciousness, otherwise you will start committing suicide. What will you do?

Marcel has written that suicide is the only important question, the only metaphysical question. It is, because if the whole boredom becomes clear to you, what are you going to do then? If life is just a rut, then what is the point of it all? You go on avoiding it.

In a religious community it is brought to your notice; it is not allowed that you should avoid it. In a Zen monastery they have a very boring routine – fixed, fixed forever, for centuries. Never a thrill, never a sensation. In the morning they get up, they do their *zazen*, they take their tea, they do their walking meditation, they go for their breakfast. And everything is the same: the breakfast is the same, the tea is the same; again they do *zazen*, again they go into the garden to work. And have you looked at the Zen garden?

They don't allow trees around their meditation hall. They make a rock garden – to bore you completely. Because trees change: sometimes it is spring and there are flowers and greenery, and sometimes it is fall and the leaves are dropping. Trees change. Trees are not monks. Trees go on changing round the year. In a Zen monastery they make a rock garden, so nothing changes. You go on doing the same thing every day, and you look out and there are rocks and sand, and the same pattern. Why?

Boredom has been used as a technique, it is a device. In Zen, boredom is used as a device: you are bored to death, and you are not allowed to escape. You are not to go outside, you are not to entertain yourself, you are not to do, you are not to talk, you are not to read novels and detective stories. No thrill. No possibility to escape anywhere.

All the monks look alike: shaved. Have you noticed it? If you shave your hair, mustache, beard, you become almost a nonentity. Your face loses individuality. The monks all look alike, you cannot make out any difference. You see the shaven heads and you are bored. Hair gives a little style, a little difference – all heads shaven look alike; with hair you can have a style. Somebody has a long hairstyle, somebody a short hairstyle; somebody is a square and somebody is a hippie. There are a thousand ways to do something with hair. What can you do with the head? It is just the same – the dress is the same, the head is the same, the food is the same, the rock garden is the same, and the meditation is the same. Year in, year out, for twenty years.

The work is to bring boredom to such a point where no escape is possible and you have to go through the breakthrough. When it is unbearable, when it comes to a crescendo and you cannot bear it, then it explodes. From that extreme, you jump. Suddenly all boredom disappears, because the mind itself disappears.

Boredom is an indication of mind. That's why animals are not bored. If you go to the very extreme, if you go on putting pressure, more and more pressure, then there comes a climax when you simply cannot tolerate anymore, and the boredom disappears – and with the boredom, the mind. That's what in Zen they call satori.

Laughter can also be used in the same way. Bodhidharma used it. There have been Sufi masters who have used it. There are a few Zen sects which use laughter also. If you can go on laughing at the ridiculousness of things, one day or other you will come to the extreme when suddenly you will see that laughter is not coming. That's the point. You go on laughing, still you go on trying to laugh, and laughter is not coming. Everything seems to be stuck, but you go on trying. Much effort is needed now; force it to the very extreme, and one day laughter disappears, and with the laughter, the human mind disappears.

Boredom or laughter, both can be used. I use both together. First I bore you, then I help you to laugh. And I go on throwing you from one extreme to another, just like a tightrope-walker: when he is falling toward the left, he leans toward the right; when he leans toward the right too much and feels now he will fall, he leans toward the left. And by and by a balance arises. Now this is the third point of transcendence.

Either you go to the left, far left, as much as you can go; or you go to the right, far right; or you just be in the middle, in the extreme middle, and there is transcendence. These three points are the points of transcendence. Either birth or death or love – these three are the transcendence points. My whole effort is not to use any extremism, but to give you a balance.

So I go on moving from left to right, but the whole idea is to keep you balanced on the rope. One day, balancing will bring you to a point where suddenly you are so balanced that the mind cannot exist. Mind can exist only either leaning to the right or leaning to the left. Mind can exist only with extremes. Mind can never exist with the middle, with the balance.

Buddha has called his path *majjhim nikaya* – the middle way. My path also is the middle way. In many, many ways I am trying to help you to come to the absolute middle where everything disappears.

Now you say "When I laugh at your jokes in the lecture I feel it is just a reflex, that my laughter is happening on the surface and not penetrating into my being."

Go on trying. Don't be worried. Let it be a reflex. Go on trying. Sometimes you will even feel that the laughter is just in the body or in the mind and you are a witness. Those are beautiful moments. You have become a little transcendental to your laughter, and that's good.

"I am laughing less and less" – it will happen, but you have to try hard. It is one of the most arduous things, to try hard for laughter, because how should one try? Laughter seems either to be coming or not coming – how can you try for it? The more you try, the more you will find it is difficult to bring; but try, let it be difficult.

Listen to my jokes now more consciously, more deliberately.

When I am telling a joke, just forget the whole world. Meditate deeply on it so you can have the whole flavor of it and it penetrates to your very heart. And when laughter comes, even if it is slight, just a flicker, a ripple, cooperate with it, allow it to become a big wave. Sway with it, go with it – be in a let-go. It will take you over.

Sometimes it is possible, listening to me so much, laughing with me so much, by and by even laughing may look like a boredom. Every day laughing again and again also creates boredom. Every day listening to jokes again and again, and you have a very small quality of laughter, a very small quantity of laughter in you – it feels exhausted. But you have to learn now a few more things.

Listen to the joke more alertly, and when the ripple arises in you cooperate with it, even exaggerate it, go with it. The question is from Bodhi, and I will suggest for him a special meditation: every morning he has to laugh for three minutes for no reason at all. When you get up, the first thing – don't open your eyes first. When you feel the sleep is gone, just start laughing in your bed. For the first two, three days it will be difficult, then it comes, and then it comes like an explosion.

First it is difficult because you feel foolish: why are you laughing? There is no reason. But by and by you will feel foolish and you will start laughing at your foolishness, and then it takes over. Then it is irrepressible. Then you laugh at the whole absurdity. And then somebody else – your wife, your girlfriend, the neighbor – may start laughing seeing that you are a fool, and then that will help you.

Laughter can become epidemic. You just try, and you report to me after one month. Laugh every morning, and if you enjoy it then every night before you go to sleep. Then there is a possibility that in your dreams I may tell you a few jokes.

Now let me tell you a few jokes for no reason at all:

The beautiful girl was one candidate for the job at the zoo as a lion-tamer. The other was an eager young man. The manager said he would give them both a chance and told the girl to go into the cage.

The girl, wearing a big fur coat, did so. The huge lion was let in with her and he immediately started to charge at her. Suddenly she stood upright, opened her fur coat and stood there completely naked. The lion stopped dead, spun around, and went meekly back to the corner.

The manager was properly amazed. He turned toward the young man. "Well, pal, do you think you can top that?"

"I'd like to try," said the guy. "Just get that crazy lion out of there."

The father took his two teenage sons to Miami for their first visit. "I want you to get plenty of sunshine," said the old man, "and to make sure you do, I'm going to fine you a dollar an hour if you're out after midnight."

The first son arrived home at two a.m. and the next morning gave his dad two dollars, saying, "It was worth it. Was she beautiful! Was she romantic! Was she passionate!"

The next day the second son came home at five a.m. and gave his father five dollars, sighing, "It was worth it. Was she beautiful! Was she romantic! Was she passionate!"

The third night the father stayed out all night – twenty-four hours. When he got home he threw his wallet on the table and said to his sons, "Take the whole thing. It was worth it. Was she beautiful! Was she romantic! And boy – was she patient!"

The fourth question:

Osho,
I am confused. When you talked about the two-
arrowed love I felt pierced to the heart and a beautiful
pain arose in me. Is love painful?
Where am I and where do I go from here?

Love is painful, but the pain is certainly a blessing. Sex is not painful. Sex is very convenient, comfortable. People use it almost as a sedative, a tranquilizer.

Love is painful because love brings growth. Love is painful because love demands. Love is painful because love transforms. Love is painful because love gives you a new birth.

Sex does not touch you at all. It is mechanical. It is just

physiological. Love brings your heart into relationship, and when the heart is in relationship there is always pain. But don't avoid the pain. If you avoid the pain you will miss all pleasures of life.

In sex there may be relaxation. In sex there may be physiological health and hygiene, but there is no growth. You remain animal. With love you become human. With love you become upright. With love you stand erect on earth. With sex you are again animal, you are horizontal on the earth, just moving like other animals, crawling. With love you are erect, vertical.

With love there are problems. With sex there is no problem at all. But with problems is growth. The greater the problem, the greater the opportunity.

So you ask me: "Is love painful?" Certainly love is painful, but that pain is a blessing. And you have felt it, the questioner has felt it.

She says: "I am confused. When you talked about the two-arrowed love I felt pierced to the heart and a beautiful pain arose in me."

She is aware that it was beautiful. Now don't recoil from it. More and more blessings are waiting for you, but of course more and more pain too. That's why many people never love — it is so painful. They choose not to love but then they remain animalistic, they never become human, they never become vertical. They never take their life in their own hands. They are never of any worth — they are worthless. Love makes you precious.

And if you are in love, then you will see that there is a still deeper pain that is of prayer. It shatters you completely. Love never shatters you completely. It simply shatters you a little, a little bit. It shatters the crust of your ego, but the center of the ego remains intact. Then there is a deeper pain, deeper than love, and that is of prayerfulness. It shatters you utterly. It is a death. When you have learned how to love, and you have learned that the pain that love brings is a blessing in disguise, it is beautiful, it is tremendously beautiful, then you become able and you take another step, and that step is prayerfulness.

With a human lover you can exist, but with the divine as your love you cannot exist. That passion is so great, it simply burns you utterly. No residue is left. In love you are simply burned, but you are there. Lovers remain, overlapping each other, burning each other a little in their fire, but not burned completely. That is the beauty of love, and that is its misery too. Unless you are completely shattered, no residue remains, the ego is gone, totally gone, there will remain a little misery.

All lovers feel a little miserable. They would like to disappear completely, but it is not possible in human relationship. Human relationship is limited. But one learns from it, that there is a possibility: if it can happen so much in a human relationship, how much more can happen in a relationship with the divine?

Love makes you ready to take the final jump, the quantum leap. That's what I call prayerfulness, or you can call it meditation. If you use Buddhist terminology it is meditation; if you use Hindu, Mohammedan, Christian terminology, it is prayer. But the meaning is the same. You have to disappear for godliness to be. Love is a training ground, a school to learn first lessons – of the beauty, of the blessing and benediction of disappearance; to learn that pain is blessed. And then a desire arises to feel the ultimate pain. The Hindu devotees have called it *virah* – ultimate pain; the pain that will remain unless one is consumed by godliness, consumed in godliness.

So when you are in love, or when love arises, cooperate with it, don't try resisting. People come to a compromise. Lovers – I have watched thousands of lovers. Every day they come to me; they bring their problems. But the basic problem that I have been looking at is that lovers by and by come to a compromise. The compromise is: You don't hurt me, I will not hurt you. That's what marriage is. Then people become settled. They become so afraid of pain that they say, "Don't hurt me and I will not hurt you." But then when pain disappears, love also disappears. They exist together.

I have heard...

The male patient complained to the dentist that he was in terrible pain, but he insisted on saving the tooth. The dentist put on his white coat, adjusted the light on his forehead, started his drill, and said, "Okay, now open your mouth and we'll see what we can do."

Just then the patient grabbed him below the belt. "What the hell are you doing?" the dentist screamed.

"Now," the man said quietly, not letting go, "we're not going to hurt each other, are we?"

Now this is what happens. When you are in love, love hurts, it hurts terribly. Then you grab each other and you say, "What! Make a compromise: let it no longer be a love affair, let it be a marriage, make it legal, and I will not hurt you if you don't hurt me." Then husbands and wives live together without being together. They live together alone. They tolerate at the most. They are patient with each other, but love has disappeared.

Love is painful. Never resist, never create any barrier for pain, allow it, and by and by you will see that it was a wrong interpretation. It is not really pain, it is just that something is going so deep in you that you interpret it like a pain. You don't know anything else. You are only aware of pain in your past life, in your past experience. Whenever something penetrates deep, you interpret it as pain.

Don't use the word *pain*. When love and love's arrow goes deep into your heart, close your eyes and don't use words, just see what it is, and you will never see it is pain. You will see it is a benediction. You will be tremendously moved by it. You will feel joyous.

Don't use words. When something new happens to you, always allow a deep look into it without any language.

The last question:

Osho,
Are you not a rich man's guru?

I am because only a rich man can come to me. But when I say "a rich man" I mean one who is very poor inside. When I say "a rich man" I mean one who is rich in intelligence; I mean one who has got everything that the world can give to him and has found that it is futile.

Yes, only a rich person can become religious. I am not saying that a poor person cannot become religious, but it is very rare, exceptional. A poor person goes on hoping. A poor person has not known what riches are. He is not yet frustrated with it. How can he go beyond riches if he is not frustrated with them? A poor man also sometimes comes to me, but then he comes for something which I cannot supply. He asks for success. His son is not getting employed; he asks, "Bless him, Osho." His wife is ill, or he is losing money in his business. These are symptoms of a poor man, one who is asking about things of this world.

When a rich person comes to me he has money, he has employment, he has a house, he has health, he has everything that one can have. And suddenly he has come to a realization that nothing is fulfilling. Then the search for "God" starts.

Yes, sometimes a poor man can also be religious, but for that very great intelligence is needed. A rich man, if he is not religious, is stupid. A poor man, if he is religious, is tremendously intelligent. If a poor man is not religious, he has to be forgiven. If a rich man is not religious, his sin is unpardonable.

I am a rich man's guru. Absolutely it is so. Let me tell you one anecdote:

They were married for twenty-five years and had their biggest argument on the day of their silver anniversary. She never hit harder or lower: "If it weren't for my money, that TV set wouldn't be here. If it weren't for my money, the very chair you're sitting on wouldn't be here!"

"Are you kidding?" he interrupted. "If it weren't for your money, I wouldn't be here!"

And let me say this to you: If it were not for your money, you would not have been here. You are here because you are frustrated with your money. You are here because you are frustrated with your success. You are here because you are frustrated with your life. A beggar cannot come because he is not yet frustrated.

Religion is luxury – the last, ultimate luxury I call it because it is the highest value. When a man is hungry, he does not bother about music, cannot; if you start playing a sitar in front of him, he will kill you. He will say, "You are insulting me. I am hungry and you are playing a sitar – is this the time to play a sitar? Feed me first. And I am so hungry I cannot understand music. I am dying." When a man is dying of hunger, what use is a van Gogh painting? Or a buddha's sermon? Or beautiful Upanishads, or music? They are meaningless. He needs bread.

When a man is happy with his body, has enough to eat, has a good house to live in, he starts becoming interested in music, poetry, literature, painting, art. Now a new hunger arises. The bodily needs are fulfilled, now psychological needs arise. There is a hierarchy in needs: the first is the body; it is the base, it is the ground floor of your being. Without the ground floor, the first story cannot exist.

When your bodily needs are fulfilled, psychological needs arise. When your psychological needs are also fulfilled, then your spiritual needs arise. When a person has listened to all the music that is available in the world, and has seen all the beauty and has found that it is all dream; has listened to all the great poets and has found that it is just a way to forget yourself, just a way to intoxicate yourself, but it does not lead you anywhere; has seen all the paintings and the great art – amusing, entertaining, but then what? Then hands remain empty, more empty than they ever were before. Then music and poetry are not enough. Then the desire to meditate, the desire to pray, a hunger for the ultimate, a hunger for truth arises. A great passion takes possession of you and you are in search of truth, because you now know that unless you know what the secret-most truth of this existence is, nothing can satisfy. All else you have tried and it has failed.

Religion is the ultimate luxury. Either you have to be very rich to come to this luxury, or you have to be tremendously intelligent, but in both cases you are rich, either rich with money or rich with intelligence. I have never seen a person who is really poor – poor in intelligence, poor in riches – ever become religious.

Kabir became religious. He was not a millionaire, but he was tremendously intelligent. Buddha became religious because he was tremendously rich. Krishna and Ram and Mahavira became religious because they were tremendously rich. Dadu, Raidas, Farid became religious because they were tremendously intelligent. But a certain sort of richness is needed.

Yes, you are right: I am the rich man's guru.

Enough for today.

OSHO INTERNATIONAL MEDITATION RESORT

Each year the Meditation Resort welcomes thousands of people from more than 100 countries. The unique campus provides an opportunity for a direct personal experience of a new way of living – with more awareness, relaxation, celebration and creativity. A great variety of around-the-clock and around-the-year program options are available. Doing nothing and just relaxing is one of them!

All of the programs are based on Osho's vision of "Zorba the Buddha" – a qualitatively new kind of human being who is able *both* to participate creatively in everyday life *and* to relax into silence and meditation.

Location
Located 100 miles southeast of Mumbai in the thriving modern city of Pune, India, the OSHO International Meditation Resort is a holiday destination with a difference. The Meditation Resort is spread over 28 acres of spectacular gardens in a beautiful tree-lined residential area.

OSHO Meditations
A full daily schedule of meditations for every type of person includes both traditional and revolutionary methods, and particularly the OSHO Active MeditationsTM. The daily meditation program takes place in what must be the world's largest meditation hall, the OSHO Auditorium.

OSHO Multiversity
Individual sessions, courses and workshops cover everything from creative arts to holistic health, personal transformation, relationship and life transition, transforming meditation into a lifestyle for life and work, esoteric sciences, and the "Zen" approach to sports and recreation. The secret of the OSHO Multiversity's success lies in the fact that all its programs are combined with meditation, supporting the understanding that as human beings we are far more than the sum of our parts.

OSHO Basho Spa
The luxurious Basho Spa provides for leisurely open-air swimming surrounded by trees and tropical green. The uniquely styled, spacious Jacuzzi, the saunas, gym, tennis courts...all these are enhanced by their stunningly beautiful setting.

Cuisine
A variety of different eating areas serve delicious Western, Asian and Indian vegetarian food – most of it organically grown especially for the Meditation Resort. Breads and cakes are baked in the resort's own bakery.

Night life
There are many evening events to choose from – dancing being at the top of the list! Other activities include full-moon meditations beneath the stars, variety shows, music performances and meditations for daily life.

Facilities
You can buy all of your basic necessities and toiletries in the Galleria. The Multimedia Gallery sells a large range of OSHO media products. There is also a bank, a travel agency and a Cyber Café on-campus. For those who enjoy shopping, Pune provides all the options, ranging from traditional and ethnic Indian products to all of the global brand-name stores.

Accommodation
You can choose to stay in the elegant rooms of the OSHO Guesthouse, or for longer stays on campus you can select one of the OSHO Living-In programs. Additionally there is a plentiful variety of nearby hotels and serviced apartments.

    www.osho.com/meditationresort
    www.osho.com/guesthouse
    www.osho.com/livingin

FOR MORE INFORMATION

For any information about OSHO books, please contact:

OSHO Media International

17 Koregaon Park, Pune - 411001, MS, India

Phone: +91-20-66019999 Fax: +91-20-66019990

E-mail: distribution@osho.net

Website: http://www.osho.com

For More Information

For a full selection of OSHO multilingual online destinations, see

www.OSHO.com/AllAboutOsho

The official comprehensive website of OSHO International is

www.OSHO.com